D0868344

High-Tech Betrayal

High-Tech Betrayal

Working and Organizing on the Shop Floor

VICTOR G. DEVINATZ

DISCARDED

WIDENER UNIVERSITY

MICHIGAN STATE UNIVERSITY PRESS
East Lansing

© 1999 by Victor G. Devinatz

The paper used in this publication meets the minimum
requirements of ANSI/NISO Z39.48–1992 (R 1997) ∞.

Michigan State University Press
East Lansing, Michigan 48823-5202

03 02 01 00 99 1 2 3 4 5 6 7 8 9

LIBRARY OF CONGRESS CATALOGING-IN-PUBLICATION DATA

Devinatz, Victor Gary
    High-tech betrayal: working and organizing on the shop floor /
Victor G. Devinatz.
    p.   cm.
    Includes bibliographial references and index.
    ISBN 0-87013-493-0
    1. Employees—Effect of technological innovations on—United
States.   2. Technolgy and civilization—Forecasting.
    3. Occupational training—United States.   I. Title.
    HD6331.2.U5D48   1999   98-52237
    331.2'042—dc21   CIP

Visit Michigan State University Press on the World-Wide Web at:
www.msu.edu/unit/msupress

For my parents,
Allen and Pearl Devinatz

Contents

ACKNOWLEDGEMENTS
ix

PREFACE
"The High-Tech Future Doesn't Work"
xi

CHAPTER 1
The Nature of High-Tech Factory Work
1

CHAPTER 2
A Brief Corporate History of Biomed
19

CHAPTER 3
Searching for and Beginning Work at a Factory Job
27

CHAPTER 4
Adapting to High-Tech Factory Work
41

CHAPTER 5

The High-Tech Labor Process

57

CHAPTER 6

The Dictatorship of High-Tech Management

81

CHAPTER 7

Factory Life

115

CHAPTER 8

Rank and File Discontent

137

CHAPTER 9

Talking Union

151

CHAPTER 10

The Return of the Despotic Factory Regime?

187

ENDNOTES

205

BIBLIOGRAPHY

227

INDEX

241

Acknowledgements

THIS BOOK WOULD NOT HAVE BEEN POSSIBLE WITHOUT THE HELP AND SUP-port of many people. Martha Bates, my editor at Michigan State University Press, was extremely supportive of this project and was instrumental in the publication of this book. Her professionalism and good cheer during this process was most refreshing for a novice author. Dick Stivers convinced me that I had a story worth telling and was both incredibly encouraging and helpful with his knowledge and experience in the book-writing process. As a mentor he has provided me with invaluable advice countless times and has served as a role model for what a dedicated scholar can and should be. I hope that someday I can measure up to his high standards.

Jackie Scruggs, Bruce Laurie, David Roediger, Frank Annunziato, Ken Gagala, Laurie Clements, and Jennifer Carton read various versions of the manuscript and were more than generous in the time they spent providing written comments and discussing my manuscript with me. The book is much improved because of their efforts. Sandy Judd did an excellent job copyediting the manuscript and Annette Tanner was superb in handling all of the production-related tasks.

I am deeply grateful to a number of people who, although not directly responsible for either the writing or the publication of this book, have provided me with emotional, moral, or intellectual support over the years. As I proceed in my academic career, I become ever more appreciative of the excellent graduate training that I received at the University of Massachusetts Labor Relations Research Center and the University of Minnesota Industrial Relations Center. Faculty members at these two universities who have positively influenced my thinking include the late Harvey Friedman, Curt Tausky, James Scoville, Barbara Laslett, Hyman Berman, John Fossum, and Avner Ben-Ner. Friends who have supported my work, in one way or another, over the years include Chuck Davis, Richard Soderlund, Kate McCarthy, David Johnson, Steve Kolodrubetz, Tom Lambert, Farzaneh Fazel, Jack Howard, Lee Graf, and Dan Rich. Besides supporting my work, Dona Warren was there to share and enrich my life in innumerable meaningful ways. Although a scholar in a completely different field, my brother, Ethan Devinatz, always expressed interest in my various projects and endeavors.

Finally, I would like to thank my parents, Allen and Pearl Devinatz, who taught me to value education and raised me in an environment that ultimately made the writing of this book possible. It is them to whom this book is dedicated.

As in any scholarly work, this text is the product of many contributors, yet any errors are mine alone.

Preface

"The High-Tech Future Doesn't Work"

THINKING ABOUT FACTORIES

I REMEMBER THE FIRST TIME THAT I THOUGHT ABOUT FACTORIES, OR AT LEAST about one in particular. It was late in August 1971 and I was a thirteen-year-old high school freshman running a late afternoon cross-country workout on the school's quarter-mile track. The team was running repeat quarter-miles that day. We ran one lap of the track fairly hard, rested for ninety seconds, ran another lap, and rested, repeating this procedure a total of ten times. Although it was late in the afternoon, the day was still hot, humid, and hazy. The air was stagnant. It was the kind of day in which you would even sweat in the shade. Under these conditions, running was extremely uncomfortable, and awareness of the Mystik Tape Corporation, a company that produced a variety of adhesive products, located across the street from the track, entered our consciousness.

In each repetition, as our legs pumped and as we gasped for air, heading into the final turn, we received a whiff of the terrible odor that emanated from the tape factory, less than fifty yards away. The smell was extremely bad that day because there was no wind to disperse it, and the stench clung to the synthetic track better than the spiked shoes used for racing during the spring track season.

"God-damn Mystik Tape!" the runners cursed, between gasps, after each lap on the track. "They ought to do something about that smell!" I joined in, as I tried to recover from each quarter-mile segment. Mystik Tape was clearly an enemy that made our running that much more difficult.

I did not think about Mystik Tape again for nearly nine years after leaving high school. In March 1984, however, while working the second shift at a food-processing plant, I met an African American worker in his late thirties who had just recently been laid off from Mystik Tape after working there for nearly nineteen years.

Bennie, a tall, broad-shouldered man with curly hair and a slight mustache, had been a machine operator at Mystik Tape from November 1964 until September 1983. "I remember when I went to apply for the job," he told me. "It was snowing and I had just gotten married." When I asked him to describe his old job, he said, "I ran this machine that put the adhesive on the tape. Every kind of tape that you could imagine. After a thousand feet of tape went through the machine, I'd have to stop the machine and cut the roll off." He continued, "I did this job until I was laid off. I was one of the last five employees in my department. There were people who were laid off who had worked for thirty-five years for the company. When I went, the factory closed."

It was hard for me to conceive of Bennie working at the same machine for nineteen years. Day in and day out. Winter and summer. Through the Vietnam War and five American presidents. Through economic recessions and booms and back again.

What was harder for me to imagine was that I had spent four years only a few hundred yards away from Bennie, although we had had two completely different experiences. While I had thought of how Mystik Tape had affected my running, I had never considered what Mystik Tape had done to the workers who spent a good portion of their waking hours there.

THEORETICIAN AS FACTORY WORKER

I cannot remember when the idea of obtaining a factory job first entered my mind. Through my involvement in political activity (including labor support work) as both an undergraduate and a graduate student, I had become interested in trying to understand the meaning of what I viewed as the major component of one's economic experience: the work situation"[1] under an economic system, known as capitalism, guided solely by profits. While I had done a considerable amount of reading in the area of industrial sociology, I felt that the only way to acquire a true understanding of the labor process under capitalism was to immerse myself in a "suitable" environment for a period of time—that is, to become a participant observer in a factory.

Participant observation has a rich historical tradition in both the social and cultural anthropological and sociological literature, as well as in industrial sociology.[2] Although I wished to be a participant observer in a factory, I did not want my role as a worker to be strictly limited to observation. My interest in becoming a factory worker also stemmed from a deeply felt need to act as a social change agent—that is, to improve the working conditions in the factory by mobilizing the workers to work collectively toward such a goal. Convincing workers that it is their right to engage in such a struggle is extremely difficult (especially during an economic recession) when they have been beaten down by a system that constantly tells them just the opposite.

With the goal of organizing workers in mind, the best thing, I felt, that could be done for the workers, and by the workers themselves, was to organize a union that would be both militant and democratic, fighting hard for the workers both before and after the first contract was hammered out. Organizing any union, much less such a union as I had envisioned, at a time when corporations were aggressively busting unions and the National Labor Relations Board (NLRB) had little inclination to stop such behavior, was, needless to say, Sisyphean labor.

I dropped out of a doctoral program in the summer of 1982 and I began to look for factory work in the Chicago metropolitan area. I worked briefly as an assistant boycott organizer for the United Furniture Workers of America, AFL-CIO, before finding two part-time jobs early in the autumn of 1982. I did not find full-time factory work until nearly five months after withdrawing from graduate school.

In the middle of December 1982, I landed a job at a small medical electronics factory located in the Chicago metropolitan area. At the time I was hired, there were approximately sixty production workers at the plant. This figure remained fairly stable throughout my seven months of work there although it varied slightly at times due to workers being hired, being fired, or in rare instances quitting.

According to the "General Summary" of the 1992 Census of Manufactures, 3,625,500 out of the 11,640,800 production workers in this country were employed by industrial establishments that had fewer than one-hundred employees.[3] Therefore, just over 31 percent, or almost one in every three, of the production workers in the United States in 1992 labored for a company that was approximately the same size as the firm for which I worked.

In terms of specific location, the medical electronics factory at which I worked was situated in a heavily industrialized area that contained factories and warehouses ranging in size from only a handful of workers to several thousand employees. Nearby, there were several industrial parks manufacturing a wide variety of products.

Although there are a number of industrial ethnographies depicting work in the service industry, most such works with the exception of one written by Juravich, have described the work and working conditions of relatively large factories, both unionized and nonunion.[4] These descriptions contrast with the working conditions in a small, nonunion plant, such as my place of employment. The presence of a trade union in a plant does not mean that the work done on the shop floor will be any better than the work done in a nonunion shop. Unionization, however, usually provides such benefits as higher wages, paid holidays and vacations, a seniority system, and a grievance procedure—benefits that are often absent in nonunion factories.

However, the medical electronics factory for which I worked should generate interest not only because as a small, nonunion shop it belongs to a group that has been rarely treated in the industrial ethnographic literature, but also because of its location in the high-technology sector of the economy. At the time that I was working in this factory (1982–83), employment in high-tech industries was beginning to be touted as a positive alternative to work in the declining "smokestack" (auto, steel, rubber, etc.) industries. This view is still being promoted in the late 1990s, as we head toward the twenty-first century.

As will be discussed in greater detail in the next chapter, the prototypical high-tech (electronics) manufacturing company is small, is nonunion, pays its production workers very low wages and is managed in an authoritarian manner, with the workers being subjected to both harsh and arbitrary discipline. Based on these characteristics, the medical electronics factory in which I worked was a quintessential example of a high-tech manufacturing firm. While this book is an exposé of one particular high-tech factory, it should be read more as an indictment of the way high-tech manufacturing firms operate as a whole, as well as of the economic system that allows for the proliferation of such factories throughout the United States.

The purpose of this book is twofold. Those who are not familiar with high-tech factory work may possess a number of misconceptions about the nature of such work. They may be under the impression that this type of factory work, where "sterile-clad workers [are] peering through microscopes in microelectronic assembly rooms,"[5] is preferable to the industrial work performed in auto factories and steel mills. They may also believe the myth that high-tech manufacturing work offers more promotional opportunities for employees, requires higher skill levels, and pays better than the work found in "low-tech" industries. This sanitized view is far from reality, and this book should dispel these myths. In addition, I hope that the text provides the reader with a degree of historical understanding of what it was like to work in, as well as to try to organize, a small, nonunion plant in the early 1980s, when the United States was just beginning to emerge from the most severe recession since World War II and the most conservative, antiunion administration since the New Deal era of the 1930s and the 1940s was firmly entrenched in the White House.

As a participant observer in this medical electronics factory, I have written this book in the tradition of the industrial ethnographic studies of Pfeffer, Linhart, and Cavendish.[6] All three of the above authors not only attempted to arrive at a theoretical understanding of the nature of factory work under capitalism through their roles as participant observers but also sought to become active in union politics or sought to intervene in the shop floor struggles in these unionized factories. My goals were similar. Besides attempting to achieve this same theoretical understanding, I adopted the role of shop floor organizer in order to attempt to organize a union at this factory.

The book is based on approximately 450 pages of handwritten notes that I made over the seven months that I worked at the plant. I was able to record a few notes while at work—usually in the bathroom—during the breaks and lunch periods. Every evening, after arriving home from work, I briefly outlined the day's events, and several hours later, I fleshed out the details in a daily journal. I often wrote for at least an hour in this journal, but it was not uncommon for me to spend two hours writing.

The name of the company and the identities of the workers have been changed to protect those workers who may still be working at this particular factory, even after this relatively long period of time. Furthermore, the names of the products and their model numbers have been altered in order to make it more difficult to identify the company. I have used the real names of the unions involved, although union staff organizers' names also have been changed.

While high-tech manufacturing plants are located throughout the United States, California's Silicon Valley has entered the public's consciousness as the epitome of high-tech industry. In 1981, Diana Hembree served a brief stint as an assembler in one of these small electronics companies located in Silicon Valley. In 1985, writing about her experiences for an article in *The Progressive* entitled "Dead End in Silicon Valley: The High-Tech Future Doesn't Work," she stated:

> In the high-tech fever that's sweeping the United States, California's Silicon Valley stands out as a vision of the future—a seemingly clean and safe successor to the declining smokestack industries of the Rust Belt. Some 1,800 electronics firms operate in Silicon Valley, chalking up more than $25 billion in sales last year.
>
> But high technology is no bonanza for the people who make it possible. The Silicon Valley production workers generally labor in low-paid, tedious, dead-end jobs. I took a position as an electronics assembler to get an inside look at the nation's most touted industry. I saw the future, and it does not always work.[7]

I, too, took a job as a production worker at one of high-tech's "factories of the future."[8] This is the story of one of those places.

1.

The Nature of High-Tech Factory Work

THE UNITED STATES, WHICH WAS AT ONE TIME THE MOST POWERFUL INDUS-
trial nation in the world, is in the middle of a transformation from a
manufacturing-based economy to a service-based economy. Traditional
manufacturing industries, such as the automobile, steel, and rubber industries, which created a middle-class lifestyle for many in the United
States, are shrinking and being replaced with service-sector jobs. These new
service sector jobs are sharply dichotomous with respect to skill. High-skill
occupations, such as software design, are being created at the same time
that low-skill jobs, such as fast food workers, are proliferating. With these
changes in the occupational structure, there is an increasing divergence
between the living standards of the upper and working classes, which has
led to the growth of more dual-income families. The public optimism
generated by the growth of the industrial economy in the post–World War
II years has dissipated and been replaced by anxiety and doubt as we approach the twenty-first century.[1]

However, there is one industrial sector that is rapidly expanding in the
1990s. Although it employs at most 10 percent of the workforce, high technology is an industrial sector that many people hope will revive the U.S.
economy and restore it to its leading role in the world. According to Sten
Thore, this sectoral growth has resulted in the emergence of a new form
of capitalism since 1970, which he labels "high tech capitalism," and
which he predicts will continue well into the twenty-first century:

The last quarter of this century has witnessed the emergence of a new economic order. That new order is the capitalism of Intel Corp., Microsoft Corp., and Genentech Inc. It is the capitalism of a new kind of turbulent American entrepreneurship. In retrospect, in the course of world history, the emergence of this new economic order may very well turn out to be as important as, say, the advent of enlightenment or the renaissance. It marks the arrival of a new age—an age of artificial intelligence, robotics, space research, biotech, and environmental technology.[2]

It is also predicted that small high-tech companies will come to dominate the economic landscape in the twenty-first century. According to Hage and Powers:

> It may be difficult to demonstrate, but it is our belief that the small high-tech company, the small high-tech profit center within multi-divisional companies, and the joint venture will become the archetypal organizational forms in post-industrial society, in much the same way that the large corporation came to be the symbol of society a century ago.[3]

In addition, Hage and Powers predict that by the turn of the twenty-first century, "high-tech firms, universities, hospitals, and other post-industrial organizations" will account for most of the jobs in the U.S. economy.[4]

Although Etzioni and Jargowsky argue that high-tech industries will not replace the more traditional manufacturing industries in the United States in the near future, many high-tech industries did experience dramatic growth from 1972 to 1984. For example, employment connected with communications services increased more than fivefold during this era. Growing almost as fast were computer and data processing services (34 percent), while five other high-tech industries grew in excess of 80 percent from 1972 to 1983—surgical, medical, and dental instruments and supplies; optical instruments and lenses; office computing and accounting machines; crude petroleum and natural gas; and engineering and architectural services. In addition, in approximately the same time period (1974–84), employment in microelectronics almost doubled. Figures from 1986 indicate that high-tech industries employed 14 percent of the total U.S. manufacturing workforce, as well as 10 percent of all manufacturing production workers.[5]

Many have praised high-tech as "a clean industry that creates few health and safety problems for its workers or threats to the environment."[6] Mahon speaks of Silicon Valley, the embodiment of high-tech industry, in more glorious terms:

> Silicon Valley is symbolic of more than the latest developments in electronic and computational wizardry. It marks as well an economic and cultural frontier where successful enterpreneurship and venture capitalism, innovative work rules and open management styles provide the background for what is perhaps the most profound and far-reaching inquiry ever into the nature of intelligence. Combined with research here in bioengineering and "artificially intelligent" software, this inquiry may extend dramatically our sense of who we are and what we can do, and affect our very evolution. . . . But a visitor who spends some time here . . . would come away with the sense that a time, a place and a group of people have come together as in Periclean Athens, Renaissance Florence or postwar Paris to affect world culture.[7]

Significantly, on the eve of the twenty-first century, the company that threatens to reshape the education, business, and entertainment industries in its own image is a high-tech company, none other than the giant software manufacturer, Microsoft. Late in 1996, Silicon Valley investor Michael Moritz spoke quite reverentially of the importance of Microsoft: "It's difficult to think of a company in the history of the world that's positioned to influence so many aspects of life as Microsoft is at the end of the twentieth century. In terms of a civilized world, you'd have to go back to the Roman Empire to find any organization that had as great a reach as Microsoft has today."[8]

Even President Clinton has expressed faith in a high-tech future and has plans to develop an industrial policy for "preserving high-tech industries and their high-paying jobs." Clinton also has stated that this industry "will move America forward to a stronger economy, a cleaner environment and technological leadership." The popular media still speaks of "high-tech, high-skill, high-wage jobs" as the economic salvation of the United States.[9]

Part of this enthusiasm for high-tech industry revolves around the perceived working conditions in the industry for both the professionals and the production workers. Dan Cook, of the American Electronics

Association (AEA), states, "It's a high-quality workplace. You're not going to come home covered with dirt and grease and god knows what else." In addition, a typical high-tech workplace is "air-conditioned and well-lit, with workers dressed casually or wearing laboratory-like smocks" and is located in "verdant industrial parks," where "no sooty smokestacks or shabby old factories mar the scenery."[10]

Besides the perception of improved working conditions, there is also the belief that work in high-tech industries is more informal and relaxed. For example, at Hewlett-Packard, the company founders, the late David Packard and William Hewlett, even when in their seventies, still preferred to be called by their first names, even by recently hired employees. Robert Noyce, Intel's cofounder and vice-chairman, labors at an open work-station "with only shoulder-high partitions," which is similar to the one hundred employees' work spaces which surround him. At ROLM, unlike in other companies, where use of such facilities is limited to employees who occupy a senior-level position, there is a $1.5 million recreation center that is open to *all* employees, as well as their families on the weekends.[11]

Although when people think of concentrations of high-tech industries, they immediately think of Silicon Valley or the Route 128 complex around Boston, high-tech industries and centers have expanded throughout the nation. By the mid-1980s, a number of small "Silicon Valleys" had emerged around Dallas and Austin ("Silicon Prairie"); Phoenix ("Silicon Desert"); Minneapolis-St. Paul; Colorado Springs ("Silicon Mountain"); Portland, Oregon ("Silicon Valley North"); Seattle; and Los Angeles. These high-tech complexes include manufacturing plants of microelectronic companies that are based in Silicon Valley. Because of space limitations and exorbitant housing prices on the San Fransisco peninsula, these firms, such as Hewlett-Packard, Intel, AMD, and Apple, have opened new factories in Texas, Colorado, Arizona and Oregon.[12]

Now that a brief introduction to high-tech industry has been provided, how should this industry be defined in the first place? Although there is no standard definition of high-tech industry, Markusen, Hall, and Glasmeier define high-tech industries as "those in which the proportion of engineers, engineering technicians, computer scientists, life scientists, and mathematicians exceeds the manufacturing average." They argue that this definition is an accurate measurement of "the technical capacity of an industry to harness scientific and technical expertise in the development of new products."[13]

An equally useful definition of high-tech industry has been provided by Hadlock, Hecker, and Gannon. They consider the high-tech industry to be one that has "a significant concentration of R & D [Research and Development] employment." These researchers label an industry as high technology if its "proportion of R & D employment is at least equal to the average proportion for all industries." If an industry meets this criterion, it is then classified into one of two groups. A Level I, or R & D intensive, industry is considered to be one in which the "proportion of R & D employment is at least 50 percent higher than the average proportion for all industries." A Level II, or R & D moderate, industry would include all the high-tech industries that do not make the cutoff for the Level I group.[14]

Based on either of these two equally relevant definitions, the small medical electronics manufacturer at which I was employed falls into the high-tech category. According to Markusen, Hall, and Glassmeir's listing of the twenty-nine high-tech sectors based on three-digit standard industrial classification (SIC) codes, the medical and dental supplies industry (SIC 384) is ranked twenty-eighth with 6.03 percent of total employment composed of engineering, engineering technicians, computer scientists, life and physical scientists and mathematicians. In terms of Hadlock, Hecker, and Gannon's definition, the medical and dental supplies industry (SIC 384) would be considered a Level I, or an R & D intensive, industry because 2.4 percent of total employment is involved with research and development.[15]

However, when people think of a "typical" high-tech company they probably think of the numerous electronic components and assembly firms that make up Silicon Valley in northern California. These companies would be classified under SIC 367 and, as would be expected, this three-digit classification code does qualify as a high-tech industry based on the criteria established by the two definitions mentioned above. Although the medical electronics company for whom I worked does not fall into the same three-digit SIC code as the "typical" Silicon Valley electronics assembly firm, my company and the Silicon Valley electronics firms are high-tech production facilities that are very similar in terms of firm size, demographic characteristics of the workforce, pay, and union status. Because much of the high-tech research literature deals with the electronics industry in either California or Silicon Valley, I will discuss the nature of this electronics assembly work with heavy reference to California/Silicon Valley as a point of comparison to show how similar this work is to the factory work that I performed in the medical electronics firm in the

Chicago metropolitan area. Since I worked at Biomed during 1982–83, as a point of comparison, much of the information presented in the following sections will focus on the relevant data from the early to mid-1980s, although more recent information will be presented when and where it is available. Nevertheless, as the reader will discover, the more recent data reinforces the trends and supports the conclusions outlined by the earlier data.

The electronics assembly industry in California has been described by one researcher as an industry that is "a typical example of an unstable, low-skilled sector" and that can be characterized as "part of the lower stratum of sweatshops and secondary labour market activity" within California's "high technology industrial complex." By the mid-1980s, there were approximately 2.5 million workers employed by electronics firms throughout the nation. California had the largest number of electronics workers of any state, with 97,100 workers involved in the industry. More than half of these workers, (50,400) were employed in Silicon Valley (the San Jose Standard Metropolitan Statistical Area).[16]

During 1993, 118,400 workers were employed by electronics firms in California and by 2005, the state's employment in this industry is projected to be 133,100, an increase of 12.4 percent. In 1996, California achieved its largest growth in high-tech manufacturing jobs since 1985. According to an American Electronics Association (AEA) report, in 1996, the state experienced an increase of twenty-eight-thousand high-tech manufacturing jobs which is more than the twenty-seven-thousand jobs added that year in the software and computer services industries. With respect to Silicon Valley, preliminary figures from May 1997 indicate that 90,400 workers were employed in the electronic equipment industry.[17]

Most of the companies involved in electronics assembly in California are fairly small. During 1977, only 408 out of 1,175 firms employed more than twenty workers. In Silicon Valley (San Jose), however, 8 percent of the companies (or 38 firms) employed more than five-hundred workers each. In 1979, these 38 firms employed 75 percent of the total local electronics workforce. According to 1984 figures, approximately half of the high-tech manufacturing firms in Silicon Valley had fewer than ten employees and more than one-fifth of these firms had fewer than five employees. More recent figures indicate that more than two-thirds of Silicon Valley firms have fewer than ten employees, while 85 percent of the firms employ fewer than fifty workers. For Southern California in 1989, the average size of the 196 assembly companies was 34.2 employees, with the median number of employees per firm being 15.[18]

There is a two-tier occupational structure that operates in Silicon Valley's electronic assembly firms. Howard argues that the high-tech workforce in Silicon Valley "is economically and sociologically the most *divided* in American industry today." The elite portion is composed of the highly paid engineers and computer scientists who reside in the North County communities of Palo Alto, Mountain View, Sunnyvale, and Cupertino. In 1980, the median family income in these communities was $48,000. The other half of Silicon Valley's workforce, the production workers, live in the South County communities of San Jose and the city's suburbs of Milpitas and Gilroy. The median family income in these communities was between 40 and 48 percent of that in North County in 1980, with that of San Jose ($22,886) registering slightly higher than that of Gilroy ($19,139).[19]

Figures from the 1990 census indicate that there is still a substantial income disparity between the North County and the South County communities although this difference has narrowed since 1980. For example, the North County communities (Palo Alto, Mountain View, Sunnyvale, Cupertino) had an average per capita income of $26,588 and the South County communities (San Jose, Milpitas, Gilroy) had an average per capita income of $16,222, an income of only 61 percent of the richer North County communities. However, if certain individual cities within the North and the South County communities are compared, the disparity is closer to the 1980 levels. For example, Palo Alto's per capita income was $32,489 while Gilroy's per capita income was $14,241, or approximately 44 percent of Palo Alto's income.[20]

Lenny Siegel, whose Pacific Studies Center researches "the social impact" of high-tech industries, succinctly summarizes these views concerning the economic division of Silicon Valley:

Silicon Valley is two worlds. There's the world of the Yuppie, the programmer, the manager—affluent people doing interesting things. The other world is the production worker—mostly women, half of them minorities, earning not much more than the minimum wage.[21]

Wage rates for production workers in the electronics assembly industry have been notoriously low. According to the 1977 national figures,
assembly workers averaged $4.08 per hour, with a range of $3.90 (unskilled) to $4.53 (skilled). In 1984 and 1985, the starting wage of assem-
bly workers in Silicon Valley was $4.50 per hour. Production workers in
electronics assembly were making approximately 15 percent less than
comparable workers in other industries while average hourly wages were
approximately $2 to $5 less than the wages of workers in comparable
unionized jobs. Figures from 1995 indicate that unskilled electronic assemblers in Silicon Valley were earning between $5.00 and $7.00 per hour
with a median wage of $6.55 per hour.[22]

These low wage levels are due, in part, to two reasons—the threat of
capital mobility and the extremely low levels of unionization in the electronics industry. Since the production process involved in much of the
work of high-tech companies can be fragmented into standardized tasks
that require little skill to adequately perform, firms can move certain parts
of the production process to geographic areas where labor costs are
cheaper. Much of the time, this production work is sent overseas.[23]

Concerning the union density of high-tech firms, by 1982, an American Electronics Association (AEA) survey indicated that of its 1,900 member companies, only 90 had collective bargaining agreements with unions.
This survey also indicated that union contracts did not necessarily exist
at only the larger firms in the industry. The survey also inquired about the
extent of union organizing activity at these firms between 1971 and 1982.
These companies reported that there were fewer than one-hundred National Labor Relations Board (NLRB) elections held during this time period and that unions won only twenty-one of these representation
elections. During the last five years of this period, from 1977 to 1982, the
AEA survey indicated that the unions won only seven of thirty-seven NLRB
elections at member firms across the United States. This union victory rate
of 21 percent from 1971 to 1982 is considerably lower than the overall
yearly union certification election success rates, which gradually declined
from 55.1 percent in 1971 to 44.9 percent in 1982.[24]

Unionization figures from Silicon Valley are generally consistent with
the AEA survey figure. Although Sawyer states that none of the 1,500 firms
involved in either manufacturing or research and development in Silicon
Valley are unionized, this appears to be an unrealistically low figure in-

consistent with two academic studies. One study estimated that 5 percent of electronics workers were organized into unions in Silicon Valley while another study noted that less than 6 percent of production workers in Silicon Valley were represented by unions.[25]

The jobs in Silicon Valley are largely segregated by race and gender. White men in Silicon Valley occupy the engineering and managerial positions that hold the greatest power and have the highest incomes. Keller reports that approximately 83 percent of all professional workers and technicians employed in Silicon Valley semiconductor companies are Anglo-American males. Nonwhite men, composed largely of Third World immigrants and African Americans, occupy the next rung on the wage structure, with minority women (mostly Third World immigrant) holding the least skilled and lowest paid jobs in the industry. In addition, according to Keller, half of all unskilled production workers in Silicon Valley electronics firms are minority women. However, Hossfeld claims that this figure is probably closer to 80 percent.[26]

As can be seen from the preceding comments, the Silicon Valley electronics assembly industry depends heavily on women, a large segment of them from the Third World. It is estimated that 70,000 women comprise the bulk of the production workers in Silicon Valley with the lowest skilled operative and laborer jobs on the shop floor composed of between 80 and 90 percent women. Of this group of production workers, 45 to 50 percent are Third World women, many of whom are Asian immigrants to the United States.[27]

However, this dependence on women production workers is not a phenomenon limited only to the Silicon Valley electronics plants, but to the U.S. and the global electronics industry as a whole. According to Snow, as electronics production jobs have moved overseas, the proportion of minorities in the domestic electronics industry has increased although there has been a slight drop in the percentage of women workers in the industry. Despite this decrease, Green reports that 76 percent of all electronics operatives are women.[28]

Why are there so many women production workers in the electronics industry? From an economic perspective, the "labor-intensive" production jobs of many high-tech companies display what Colclough and Tolbert refer to as the "classic characteristics of secondary labor market jobs—low skill, low wages, few benefits, little job security, and limited opportunities for mobility."[29] Women have traditionally been employed in these secondary labor market jobs and, increasingly, this is also becoming true of both racial and ethnic minorities.

High-tech employers offer a different reason for their overdependence on women as electronics production workers. Based on a sexual stereotype of women as production workers, these employers claim that women are more patient, and have better eye-hand coordination and manual dexterity than men.[30] When discussing why women are more suited for performing repetitive assembly and inspection tasks in a high-tech factory, one employer stated:

> You couldn't get a man to stare into a microscope for eight hours a day and do this. They just wouldn't, but the women do it very well. It's not sexual discrimination but physiological and psychological advantages that women have in this work.[31]

In order to summarize the discussion up to this point, it appears that the "average" high-tech production worker is a minority man or woman, works for a small firm, is poorly paid and lacks union representation. As will be illustrated in my industrial ethnography of working as a production worker in the medical electronics industry during 1982–83, the demographic characteristics of the medical electronics plant at which I worked were strikingly similar to those of the California/Silicon Valley electronics production industry.

THE ORGANIZATION OF PRODUCTION WORK IN HIGH-TECH FIRMS

There are a number of studies that examine certain aspects of how production work is organized and how workers are controlled within high-tech firms. According to Colclough and Tolbert, the organization of production work in many high-tech firms is based on management's inherent distrust of the workers. This distrust is reflected in management's attempt to deskill the workers, to replace, and then ultimately to control them on the shop floor. This strong managerial control is manifested through a top-down hierarchy of authority where management is fundamentally responsible for deciding policies that the workers are then required to carry out.[32]

The research that has been done on the work organization of high-tech industries indicates that new managerial strategies have not been developed but rather that managerial strategies from the more traditional industrial sectors have been applied to these industries. Colclough and Tolbert found that in spite of the fact that high-tech industries utilize complex production processes and technologies, the production process is still organized according to scientific management (or Taylorism which is the process of breaking a job into its component parts in order to devise a method for performing the job more efficiently), where planning is separated from execution and the production process is fragmented and routinized. According to these researchers, this organization of the labor process, along the principles of Taylorism allows managers to deskill the workforce, pay the workers extremely low wages, and make the workers easily replaceable. Since high-tech firms desire maximum flexibility in terms of laying off production workers, once these employees are made replaceable, this goal can be easily accomplished.[33]

Mohseni's findings concur with those of Colclough and Tolbert. He argues that production workers in high-tech firms are controlled through Taylorist and Fordist principles while scientists and engineers in the industry are controlled through variations of post-Fordism that emphasize both teamwork and decentralization in the organization of this type of knowledge work.[34]

Consistent with the use of Taylorism is the finding that management practices in high-tech firms are based on bureaucratic rules and procedures combined "with close supervision of production workers." In addition, productivity is viewed in terms of an individual worker's performance, and time and motion studies, a major component of scientific management, are used for measuring an individual's productivity.[35]

In addition to tight managerial control on the shop floor, Hodson discovered the presence of managerial incompetence in high-tech firms. He found that high-tech managers often lack human relations skills and that their managerial styles are more authoritarian and less professional than those of managers in other industries. Not surprisingly, production workers surveyed in Hodson's study viewed this managerial incompetence as a major reason for their work dissatisfaction.[36]

However, in the unionized high-tech companies that Hodson studied, he found that the workers still complained about managerial incompetence although their concern was somewhat attenuated. Although they did not display confidence in management practices, the unionized workers "did not feel as individually vulnerable" to management's actions, largely due to the grievance procedure. The grievance process, which was able to protect the workers from the worst abuses of management behavior, was the reason for the reduction in the workers' resentment. They did not feel as much fear and anger over what they often viewed as arbitrary and capricious behavior on the part of management.[37]

A PRIMARY MANAGEMENT CONTROL STRATEGY: UNION AVOIDANCE

Because of the nature of managerial control of the shop floor and the fear that unions, with their contractual clauses concerning working conditions and their threat of strikes, will undermine this control, it is not surprising that high-tech industry is one of the most union-resistant sectors of the U.S. economy. High-tech firms have opposed unionization *even more vigorously* than have other industries. Based on this fact, it is not surprising that, in recent years, there have been no successful votes in favor of unionization among the workers at any Silicon Valley electronics production firm although a number of certification elections have been held. Managers at Silicon Valley production firms have harassed, fired, and blacklisted a large number of union activists and supporters in an attempt to curtail union organizing activity. A detailed account of union organizing drives conducted by the United Electrical Workers (UE) between 1971 and 1984 involving workers at more than ten Silicon Valley firms indicates that most of the UE campaigns never were able to obtain an NLRB election because of employer behavior that involved "intensive surveillance, threats, discriminatory discharges, and other illegal employer conduct."[38]

Concerning specific situations in these UE organizing drives, in 1973 the workers at Tomco voted 24 to 1 in an NLRB election to join the UE. After two months of negotiating a contract with the union, the company locked out its employees and then closed down its facility. At Siltec, a majority of the 160 employees signed union authorization cards but the organizing campaign was irreparably harmed when the company fired fifteen union activists.[39]

In addition, there are incidents of termination during organizing drives in high-tech industries even for minimal union activity. Rogers and Larsen report that a pro-union employee who distributed union literature to her coworkers was immediately fired on trumped-up charges. In another incident, they also point out that a Filipino employee who worked at Fairchild Semiconductor Corporation in Santa Clara County "had been fired for reading a union leaflet, printed in English, to a Tagalog-speaking" employee, who also was promptly discharged.[40]

Goss reports of a woman who worked at Digital's Roxbury plant in Boston who was fired in 1983 when she wrote a lead article in the newsletter of the High Tech Network (HTN) and then "discreetly distributed" the newsletter to ten coworkers. The HTN was an informal group of Boston-area workers organized by the Communication Workers of America (CWA) and three other major unions that was involved in publishing a newsletter and sponsoring workshops about working conditions in their companies. The article that led to the firing concerned President Reagan's visit to the Roxbury plant in 1983 and criticized his administration's affirmative action policies.[41]

In an attempt to understand the low success rate of unionization in high-tech firms, Robinson and McIlwee studied two high-tech manufacturing companies located in the Sunbelt. Although over half of the workers interviewed stated that they would vote for a union if an election was held, the researchers felt that a successful unionization drive was unlikely because of the managerial control strategies employed. The shop floor was run in a very bureaucratic manner, based on using punishment (frequently discharge) as a managerial control strategy. In addition, the workers were closely supervised and management played on their high levels of fear about their job security. Among the largely female and Latino workforce, there were many employees who had "intermittent work histories," as well as "extended periods of unemployment" or other time absent from the labor force.[42]

Mike Eisenscher, a former UE organizer who spent ten years during the 1970s and 1980s trying to unionize high-tech workers in Silicon Valley, argues that the organization of high-tech production work provides an additional obstacle to unionization of the industry by isolating and separating workers from one another. He states:

> Unlike auto factories, steel mills, and other basic manufacturing facilities, semiconductor and computer manufacturing plants generally do not have large numbers of employees performing functions on an integrated assembly line or manufacturing process.[43]

13

According to Early and Wilson, high-tech work is performed in small groups within departments that have between six and thirty workers. In addition, these jobs are highly compartmentalized and closely monitored by supervisors, with the ratio of supervisors to employees on the order of one to five or ten. In the individual manufacturing facilities, there is little opportunity for workers to have prolonged contact with other workers outside their own group.[44]

Finally, the instability of high-tech industries might also be a contributing factor in the difficulty confronting employees who want to unionize. High-tech firms appear to be extremely vulnerable to economic and environmental uncertainty and "the normal condition of high-tech firms" is "one of chronic upheaval related to *constant restructuring*, shifting job demands, and cycles of growth and decline." In addition, high-tech firms are characterized by a constant capital (machinery, tools and plant equipment) which is lightweight and mobile and a low capital/labor ratio, which necessitates that "the organization of labor be based on temporary hiring and maximum flexibility in conditions of work."[45] Therefore, such industry characteristics make it easy for many high-tech companies to shut down their operations and move to other locations whenever product demand declines.

PROMOTIONAL OPPORTUNITIES IN HIGH-TECH PRODUCTION WORK

In addition to having to cope with a harsh workplace environment, high-tech production workers have few opportunities for being promoted off of the shop floor. Historically, women workers occupying either professional or technical positions in electronics firms were vastly underrepresented based on their numbers in the industry. For example, in electronics firms in Silicon Valley from 1950 to 1970, Keller reports that women professional and technical workers increased their percentage of total employment from only 0.9 to 4.0 percent.[46]

Hodson states that advancement opportunities for production workers are rather limited. Green argues that for women production workers, there is limited opportunity for promotion to a higher-paying technician's job. Although the women electronics assemblers interviewed by Green had aspirations for advancement within the firm, a minimum of a two-year college degree with an emphasis in mathematics, physics and electronics was required and most often used as a screening device by the companies.

However, most of these women did not have the necessary time and resources for obtaining these degrees. Hodson found that when there were mobility opportunities for women production workers in high-tech firms, the mobility was in a lateral direction, within their own companies or between companies in search of "10 to 15 percent hour wage differentials," rather than in an upward direction.[47]

A NEW KIND OF FACTORY WORK OF THE FUTURE?

If one considers the combination of the previously discussed working conditions for high-tech production workers, the late twentieth-century high-tech workplace hardly appears to be one where empowered, highly paid, and independent employees find self-fulfillment in their work. In fact, these new "high-tech regimes" may be characterized by just the opposite: a workplace where the decentering of both "work" and "skill" has occurred and where "knowledge" becomes central for only a tiny part of the workforce.[48] In addition, although the public might be led to believe that high-tech production workers have better working conditions than manufacturing workers laboring in the hot, dirty, and dangerous factories of basic industry, this is hardly the case. In reality, the high-tech workplace is much more similar to the sweatshops of the late nineteenth- and early twentieth-century industrial America, where poorly paid production workers toiled in the shadows of brutal foremen without the benefits of union protection. Instead of approaching the dawn of a new and exciting workplace of the future, for most production workers laboring in high-tech firms, the working conditions indicate that these firms are marching boldly back to the past. In comparison to these working conditions, the unionized automobile and steel plants of the mid-twentieth-century offer a *progressive* alternative to the high-tech factories of late twentieth-century America.

Consider this description of Marie Van Vorst's work (in her own words) in a pickle factory in Pittsburgh at the turn of the twentieth century:

My hands are stiff, my thumbs almost blistered. . . . Cases are emptied and refilled; bottles are labeled, stamped and rolled away . . . and still there are more cases, more jars, more bottles. Oh! the monotony of it! . . . Now and then someone cuts a finger or runs a splinter under the flesh . . . and still the work goes on. Once I pause an instant, my head dazed and weary . . .

Quickly a voice whispers in my ear: "You'd better not stand there doin' nothin'. If she catches you she'll give it to you."[49]

Except for the different industry involved, this description of the work process easily could have been made by myself when describing how I felt while working as a production worker at the medical electronics plant during 1982–83.

As I mentioned in the preface, the industrial ethnography that follows is the story of my work in and attempts to organize a small medical electronics factory in the metropolitan Chicago area in 1982–83. While the metropolitan Chicago area is not widely viewed as a high-tech center, in terms of absolute numbers of high-tech jobs as well as manufacturing plants, the Chicago Standard Metropolitan Statistical Area (SMSA) ranked second in both categories to the Los Angeles–Long Beach, California SMSA in 1977. In addition, the manufacturing of medical instruments and supplies is one of the fastest growing high-tech industries. The employment of 244,000 workers in this industry in 1990 is predicted to grow to between 300,000 and 356,000 workers by 2005, an increase of between 22.8 and 46.0 percent.[50]

Although there have been a number of industrial ethnographies written about factory work in the United States, this is the first one to discuss what it was like to work in a small, nonunion high-tech factory as an unskilled production worker. As will become apparent from my discussion of this industrial establishment, this factory is not an aberration but is typical of the high-tech manufacturing firms described in the small, but growing, research literature.

An early reviewer of a preliminary draft of this manuscript stated, in part, "the story he tells is one of conflict and backbiting among the underclass, of racial and ethnic divisions and the general perversity of small gauge individuals. I found the account both revealing and depressing, the latter because the author encountered so little that was uplifting." But this story should not be interpreted as merely what happens when sadistic, cruel, and petty-minded line foremen and production and plant managers are given control of a small factory where a largely minority workforce engaged in production work within the secondary labor market experiences the brunt of management's whims. Rather, it is the story of managerial decision-making and the control of production workers in high-tech companies, which is *structural* in nature and endemic to many high-tech manufacturing concerns. My story is not unique and my experiences and feelings have probably been shared by thousands of high-tech assembly workers in the United States, whether they have labored in factories in Silicon Valley, along Boston's Route 128, in North Carolina's "Research Triangle," in Texas' "Silicon Prairie," in Colorado's "Silicon Mountain," or in Oregon's "Silicon Forest."

2.

A Brief Corporate History of Biomed

IN THE EARLY 1950S, DR. PAUL ZOLL OF THE HARVARD MEDICAL SCHOOL WAS the first person to successfully perform ventricular defibrillation by means of external countershock. In addition, in 1956 Zoll reported on his pioneering work with an artificial "Pacemaker." This "Pacemaker" was a small electronic device attached to heart patients' skin which provided the required pacemaking electrical signals for abnormal hearts.[1] Due to the work of Zoll and other investigators, within a decade defibrillators had become commercially available and were commonly utilized throughout the United States.

By the late 1970s, the defibrillation procedure was still very similar to what it had been in the late 1950s: two metal electrodes or paddles were placed on the patient's chest and a countershock was administered through these paddles in an attempt to defibrillate the victim's heart. Although the machines used in this procedure were much smaller due to technological advances, the basic process was substantially the same as that performed nearly two decades previous.

THE BIRTH OF BIOMED: THE LATE 1970S

In the late 1970s, Robert Leon Herman, a self-taught biomedical engineer in his mid twenties, concluded that the current method of defibrillation was not as efficient or efficacious as it might otherwise be. Based on this conclusion, he immediately established the Biomedical Electronics Corporation (Biomed) in order to design, manufacture, and market a new defibrillation system.

Described by people in the medical community as a "bona fide genius" in the area of physiological interface with electronic equipment, Herman attended engineering school at a large midwestern state university for one year. Upon leaving school, Herman worked for a small medical electronics manufacturer located in the metropolitan Chicago area for several years, primarily in the area of sales and service although his last position with the company was as director of biomedical engineering. Upon the formation of Biomed, one of the leading pacemaker cardiologists in the world had strong praise for Herman and his abilities:

> I thought I was aware of the problems presently facing cardiologists and the potential solutions to those problems but Robert really buried me. Not only am I impressed with his existing product development, but I am tremendously excited about the products he will develop and the problems he will help solve in the future.

In addition to being chairman of the board of Biomed, Herman was also the largest single stockholder of the privately owned firm, as well as being the director of research and development and technical services. In this last capacity, he was the designer and inventor of the company's products.

Shortly after Biomed's formation, a number of national hospital supply distributors expressed strong interest in distributing Biomed's products throughout the United States. A division of a leading pharmaceutical manufacturer studied Biomed for six months and projected sales volume of $100 million within a five-year period and pretax profits between $125 and $250 million over an initial ten-year period. These figures were based on the assumption that this division would distribute Biomed's products through a national sales force to be created by them. However, Herman did not feel that this distribution arrangement was advantageous to himself so he suspended discussions and decided to raise private capital to exploit the market potential for Biomed's products.

In order to raise start-up capital, a Chicago area venture capital firm was retained in an effort to develop a sufficient funding plan. Venture capital can be defined as "money placed in new or young high-technology companies with a high potential for growth,"[2] and the expansion of venture capital firms has been intricately connected with the growth of high-tech industries.[3] This venture capital firm put together an initial package that included more than $250,000 of private capital along with a Small Business Administration Loan of approximately $500,000. However, with this financial package, the venture capital firm insisted on the addition of a new chief executive officer (CEO), Mr. Harry Williams.

In addition to becoming CEO, Williams also became president of the new corporation. Prior to his involvement with Biomed, Williams had served as executive vice president of a major producer and distributor of specialty frozen foods that had annual sales of $150 million. In addition, he had also served for a number of years as executive vice president of a large producer and distributor of food and chemical products. Besides holding an undergraduate degree in business administration from a private midwestern university, Williams had earned an MBA degree from the University of Chicago Graduate School of Business.

In the first eight months of Biomed's existence, a series of start-up problems affected the company's overall performance. Specifically, late deliveries of essential materials (cables necessary for production were delayed four months) and supplier errors (product not up to specification was delivered and months were spent correcting these parts) hampered the corporation's initial plans. In addition, another major problem involved the training of a knowledgeable sales force for Biomed's products. Since there were no sales personnel who were trained to sell and service this new cardiac care system (such sales personnel needed to be qualified in *all* areas of emergency medicine, anesthesiology, the cardiovascular disciplines and surgical procedures), a sales force had to be assembled using only Biomed's resources. These problems led to a delay in repeat orders and exerted serious financial pressure on the company's working capital.

These problems, taken together, resulted in the need for a private placement, the selling of shares of private stock to raise capital, which generated approximately $1.5 million for the company. This offering was oversubscribed, that is, demand for the private stock exceeded supply, largely due to individuals who had had experience working with Biomed's products, such as medical doctors, paramedical personnel, sales representatives and others associated with the hospital supply industry.

With this infusion of capital, major production (as well as other) problems were ironed out and Biomed was able to embark on a period of rapid growth. By the early 1980s, Biomed had in excess of three-hundred customers (fire departments, ambulances, paramedics, and hospitals) and was adding to this total weekly because of the hundreds of conversion cables that were being shipped to new customers. At this time, Biomed was also expanding into foreign markets. The company had received solicitation of its account from twenty-three foreign countries that were suitable for export of Biomed's products and had begun to screen potential foreign distributors. In addition, an arrangement had been made with a large Swedish medical distributor to represent Biomed in the Scandinavian countries. Summing up Biomed's future prospects, two senior medical industry analysts commented to Herman at an American Heart Association symposium, "If you screw it up, you'll still be $30,000,000 in two years."

Because of the company's rapid growth and success in the marketplace, it was decided late in 1982 that a public offering should be underwritten. With sales for fiscal 1984 projected to be $9 million, Biomed felt that the time was ripe for maximizing its growth through controlled financing. Plans were established that set 1 May 1983 as the latest date at which this underwriting would be completed. However, due to a minor sales downturn, the investment firm that was supposed to underwrite Biomed's public offering withdrew their services in early May. After this withdrawal, Biomed was forced to make other plans in an attempt to complete the underwriting of this public offering for late in 1983. However, this second attempt was also not successful and Biomed did not become a publicly traded company until the early 1990s.

THE MANAGEMENT TEAM: OFFICERS AND DIRECTORS

Besides Herman and Williams, there were five other officers and directors in the early 1980s who provided leadership for Biomed—Albert Coolidge, Edward Killingsworth, Matt Ordway, Gary Wilson, and Robin Sexton. Although the occupations and interests of these officers and directors might seem heterogeneous at first, these people (except for Sexton) were extremely homogenous in terms of their undergraduate and graduate educations, which took place at elite private and public universities.

The secretary, as well as a director, of Biomed was Albert Coolidge. He was a member of a Chicago area law firm who held an undergraduate degree in economics from Harvard University and a J.D. degree from a prestigious midwestern law school. Edward Killingsworth was a director of Biomed and was also a professor of policy studies at a Chicago metropolitan area university. In addition to being a psychologist in private practice, Killingsworth had also served as vice president, and later as president, of a consulting firm that provided psychological services in the workplace. He held an A.B. degree in psychology from Harvard University as well as a Ph.D. degree in psychology from an elite private midwestern university.

Matt Ordway was the only M.D. who was serving as a director of Biomed. At the time, he was working as a director of emergency services at a hospital in a small midwestern city as well as being an assistant professor of emergency medicine and internal medicine at the public university's medical school located in that city. Prior to accepting this position, Ordway had worked as an associate director and education director of emergency medical services at a Chicago area hospital and had been a faculty member in internal medicine at a Chicago-area medical school. Gary Wilson was another of the company's directors who was also a partner in a Chicago area law firm. Biomed utilized his firm for their legal services. He held an undergraduate degree from Yale University and a J.D. degree from an elite eastern law school.

Robin Sexton was the vice president, treasurer and assistant secretary of Biomed although she was not a director. Besides Herman, she was the only officer who did not have a college degree. She had become the secretary of the company shortly after its formation and was, at the time, Herman's girlfriend. Prior to her employment with Biomed, Sexton worked as a credit and collections supervisor for a major electronics manufacturer and as a national credit administrator at another smaller firm. She had attended a technical/vocational school for one year in a small city in Wisconsin.

OTHER MANAGEMENT TEAM MEMBERS: OFFICE AND PLANT PERSONNEL

In addition to the officers and directors, by the early 1980s Biomed had hired four other management personnel to run the daily operations of the firm. In the front office, a national sales manager was hired to recruit, train, and supervise the sales force while an office manager was responsible for handling order entry, accounting, invoicing, payables, and administrative procedure. Two additional managers were hired to oversee factory production. A production supervisor for the disposable electrodes was responsible for installing manufacturing equipment as well as for supervising the efficient hand production of the product by the unskilled workers. Finally, a production supervisor for permanent adapter cables was responsible for hiring, training, and supervising the skilled technicians in the assembly of the Biomed adapter cables.

The advisory boards were established within a few years of the formation of Biomed to assist the Board of Directors and the management of the company by providing professional assistance to the company in terms of evaluating the firm's products, product testing results, and product literature. The first of these advisory boards was specifically responsible for analyzing Biomed's current products by offering suggestions for how to properly evaluate them. The second advisory board was responsible for helping Biomed in its research and development program on developing an external pacemaker. Specifically, this board was asked to provide professional input into the testing and evaluation of this new device. Both boards were composed of medical doctors, biomedical engineers, and paramedics—professionals who were likely to have knowledge of the operation of the products in a clinical setting.

CHANGES IN BIOMED: THE LATE 1980S AND 1990S

Biomed's sales did not expand as rapidly as the company projected in the early to mid 1980s. By the late 1980s, Biomed had become the Critical Care Products Division of a larger firm in the industry. Biomed severed its relationship with this parent corporation in the early 1990s, reorganized itself, and completed an initial public offering of the company's common stock shortly thereafter.

Throughout the late 1980s and the early 1990s, Biomed continued to steadily increase both its sales and its profit margins. By the early 1990s, the company's electrode pads, cables, and adapters were incorporated into almost 50 percent of the defibrillators purchased each year. Biomed had also negotiated licensing and Original Equipment Manufacturer contracts with approximately twenty defibrillator manufacturers in the United States and Europe, including agreements with six of the top ten defibrillator manufacturers worldwide. In the Pacific Rim, the company continued to penetrate the Japanese market through a licensing agreement with Japan's largest defibrillator manufacturer. By the mid-1990s, it was reported that the company's sales were in the five to ten million dollar range. After the company went public, Biomed's strategy was to increase growth through acquisition and building strategic alliances with other medical equipment manufacturers' distributors. Based on this strategy, Biomed reached an agreement on a joint venture with a small surgical and medical instruments manufacturer to manage the clinical research and marketing of its cutting-edge technological products on an exclusive basis in both the United States and Canada. Another strategic partnership was reached with a medical research firm for penetrating the advanced life support prehospital defibrillator market.

In terms of acquisitions, approximately one year after Biomed went public, the company announced that it had reached an agreement in principle to acquire one of the largest medical equipment manufacturers/distributors of products in the prehospital market. However, several months later, Biomed announced that it had ended negotiations to acquire this company.

Once these negotiations had ended, a smaller medical electronics manufacturer that competed directly with Biomed in certain market segments offered to acquire Biomed. The company responded that Biomed's board was prepared to consider any equitable offer for the firm but that it was not up for sale. Biomed then rejected the above company's offer as inadequate. Nevertheless, Biomed was advised by its investment firm that this smaller manufacturer had purchased more than 5 percent of Biomed's stock as part of its attempt to purchase the company.

At the time of Biomed's reorganization in the early 1990s, none of the original officers or directors of the company remained. However, Liz Bordman, a line foreman who had supervised the snap-type electrode department in the early 1980s, had been promoted to the position of the company's purchasing agent.

With the company poised to achieve even greater growth, sales, and profits in the mid to late 1990s, Biomed's current president and CEO stated, "Of course, beyond the immediate criteria we use to guide our company's future is an overriding corporate mission to help save lives. This company is succeeding in its mission."

3.

Searching for and Beginning Work at a Factory Job

THE ADVERTISEMENT IN THE "HELP WANTED" SECTION OF THE THURSDAY EDI-tion of the newspaper read: "Light Assembly. Fast growing company seeks day help. Starting salary $3.50. Call 538-7214." I had not seen many job advertisements for unskilled labor during the last few months (with the unemployment rate steadily rising, to a national level of 10.4 percent and a statewide mark of 12.5 percent), so the advertisement naturally attracted my attention. When I read the notice, I was taking a break from my part-time job as a security guard, so I decided that I would call the first thing the following morning to find out more about the job.

Finding a factory job in this economic "recession" appeared to be a rather formidable task. I had never applied for such work before, so the job hunting process was rather intimidating.

I had been lucky enough to find two part-time jobs a couple of months earlier. One job was as a security guard at an art museum and the other job was as a general factory worker at a small, family-run bindery. I usu-ally worked between twelve and twenty hours a week at the art museum but my hours at the bindery varied considerably. Some weeks I would work over thirty hours, while other weeks I would not be called in at all. The last time I had worked at the bindery had been two days before Thanks-giving of 1982. I was not called back after that.

I was beginning to think that I would never land a full-time factory job. I became increasingly discouraged each week when I read of more factories laying off workers or permanently closing their doors. The people

I contacted at the few jobs for which I was able to apply always promised that I would be called back for an interview or told me that I "had a real good chance of getting the job." I was never called back for any interviews and if I "had a real good chance of getting the job," it was never apparent to me.

With the unemployment rate hovering around 12.5 percent for the Chicago metropolitan area, my prospects seemed grim. I had given serious thought to a friend's invitation to live in his block house in a blue-collar section of Baltimore while looking for a job in the area. I was not sure, however, that I would have any better luck in another heavily industrialized region. I decided to continue looking in the Chicago area at least through Christmas. If nothing turned up by the start of the new year, I would consider my friend's generous invitation.

I had even called an employment agency out of desperation. The woman I talked to first asked me about my educational background and then inquired, "Do you like to talk to people?" I sensed that the conversation was not proceeding in a desired direction. "I'm interested in factory work," I stated bluntly. "I work part-time in a bindery."

I then asked her to explain the procedure used by this particular employment agency. "You come down, fill out an application, and pay a $70 fee," she said matter-of-factly. "And you promise each applicant a job?," I asked hopefully. "Oh, no," she continued. "We'll try to find a job that is suitable for you."

I pressed on. "All I have to pay is $70?" "If you accept a job that we find for you," she replied, "you'll have to pay us a certain percentage of your wages."

"How much will I have to pay?"

"That depends on how much you make."

"Let's say that I make the minimum wage."

"Oh, it will be a small amount. I'm not sure exactly how much it will be."

"And how long do I have to pay this small amount? Forever?"

"Nothing lasts forever," she replied. "Look, I can't answer any more questions. If you are interested, you will have to come down to the office to fill out an application."

I thanked her for both the information and her time. I immediately ruled out the use of an employment agency for finding a factory job.

Early Friday morning, I called up the company to learn more about the light assembly positions. "The hours are 8:00 A.M. to 4:00 P.M. and the starting wage is $3.50 per hour," the secretary said. "We manufacture medical supplies here. If you are interested in the job, you should come down and fill out an application and somebody will show you around the place."

After a quick breakfast, I was on my way. I caught a bus at 8:50, transferred to the "El," and boarded another bus which dropped me right in front of the factory. I had a strange feeling that I would arrive at the factory and be told, "I'm sorry. We have filled all the positions. However, if you would like to leave your name and phone number, we'll give you a call if anything opens up."

As soon as I got off the bus, I ran to the factory's front door. It was unseasonably warm for early December (the temperature was in the low 60s) and I was dripping with sweat by the time I arrived at 9:45. I checked the address. There were three large metallic letters—BEC—on the wall next to the door. This was the place.

After entering the front door, I rang a buzzer next to a locked glass door that separated the offices from the reception room. The receptionist came to the door and handed me an application. I was relieved that they were still accepting applications. I took a seat next to two young AfricanAmerican women who were already working on their applications.

The application was a standard form, which I had filled out a month earlier when I had applied for an entry-level printing trainee position. After filling out the "personal information" section (name, address, phone number), I proceeded to the "employment desired" section. For position, I wrote in "Light Assembly" and for salary desired, "$3.50/hour." The next section was the education section, and it was in this portion of the application that I first wrote in falsified information. I stated that after graduating from a local suburban high school, I had attended a state university for two years, studying liberal arts. I knew that listing my true educational background—a bachelor's degree and a master's degree from a fairly prestigious private university, as well as an additional two years spent in a doctoral program—would have automatically disqualified me from consideration for unskilled factory work.

Before I had begun to apply for jobs, I had sought out the advice of a union organizer I had become acquainted with that summer and fall. When I asked her what I should put down on job applications regarding my educational background, she advised, "You want the company to think you are smart enough to do the job, but not too smart. It depends on the kind of job you are applying for. You might want to mention that you have spent some time in college, but then again you might not." I thought that two years in college along with a working-class job for the past five years was a good compromise and combination.

The union organizer also counseled, "You have to cover your time by finding a legitimate cover. If you know of someone who will say that you have worked for him, that would be perfect. If you were a woman you could simply say that you had a baby and were raising it. But if guys don't cover their time, employers may think that they have spent it behind bars."

I had already considered finding such a cover. While working on my doctorate, I had spent my last year at school living in a boardinghouse owned by a woman who ran a small construction company. I had become friendly with her and I knew that she was quite sympathetic to my politics. When I called her to ask if I could have a "job" with her company for the past five years, she was more than happy to comply.

Thus for the former employment portion of the application, I wrote that I had been a general laborer for this small construction company for the past few years, earning a salary of $4.00 per hour. When the application asked for my reason for leaving this job, I simply wrote: "Wanted to move to the Chicago area."

For my references, I listed my "former" employer, one of my high school coaches, and a political science professor with whom I had become friendly with several years previous through a summer job. Both of these friends were informed of my "background" and agreed to corroborate my story, should they be contacted.

The final part of the application asked about my physical record. I truthfully answered that I had no physical limitations to preclude me from any work for which I was being considered.

All that was left was the signing and dating of the following statement appearing at the bottom of the application. I signed it without any hesitation:

I certify that the facts contained in this application are true and complete to the best of my knowledge and understand that, if employed, falsified statements on this application will be grounds for dismissal.

I authorize investigation of all statements contained herein and the references listed above to give you any and all information concerning my previous employment and any pertinent information they may have, personal or otherwise, and release all parties from all liability for any damage that may result from furnishing to you.

I understand and agree that, if hired, my employment is for no definite period and may, regardless of the date of payment of my wages and salary, be terminated at any time without any prior notice.

After I had completed my application, I turned it in to the receptionist, who said, "Please wait here for an interview." I was surprised to hear this because the two African American women who had handed in their applications only a few minutes earlier had left without being given interviews. The only other person waiting for an interview was a young Latino man dressed in a suit who held a resume in his hand.

"Are you applying for the technician's job?," he asked me. "I'm applying for a light assembly job," I replied. To this he responded, "Well, you can consider it to be a technician's job." The young man informed me that he was a recent graduate of an electronics program at the DeVry Institute of Technology. I told him that I thought that he was overqualified for the job.

"What are they paying?" he asked me. "$3.50 an hour," I answered. "Geez, is that all? You'll probably get the job," he retorted. "I think there are a few positions open," I acknowledged. After this short exchange, I changed the subject.

"How's your job search going?" I inquired. "Well, I'm applying for a lot of jobs. I'm just not getting any of them," he replied. After this last comment, we both sat uneasily in our chairs, waiting for our interviews.

"Poor bastard," I thought. "He goes to school to get technical training and ends up applying for a job like this." It was not until several weeks later that I learned that there also had been a couple of electronic technician positions open that paid about $5.70 an hour. The young man I had talked to did not get one of these jobs.

While waiting for my interview, I tried to relax as I examined the walls of the reception area. An electrocardiogram (a record of the heart's action currents) was painted on the walls. In addition, there were several newspaper articles about the Biomedical Electronics Corporation (Biomed), as well as brochures advertising the company's products. I tried not to appear to be too interested in these items. Even though I realized that Biomed's products had something to do with the heart, I could not figure out exactly what these products were or their respective functions.

"Victor," a young woman said as she appeared at the door of the reception area, "I'm Liz, please come with me." Liz, a young white woman who appeared to be in her early to mid-twenties, was short and slender with dark black hair cut in a boyish style, led me through the office area to a door that opened up to a short corridor. At the end of the corridor was another door that led directly to the factory. As I entered the factory, I saw approximately fifty people engaged in various stages of assembly work. Even though this was my first time in such a factory, I tried not to express my amazement at the scene before me. I was desperately hoping that I would get this job!

Liz guided me toward a desk at the front of the factory. "Have a seat," she said. "Read these work rules." I read them rather rapidly. The rules seemed to be quite straightforward. Next, I was taken on a rather quick tour of the factory. "Are you working now?" Liz inquired. "Part-time at a bindery," I replied, omitting the fact that I was also working at the art museum.

"Here's where the wires are stripped," she said. The workers looked at us with indifference. "Assembly takes place here," Liz continued as we walked to another part of the factory. Continuing on our journey, we stopped to observe the gelling process. "This is where the gelling takes place. Mary is one of our top gellers," Liz said. Mary looked at us and smiled. "We like to have men do the gelling because it's hard on the arm." We walked to another table and watched an Asian-American man gel at what appeared to be a furious pace. He was forcing a clear, viscous substance into a green foam pad with a metal spatula.

When we returned to the office, Liz stated, "We're currently low on supplies, but we will definitely call you next week. If you don't hear from us, give us a call. You can have the job if you have nothing else going."

"I don't have anything else going," I replied. "I want the job."

As I left the building, I heard someone tell the receptionist to stop taking applications because they already had too many of them. It was 10:30 A.M. I was overjoyed. It appeared that I had obtained a factory job at last!

When Biomed did not call me by the middle of the following week, I decided to call the company. I was able to talk to Liz on the phone. "We haven't hired anybody yet because it has been a slow week," she said. "We're still waiting to receive some more supplies. We'll call you at the beginning of next week." I began to lose my initial optimism. Was the company just giving me a line? I remembered what I had been told in the past when I had filled out other job applications—"We'll call you for an interview," or, "We're very interested in you." I had a feeling that the same thing was happening again. I was becoming a bit skeptical about my chances of obtaining a factory job at Biomed.

Monday of the following week passed with no word from Biomed. Once more, I decided to call Liz. At about 11:00 on Tuesday morning, I called Biomed but this time I was prepared for bad news. While I was waiting to talk to Liz, another woman came on the phone and said, "Victor, this is Debbie. Come in tomorrow at 8:00 for gelling."

"Great," I replied. "Thank you!" A factory job had come through at last!

MY FIRST DAY AT BIOMED

I arrived at the factory at 7:40 on Wednesday morning. The plant was not open yet, and only one middle-aged woman worker, wearing glasses with thick lenses, was there when I arrived. I learned that her name was Sharon and that she was originally from Iraq. Sharon spoke a halting, broken English but was friendly nonetheless. "My first job in this country," she told me. "What kind of medical supplies does Biomed make?" I asked. Apparently, Sharon did not understand the question because she replied, "My job—gelling. Good job, not too hard." We walked to the back door of the factory but it was still not open.

The other workers began arriving at 7:50. Although many of them were talking to each other, few seemed in a good mood. The back door was unlocked a few minutes before 8:00.

Inside the factory, I met Steve, the plant manager, who handed me a time card and an income tax form to fill out. Steve had very straight brownish-blond hair that covered his forehead and went down to his shoulders. His mustache made him look quite sinister and he walked with a limp. Then Debbie, the line foreman of the gelling department, assigned me to work with Joe. Joe, a young white worker in his early twenties who had crooked teeth, was supposed to teach me how to gel. Art, the young Latino line foreman who was in charge of the packing/inspecting department, brought a box of twenty medical devices to me that were to be gelled. Each device had two circular pads, one larger than the other, with the green, circular foam in each pad surrounded by soft, white, synthetic material. There was a blue and white cable attached to each pad that converged into a plastic connector that contained the firm's name.

After Art assigned me to a work table, he gave me a metal spatula and a plastic container filled with gel. My table, like the other fifteen gelling tables, came equipped with a small maneuverable lamp. Joe explained the proper procedure for gelling while he demonstrated each step. Taped on the wall, behind my table, there was a sheet of instructions (which looked like it had been printed by a computer) that outlined the gelling process step by step. The sheet read:

Gelling Procedure

Defib and ESU

1. Make sure that the foam pad is clean.
2. Shake solution, lift foam pad and spray onto element. (Omit this step for ESU products.)
3. Saturate foam pad completely with gel, forcing the gel through the green foam and down to the element. Make certain that you can see the element when done.
4. Apply an even glaze of gel on the surface.
5. Remove any excess gel from the paper ring. Peel off ring and discard.
6. Apply formed liner and remove excess air without squeezing gel onto adhesive.

ECG Old Model

Same as the above, excluding steps 2 and 6.

Apply unformed liner treated side down.

Joe made gelling look so easy. After shaking the spray bottle of solution, he quickly squirted the solution between the foam pad and the tin element. Ever so precisely and deftly, he rubbed the gel into the foam pad until it was completely saturated. Then he placed a thin glaze of gel on top of the pad. Finally, he removed the paper ring from the pad and replaced it with a circular plastic cover.

"OK, you try it now," he said. When I tried to gel, I experienced many problems. I did not adequately saturate the foam pad with gel; I was slow and clumsy with the metal spatula. The spatula felt unnatural in my hand and the gelling motion felt awkward. I also had trouble removing the excess air bubbles from the gelled pad when I replaced the paper ring with the plastic lid. Much of the gel seemed to leave the foam pad and land on the adhesive. Joe was patient and sympathetic. "I understand," he said. "You've got the first-day-on-the-job blues."

I watched Sharon and an Indian woman gel their medical devices. They worked very quickly and efficiently, completing each one without expressing any emotion. They also made the gelling procedure look very easy.

Joe patiently checked each piece that I completed. He showed me where there were air bubbles and how to successfully remove them. As the morning progressed, he gave me more tips, which I greatly appreciated. I was very concerned about working so slowly but Joe told me not to worry about speed but to be concerned with performing the operation correctly. I was concentrating quite hard on learning this "skill."

Shortly after Joe had demonstrated the proper gelling procedure to me, I asked him, "What is this medical device called that we are working on?" "It's a TR60," he replied. "Not the model number," I said. "What's the device called?" Joe looked confused and repeated, "It's a TR60. What do you mean?" Art overheard our conversation and came over to my desk and handed me a short pamphlet that explained the instrument's uses and provided some information about the device.

I learned that the instrument was called a Biomed Disc Anterior Pad, and that it was used for defibrillation and electrosurgery. I wondered how many of the other workers knew the official names and the uses of the products that they were producing. It seemed likely that they were not provided with this information.

As the minutes of the morning ticked by, I was still gelling pitifully slowly. I was apprehensive and became depressed over my lack of speed and production quality. At times, it appeared that I had succeeded in getting more gel on my hand and the desk than on the green foam. It seemed that it would take me weeks to master this skill. I was beginning to become tired; my right arm grew heavy as time seemed to proceed at a snail's pace. Finally, it was 10:00. "Break time!," yelled Debbie, signaling the start of the fifteen-minute morning break.

I spent the break recovering from the first two hours of work. The only positive comment that could be made about gelling is that you can sit while doing it. I remained in my chair a few minutes and then I walked around the factory until the break was over.

After the break, I was still having trouble gelling. Joe continued to help me out, which was quite comforting. It was at this time that I noticed that

there were slips of paper taped to each gelling table, contained the following information:

Standard Average Gelling Times

TRO1, TR60	TR21, TR80	TW13, TW82	TW92	TR50 (old)
7.3 minutes	4.6 minutes	3.9 minutes	2.7 minutes	3.0 minutes

I was shocked to see this information. I was currently taking more than
twenty minutes to gel a TR60, approximately three times as long as the
listed standard average gelling time. I could not imagine myself ever gelling a TR60 in a little more than seven minutes.

Lunchtime, 12:00, rolled around and I learned of another of Biomed's
procedures. Twice a day, once before lunch and once at the end of the day,
each production worker was required to fill out a form known as the "Production Work Report." This slip of paper contained spaces where each
worker filled in his name, the date, the model number(s) he had worked
on, the process description (the production activity performed), the time
taken to perform the production activity, and the number of pieces assembled. There was also a space for "Other" but I never discovered the use
of this portion of the form. Joe instructed me how to fill out the production work report.

"For model, write TR60. For process description, write gelling. For time,
put 3:45 because you don't count the fifteen-minute break..." I inter-
rupted Joe, "But I only worked for 3:30. I didn't start until 8:15. I had to
fill out some forms." "Just put 3:45," he replied. "That's what you are supposed to put. And for assembly, write in the number you gelled." During
the morning I had gelled only nine TR60s, which I considered to be a
rather embarrassing total.

I ate my bag lunch in the small, cramped lunchroom. There were not
enough tables and chairs to accommodate all of Biomed's workers. The
majority of the young male workers adjourned to their cars in the employee parking lot to eat their lunches, smoke cigarettes, and listen to either their radios or tape decks. I was concerned with showing some
improvement in gelling after lunch.

After this brief recess, I became slightly better at gelling. I worked more
quickly and more efficiently. I still asked Joe to check each piece, which
he graciously did. At around 2:00, right before the fifteen minute afternoon break, I became quite tired, bored, and depressed. My upper back

started to hurt and I began to look forward to the end of the day. I stopped asking Joe to check my pieces and I attempted to handle my own production problems.

At this time, I was struck by the reality of the situation. I would be gelling TR60s or some other model for at least seven hours a day. I would be performing the same motions over and over. I would have to get used to the noxious feeling of the slimy gel against my hand. How would I feel about gelling in one week? Two weeks? Two months? The prospects that lay before me were not too encouraging.

At 3:00, Debbie went around and asked the gellers if they wanted to work an extra hour, until 5:00. I agreed to stay although Joe declined Debbie's offer. "I don't need the extra money," he said. All of a sudden, the day seemed to grow much longer.

During this extra hour of work, I ran out of disc anterior pads to gel so I got up from my chair to obtain another box of pieces, which was on a nearby table, only a few steps away. Debbie became upset and she asked rather indignantly, "Victor, what are you doing?" "I'm getting some more pieces," I replied. "A worker should never get pieces by himself because the plant manager will become upset," she continued. "If you need something, call Art and he will get it for you."

Debbie looked as authoritarian as she sounded. She was a heavyset woman in her late twenties, with a pudgy face and long brown hair, who always wore flannel shirts, bell-bottomed blue jeans, and work boots. She smoked quite heavily and her breath reflected that fact if you came within a couple of feet of her.

I was not very productive during the last hour. I gelled two TR60s. Sharon and the machinelike, Indian woman were still working at a furious pace. When 5:00 arrived, I had put in nearly eight hours of gelling. I was quite relieved to depart from the factory. My first day of work had finally ended.

MAKING SENSE OF FINDING A FACTORY JOB

Applying for unskilled factory work, not to mention landing such a position in tough economic times, is no easy task. If one is fortunate enough to arrive at a factory that has advertised openings in time to fill out an application, one's academic and occupational backgrounds cannot reveal too "skilled" a background if one wants to get the job. Even a couple of years of college might make a potential employee appear "overqualified" for the job. Employers may be worried that such "educated" workers will find the work too boring and monotonous. Thus, they are afraid that these workers will leave to find better work or to go back to school.

It appears that employers desire high school graduates because this indicates, at least, regular attendance and an ability to follow a daily schedule. Having a steady occupational background—one or two jobs that the worker has held for a number of years, no matter how menial the job—is another good sign because it indicates that the worker will stick with the job for a period of time. If the worker earned relatively low wages at these jobs, all the better.

Another factor that enters into obtaining unskilled factory work is luck. I feel that I was very lucky to be hired out of the mass of applicants. I am not sure how employers choose between equally qualified or equally unqualified candidates as the matter may be, unless they make their selections by some kind of gut reaction. If a worker with no "skills" has bad luck and cannot find work, his only option is to keep searching by pounding the pavement.

My experience of searching for factory work was similar to that of Pfeffer. Pfeffer, a political science professor at Johns Hopkins University who had taken a sabbatical to work in a factory in the Baltimore area in 1974–75, reports that he falsified his employment record by stating that after he had graduated from high school, he had worked for fifteen years as a grocery store delivery truck driver and then for five years as a general maintenance worker for a construction company. In addition, Pfeffer states that when he inquired about jobs on the phone, many employers seemed to be impressed with his "seeming steadiness when [he] told them [he] had worked on prior jobs for fifteen and five years respectively."[1]

His experience with the one employment agency that he had visited in Baltimore was similar to the limited contact that I had with the employment agency in Chicago. According to Pfeffer, the contract at the employment agency, which Pfeffer eventually signed in an attempt to find factory work, was "a form of extortion, a modern indenture."[2] The agreement called for the paying of a "permanent placement fee" of $300, to be paid over a fifteen-week period, deducted from the employee's weekly wages. However, if the employment was not "permanent," things became more complicated. Pfeffer points out:

In the event my employment was terminated within ninety days, however, I was obligated instead to pay a "temporary placement fee," the amount to be determined by how much I had earned and whether the termination was my fault. If I was terminated through no fault of my own, or if I voluntarily left the job with "just cause," that temporary fee was not to exceed 20 percent of my total wages received or 75 percent of $300, whichever was less. But if, as would be more likely, I was discharged "for cause" or left the job without "just cause" within ninety days, then I was liable for up to 75 percent of the permanent placement fee, for $225.[3]

As I did, Pfeffer also found that searching for a job "willy-nilly subjects all to an intimidating introduction to the facts of work life." As Pfeffer points out, job seekers for factory work have little control over what job they will actually get or in deciding where they want to work. Their only choice is to decide whether to accept or reject the job that is offered to them.[4]

4.

Adapting to High-Tech Factory Work

After my first day of gelling, I hoped that I would do better on my second day. At the start of the day, Sharon told me that she had never seen anyone gel so well on their first day. I knew that she was just being nice.

I devised a new strategy for gelling the TR60s. Instead of piling mounds of gel in the center of the pads and then attempting to rub it all in, I placed a small amount of gel on one area of the pads and then proceeded to rub the gel into only that area. I repeated this procedure until the whole foam pad was saturated with gel. This process seemed to be very effective and I felt that I was becoming more competent at gelling. I did not feel bored and the work felt easier than the day before.

I was very productive for the first hour after lunch. After that, I began to get very tired and my back began to ache terribly. I looked forward to the afternoon break. I also began to experience the monotony, drudgery, and sheer boredom of my job. I started to lose my concentration and I was concerned that I was becoming sloppy.

Art had not returned any incorrectly gelled TR60s to me so I reasoned that I must be doing a decent job of gelling. My optimism was short-lived because after the break Art showed me that I was not putting enough gel on the edges of the pads. This flustered me a bit, so I began to overgel the pads. I was trying to compensate for my previous undergelling. Later, Art showed me a TR60 that I had over-gelled.

Late in the afternoon, I became numb for awhile. My arm and back stopped hurting and I seemed to work instinctively while my mind wandered. I was not sure that my quality-level was high but I did not give a damn. I was positive that I would have a better day tomorrow.

As I left the factory, I began to wonder how long I would actually be able to tolerate these working conditions. My final production figures for the day showed an improvement from yesterday—twenty-two TR60s and thirteen TW13s.

My third day of gelling began with the completion of eight TR60s before Art brought over some ZB3s for me to rework. I thought that I must have been doing a decent job of gelling if I was asked to fix up another worker's pieces. The only problem was that I had not been shown how to correctly use the rework rings. I removed the paper from one of these rings and placed it on the adhesive surface of a ZB3 so that two adhesive surfaces were stuck together. I could not remove the rework ring once I had regelled the ZB3. I pointed this out to Art and he said that it would have to be thrown out. I did the same thing with another ZB3 (because I did not know any better), told Debbie about it, and she said, "You shouldn't be having this problem—paper shouldn't stick to this surface." She added rather disgustedly, "Stop doing this and continue with your other work."

Instead of continuing with TR60s, I was given ZB3s to gel. ZB3s had only one circular foam pad, which was the size of the smaller pad on the TR60, and they did not require the spraying of the solution. "ZB3s are easier to gel," said Sharon. I agreed. I felt more comfortable working with the smaller pads. It was a nice break from working on the TR60s.

The day was going rather well until Debbie returned a batch of TR60s to me after lunch. The TR60s that I had gelled in the morning had gel oozing out from under the plastic lids and onto the adhesive surface. Debbie instructed me to fix them up. I was rather concerned about this because I knew it would affect my daily production output. I scraped the gel off of the adhesive and I figured that the TR60s were now in suitable shape to pass inspection. I became a bit wary when I saw Kim, another inspector, reworking some of my ZB3s, which had been delivered by Art earlier that day.

After the afternoon break, the TR60s were returned to me once more. Art told me that they were overgelled and that he would get Joe, my former tutor, to help me out. Art said, "I think you're trying too hard. Just be concerned about doing a good job. I'm sure you can be taught to do this properly. Once you get the hang of it, you'll knock them off very quickly."

He continued, "Our duty is to the medical patients. We wouldn't want to produce defective equipment that might actually kill someone. How would you like to have that on your conscience?"

I thanked Joe for coming over to help me out again. I told him that I was sorry that he had to be bothered but he said, "That's alright. I was getting lonely sitting over there." He reviewed the entire gelling procedure for me and he helped me to rework the TR60s. I had trouble performing the rework but my ZB3s improved tremendously once I became more careful. Art examined the ZB3s and told me that they were much better, but I thought that he was still concerned.

Joe reworked my TR60s while I completed more ZB3s. He checked each piece and told me that my work was much better. I knew that I could do the job correctly if I avoided the "race for production."

At this time, I became worried about losing my job because of my poor production quality. Art also criticized me for my messy workplace. Gel had been spilled on my table, and my spatula (handle and blade) was covered with it. In addition, gel was all over the inside and outside of my finished disc anterior pads. I had not adequately cleaned up these messes because I thought it would take too much time away from production.

At the end of the day, I showed Art the last few ZB3s that I had gelled. "Beautiful," he said. "Just keep on doing what you're doing—TR60s, TW13s, ZB3s." I felt better after this but still somewhat uncomfortable.

My gelling continued to improve over the next several days. Whenever I saw Art and Debbie talking together at the inspecting tables, I became concerned. I was sure that they were examining my disc anterior pads. I kept waiting for Art to return my pieces to me for regelling.

I did happen to ruin one piece, I accidentally placed the wrong side of a plastic lid on a gelled pad. I was warned not to do this by Debbie because it is almost impossible to remove the lid from this position. I then tried to remove the lid and when I realized that I could not, I considered throwing it out by hiding it under some paper towels in my garbage box. I decided against this tactic, fearing that I might be in trouble if it was discovered by a line foreman. I pushed it off to the side and decided to worry about it later. Debbie happened to be walking by at the time and stopped to look at the piece. "I put the lid on the wrong way. I think it is ruined," I said. "I think you're right," she replied, appearing not to be visibly upset.

Early in my second week of work at Biomed, Debbie approached me one morning and told me that my table was a mess and that I should try to keep it cleaner. She told me that she had spent fifteen minutes after work one day cleaning my table. I was still concerned about the quality of my gelled pieces. During the breaks, I would check the inspecting tables to see if my pieces had been approved for packing. If my pieces were not there, I knew they had passed the inspection. If they were still there, I would compare them to the other disc anterior pads to see how they fared against them. I felt that I was beginning to get the knack of gelling because none of my pieces had been returned to me recently.

Later that week, I heard Debbie state that every geller should be gelling at least fifty TR60s a day because "fifty is shit." I became alarmed because I was not even completing thirty-five a day although I was claiming on my production work reports that I was gelling 46 to 48 a day (more on this later in the chapter). I decided to spend less time rubbing the gel into the pads and I discovered that I could work more quickly with the same level of efficiency. At the end of the day I had gelled an "honest" forty-six TR60s, but I recorded fifty-eight on the daily production work report.

Art returned two undergelled pieces to me at the end of the week. I was not particularly concerned about this because I felt that I had sufficiently mastered the art of gelling. I fixed the pieces without any problem. I was much more concerned with picking up my speed.

MEETING THE WORKERS

The first worker I met at Biomed who was not a geller was Raoul. He was a young Latino in his early twenties, with jet-black hair and a mustache, and he was a close friend of Joe. Raoul was an assembler in the disc anterior pad assembly department. After eating a sandwich during the morning break of my second day, I had a brief conversation with him.

"This is a lousy job," he said. "I wonder what they are up to. They fire a bunch of people and hire a bunch of people. People seem to come and go. There were people here yesterday who aren't here today, right? Maybe they fire you if you don't work fast enough." He appeared to be angry with the entire situation.

When I returned to work after the break, I began to mull over Raoul's comments. I tried to work more quickly and I felt more pressure. If other workers had been fired, I figured it could happen to me.

That day, after I finished eating lunch, I wandered into the subassembly room and met Manuel, a Latino worker in his late twenties. Manuel, who wore glasses and was working studiously, informed me that the subassembly room was also known as the United Nations room, "because we've got a little of everything in here." He was painting coverings for some kind of medical electrode. Manuel also said, "This is a lousy job."

The following week, Manuel told me, "Biomed has an $8 million deal going if they can meet a certain deadline." He hoped that this deal would result in a raise for the workers in January. "I don't know any details but I wonder what is actually going on in the company," he said. "Nobody is talking."

Kim, a tall and solidly built young white worker, was running a sealing machine when I talked to him during an afternoon break. "So, how do you like the job?" he asked when he discovered that I had only been working a couple of days at Biomed. "It's OK," I answered. "I think this job is boring," he replied. When he saw me stretching my back, he said, "Everybody's back hurts who works here."

A week after Manuel mentioned the $8 million deal, Kim told me about the deal. He said, "The deal is about to be closed. The workers are supposed to get a raise at the start of the year, but I don't know how big or small it will be." I do not know if the deal went through but I know that no raises were given early in 1983.

One worker I would get to know fairly well was Bob. I met Bob, a white worker in his mid-twenties, who was stocky and had a bushy beard, one morning at a bus stop while waiting to catch a bus to Biomed. I recognized him immediately, so I started up a conversation with him. I learned that Bob was a machine operator and that he was hired the same day that I was. We discussed a variety of topics and seemed to hit it off fairly well.

When Bob applied for a job at Biomed, he filled out an application in the reception area at the same time that an African American man was working on his application. Both were given individual tours of the factory. When Bob saw the machine that produced the plastic lids for the disc anterior pads, he told the line foreman who was conducting his tour that he had run a similar machine at one of his previous jobs. Upon hearing this news, the line foreman became excited and told Bob that he would be hired to operate this machine.

As Bob and the African American applicant left the factory together, he mentioned to Bob that the supervisor had said to him, "We are not

doing any hiring now. We are only taking applications for the future."
Although the supervisor's comments bothered me, Bob was not concerned
about them. A few days later, Bob told me that his father was a member
of the executive board of one of the major railway unions in this country, the Brotherhood of Railway, Airline and Steamship Clerks (BRAC),
which is now named the Transportation Communication Union.

Another worker I became friendly with was Sam. Sam, who had recently
graduated from high school, had long hair and was interested in music—
both classical and rock. When he was not working at Biomed, he was either attending school or practicing his music on his classical guitar.

Sam spent much of his day at the factory gluing together ECG electrodes. We discussed how boring and tedious the work was and the physical problems inflicted on us by this work. Sam mentioned that he liked
working in a "smaller place" where he could get to know everyone more
intimately, as opposed to working in this "big" place. He stated, "This job
wouldn't be so bad if they let us rotate positions. We could do one job for
several hours, another job for a few hours, and so on." I agreed that this
would greatly help to reduce the boredom and tedium inherent in factory
work.

Since the electronic technicians had their breaks and their lunch period at a different time than the rest of the factory workers, I had trouble
meeting them. I had seen a number of technicians walk through the factory but that had been the extent of my contact with them. During the
Christmas buffet lunch, I talked to a technician for the first time.

Jim, a small white worker who was in his early twenties (although he
looked much younger) was recruited by Biomed at the DeVry Institute of
Technology. He told me that there were currently seven technicians and
that an eighth would be added after the holidays. "The work I do is not
very difficult," he said. "I solder and test equipment. But it is very boring
and tedious. Anyone could do my job after watching someone do it for
several days." Jim added, "This company is growing. They are constantly
producing new items for the market. Biomed will really take off in a couple
of years."

I did not meet another geller until my fourth day of work. Juan, a portly
Latino in his early 30s who always dressed well, asked me, "What do you
think of this job?" "It's OK," I replied. "It's not too bad because you don't
get dirty and you get to sit down all day," he said. I agreed, but added,
"My back always hurts from this job." "Mine, too," he laughed. During

the first few days of work, whenever I stretched my back while gelling, I looked at Juan and saw him stretching his back, too, with a grimace on his face.

"Are you working on Sunday?" he continued. "No," I answered. "What about you?"

"Yes, my family needs the money."

LEARNING MORE ABOUT BIOMED

Toward the end of the morning of my second day of work, Debbie and Liz began to review the job applications in order to hire a few more workers. They sat at a table just opposite me, so I overheard their entire conversation. The two line foremen brought over several thick folders of applications. I could not believe the number of applications there were!

They laughed at various applications. One person who had studied biomedical engineering at the graduate level and had applied for an unskilled assembly position was immediately eliminated as a possible candidate for a job. Another candidate was also determined to be unsuitable. "This guy wants $4.35 an hour," laughed Liz, as if that was an outrageous demand for an hourly wage. They finally located a "successful" applicant named Juan Gonzalez, whom Debbie had trouble reaching by phone.

The application review process that I had observed confirmed some of my own hunches. They did not perform a thorough investigation of the applicant's academic or employment background, or indeed any investigation at all. Neither did they attempt to contact the applicant's references. This is not too surprising because Biomed's application form did not even ask for the references' phone numbers.

Although I had been punching a time card for two days, I did not notice the white card taped next to the time clock until the morning break of my third day. The card read:

When you work in a modern factory, you are paid, not only for your labor, but for all the productive genius which has made that factory possible: for the work of the industrialist who built it, for the work of the investor who saved the money to risk on the untried and new, for the work of the engineer who designed the machines of which you are pushing the levers, for the work of the inventor who created the product which you spend your time making, for the work of the scientist who discovered the law that went into the making of that product, for the work of the philosopher who taught men how to think. . . .

John Galt (*Atlas Shrugged*, by Ayn Rand, 1957)

A few days later, Sam read the card by the time clock and said, "What bullshit! We should rip this off the wall!" I felt the same way as Sam did. This was the only comment that any worker made to me about this quotation. I am not even sure how many workers had read or even noticed this quotation on the wall.

During the first few weeks that I worked at Biomed, business seemed to be booming. There was a lot of pressure on the workers to get out the production. "Do you hear that, people? We have to produce seven cases of TR60s a day!" Debbie bellowed at the gellers one morning. The drive for increased production was on and the workers were the ones who would have to pay the price. That was all the line foremen seemed to be concerned with—production. They never stopped to ask the workers how they were feeling. They only asked them one or two questions repeatedly— "How many TR60s have you produced today?" or "Have you reached your quota for the day?"

I heard Debbie barking at a woman assembler about making the quota for assembly work. Debbie complained that the assemblers were not working fast enough. She threatened to fire them if they did not start to turn out more work. Thus, I was not surprised when Lenny, the young man in charge of shipping and receiving, told me that Biomed was looking to move its production to a bigger facility, because of the anticipated rapid expansion of the company.

I had been working at Biomed only a week before I saw my first time study. It was performed on Joe. Debbie told Joe, "OK, I want to see how fast you can gel ten TR60s." Joe treated the time study as a challenge. He whipped off ten TR60s in just under forty-five minutes! The standard average gelling time for ten TR60s is seventy-three minutes, so Joe worked more than twenty-eight minutes faster than it would take the "average" worker to complete such a task.

A time study was also performed on Art and Kim. They were timed on inspecting, packaging, sealing, and packing one box of ten TR60s. The duo appeared to be working very fast—much faster than when they normally performed these operations.

Later that day, I told Art that I was going to set a new personal production record in gelling. He said that was good because everybody would have a time study done on them in the near future.

When I walked into the factory each morning, my stomach dropped as I thought about what awaited me during the next eight hours. The sinking feeling in my stomach gradually disappeared as the months rolled by. Before the start of each day, the workers congregated in the lunchroom to drink coffee, smoke cigarettes and to make small talk. The atmosphere in the lunchroom at this time was dismal. The workers seemed constantly unhappy and they never looked forward to the upcoming day.

When I began to work at 8:00, I gelled furiously until the morning break at 10:00. I calculated that it was best to work hard early in the day, when I felt the most refreshed. I was continually concerned with my productivity, which was the major reason why I attempted to work fast. I was always worried that I would be fired for not working fast enough. The morning break began when Art yelled "Break time!" He waited until the second hand reached the twelve at 10:00 before providing us with a temporary respite from the grind of production.

The first thing that I did during these breaks was to rush off to the bathroom to wash the gel off of my hands. There was only one facility for all of the production workers of both sexes, so I often had to wait in line to use the sink. I spent the rest of the break talking with the other workers and attempting to recover from the work of the previous two hours.

From the end of the morning break until lunch at 12:00, time seemed to pass more slowly. My back began to ache during this period although the more days I spent gelling, the earlier in the day my back would begin to hurt. After a couple of weeks, my arm as well as my fingers began to hurt in the morning. Gelling became more difficult and it was often hard to concentrate. If I experienced trouble gelling a particular pad, it was easy for me to become frustrated. This would cause me to feel tense while gelling, for which I had no release. I still tried to gel at my previous pace but it was an uphill battle.

At 12:00, immediately before the workers went to lunch, the first production work report of the day was filled out and turned in to the line foremen. The first couple of days I "padded" my production output by one or two pieces each work report. I did this so I "looked" more productive. I also figured that Biomed's accounting procedure was not sophisticated enough to discover this discrepancy. I continued to "pad" my work reports, gradually increasing the "padding" until I was "padding" my daily production an additional 33 to 50 percent of my normal output.

When Art yelled "Lunchtime!" the workers began to divide into smaller groups based on either race or ethnicity for the half-hour period. The African American workers hung out together and the Indians as well as the Latino women formed their own groups. This half hour always went by much too quickly for most of the workers.

The toughest portion of the day was from 12:30 until the afternoon break at 2:00. Gelling became increasingly painful, and I would watch the minutes tick off until the break. My arm, neck, and back were very sore and sometimes I began to get a headache. I tried to maintain a decent gelling speed, but I had slowed considerably since the morning. Fatigue was now evident in the gellers' faces. Motions became strained and everyone tried to hang on. I became sick of gelling, and I did not want to gel any more disc anterior pads in my lifetime.

I finished gelling one piece and moved on to another. My arm felt like it was going to fall off. Another one was completed. I figured that there was time for two more before the break. Only three more minutes had passed; it felt like ten. Ten more minutes to go—time for me to finish just one more. I could not believe how tired and worn out I already felt. And it was only Tuesday. Somehow 2:00 arrived, Art yelled "Break time," and I slumped back in my seat. I felt too tired to move. I wished the day was already over.

After the break, there was only one hour and forty minutes left for gelling. I realized I would make it through the day. I could see the light at the end of the tunnel. I gelled without thinking and my body became numb. I still counted the minutes but now it seemed that I looked at the clock every few seconds. I convinced myself that once I made it to 3:00 it would be all downhill. Vern, a young white geller with a bad case of acne who worked near me once said, "The last hour always seems like three hours."

Once I made it to 3:00, I aimed for 3:15. Then for 3:30. Only 25 minutes of gelling left until clean-up at 3:55. It was 3:51, not enough time to start another one. I dawdled over the pad I was working on. The workers were eyeing the clock, waiting for Debbie's announcement. It was 3:55 and it finally came. "OK," she shouted. "Time to clean up." Relief was seen on all the gellers' faces as they wiped off their spatulas and tables.

Production work reports were hurriedly filled out and placed on Debbie's desk. The workers moved quickly to get their coats and their time cards. A line formed by the time clock; everyone was waiting for the last minute to tick off—for 3:59 to turn into 4:00. Tick! Cards were punched one right after another. Workers exchanged greetings as they hurried to their cars or to catch a bus. The day was over.

Working in a factory really took its toll on me, both mentally and physically. When I came home from work, my back was sore, I felt tired, and I found it hard to concentrate on anything but the simplest activities, such as eating or watching television. Sometimes I did not feel human until I woke up the following morning, only to begin the process anew.

WORKING OVERTIME

There was overtime available during the first couple of weeks that I worked at Biomed. On days that Biomed offered overtime, Lori, the assistant plant manager, who was quite heavy, wore thick glasses, and dressed masculinely, usually came around at about 3:00 to ask the workers if they wanted to stay until 5:00. Once she came by and tried to convince the workers to stay until 6:00.

If it was a Thursday, she came around to see who was willing to work on Saturday and/or Sunday. Lori even offered time-and-a-half pay for working on Christmas Eve and the day after Christmas which was a Sunday.

For the most part, the younger white workers did not work any overtime while the older workers, as well as the Indian and Latino workers, stayed when any overtime was offered. There was no doubt in my mind that they worked these extra hours out of economic necessity. The same pattern occurred concerning weekend work. A little less than half of the regular workforce came in on the one Saturday that I worked at Biomed.

That Saturday afternoon, Lori asked Anna, the slight Indian woman geller, and Sharon if they were planning on working the next day. Both said no. Earlier in the week, Anna had agreed to work on Sunday. Biomed especially wanted Anna to work on Sunday because she was the most productive of the gellers in addition to turning out the best quality pieces.

In the afternoon, I noticed that Anna was becoming increasingly fatigued. She began to rub her neck and she looked very tired. Even the gelling "machine" was not able to handle the relentless pace of Biomed's "assembly line" without feeling it. Anna appeared to be much more human now than ever before. Six straight days of gelling was too much for any human body to accept.

A DISRUPTION OF THE DAILY ROUTINE

The only company-organized disruption of the daily routine at Biomed during the seven-month period that I worked there was the company's hosting of a holiday buffet lunch. Biomed gave us an hour off (half of it paid) and provided the workers with cold cuts, bread, cheeses, potato salad, cole slaw, raw vegetables with dips, and canned soft drinks. The lunch was nice but it hardly compensated for the low wages and the harsh working conditions. I overheard one young woman worker say, "This is nice. They wouldn't have ever done this on my other job."

At the lunch, I asked Debbie if the plant manager had found my time card, which he had misplaced earlier that morning. She replied coldly, "If he hadn't, you would have heard about it."

It was hard to get back to work after lunch. I was waiting for the afternoon break. When Art yelled "Break time!" at 2:00, Debbie went into an uproar. "No break now!," she bellowed. Debbie was not sure when the break should be called, since the lunch period had lasted until 1:15. Steve had not informed her when the break would be so she was in a tizzy. When she could not find Steve, she decided that the break would be at 2:15. One could tell that Debbie enjoyed the power that she wielded and that she took it quite seriously.

ADAPTING TO HIGH-TECH FACTORY WORK: AN ANALYSIS

My experience of physically adapting to work at Biomed in 1982 was extremely similar to that of Hembree, who worked in a high-tech factory, and Cavendish, who worked in a British automobile components factory.[1] Hembree, who worked in a small electronics factory in Silicon Valley for several months in 1981, described how working in the clipping department led to continual pain in both her shoulders and her neck as well as a throbbing head by the end of each shift. After working in the clipping department for three-and-a-half weeks, Hembree states that her eyes were

52

extremely sensitive to sunlight and that it was difficult for her to read for more than fifteen minutes at a time. Cavendish complained of similar ailments. While working as an assembler in a medium-sized factory in 1977–78, she suffered from frequent backaches, and neckaches, as well as eyeaches on the job.[2]

It was hard for me also to adapt to the physical pain of gelling. Besides my back constantly aching, my neck, arm, and hand also hurt. These pains intensified rather than diminished, the more I gelled. I never expected factory work to be so physically painful.

Gelling, an activity that one would classify as "unskilled" factory work, was harder to master than I had originally thought. For many workers, it takes several weeks to acquire the proper gelling technique and speed to meet Biomed's production standards. Other workers became discouraged with having to gel for any length of time and quit.

According to Kusterer, no job is truly "unskilled," because each job requires that the worker possess important "working knowledge" in order to successfully perform the job.[3] During my first few weeks on the job at Biomed, I was acquiring "working knowledge" in two specific "subject areas of working knowledge" outlined by Kusterer: "knowledge about routine processing procedures" and "knowledge about the formal organization."[4]

Knowledge about routine processing procedures, according to Kusterer, is, in actuality, the most basic kind of working knowledge. It includes how to perform "routine procedures that are necessary to accomplish the functions that have been assigned to the particular job." In terms of this kind of knowledge, the solutions to the work problems that each employee must perform are composed of the work tasks that management assigns to each job category in order to establish the technical division of labor in the work setting.[5]

In terms of applying this knowledge of routine processing procedures to gelling, I had to devise strategies for how much gel to use and where to place the gel on the pads in addition to making sure that I was neither overgelling nor undergelling the pads. It took me several weeks to get the gelling procedure right and to learn the subtleties of using various strategies for gelling the different models of electrode pads.

Knowledge about the formal organization is considered by Kusterer to be "supplementary" to the basic knowledge about routine processing procedures.[6] Nevertheless, it is as *important* as the basic knowledge acquired about routine processing procedures for survival on the job. According to Kusterer, knowledge about the formal organization:

> includes all the knowledge that workers develop about the workers in other job categories with whom they come in contact, including management representatives. . . . Workers also develop knowledge about the formal organization as a separate subject in itself. They understand its division of labor, and they understand how this division of labor can operate, almost like an independent force, to pressure people in different job situations to behave in different ways.[7]

The most important knowledge of the formal organization, i.e. Biomed, that I acquired in the first few weeks was the knowledge that I could get away with padding my production work reports by fairly substantial amounts. This technique, referred to as a "pencil bonus," is often used in production settings where workers are required to keep track of their output or the time that it takes them to perform a job.[8]

Balzer, who worked as the lowest level bench hand in a Western Electric manufacturing facility, first learned of using the "pencil bonus" to increase one's efficiency rating from a fellow production worker. The worker told Balzer, "You'll learn to . . . pad your bogey (a record of the employee's work week), everyone does. If it takes you thirty minutes to set up, mark it down as forty-five. If you finish a job in forty minutes, put down forty minutes for the job and another twenty for material handling."[9]

Even after I had spent nearly two straight months gelling I was never able to reach the "standard average gelling time" and subsequently the daily quotas. Without giving myself generous pencil bonuses on a daily basis I am convinced that I would have been terminated quite early in my gelling career.

Although I do not know how widespread this practice was at Biomed, I have a hunch that some of the workers in the gelling department were giving themselves pencil bonuses. However, I believe that this type of behavior did not occur (or at least not to a significant degree) among all workers in all assembly departments because there were workers who did not achieve their production quotas and were subsequently fired.

Connected with this activity of giving myself pencil bonuses, I also learned some additional important knowledge about the formal organization. Specifically, getting away with padding my production work reports *on a daily basis* by 33 to 50 percent indicated the high level of managerial incompetence that existed at Biomed. After working only a few days at Biomed, I had figured out a simple procedure for how line foremen could have kept fairly accurate totals on individual workers relatively easily, but, of course, I was not going to volunteer such information. This lack of insight provides powerful support for Hodson's finding that the management of many high-tech firms are downright incompetent.[10]

As for gelling itself, I *hated* the activity. When I became the "runner" (the worker who picks up the gelled electrode pads and delivers new batches of electrode pads to the gellers), the plant janitor, and the utility man, I did everything possible to avoid having to gel. The only times that I gelled were the times when Debbie or Steve forced me to gel because I could not find anything else to do to occupy my time.

Until I performed "assembly-line" work at Biomed, I did not realize the extent to which such work is quantified. Management expected the workers to work every second of every minute of the designated work time. This attitude was reinforced by the various production schedules of each department, which stated how long (in minutes and seconds) it should take to produce one unit.

I also realized how fragmented the production process was when I asked Joe on my first day of work what the TR60s were used for and he did not know. Pfeffer argues that capitalist production, due to the current division of labor, is fragmented where workers learn only about those specific aspects of production that their jobs incorporate. Therefore, the other aspects of production including the organization and coordination of production are viewed as "a mystery and a mystification."[11] Under such circumstances, it is not surprising that Joe did not know for what purpose the TR60s were used.

Early on in my work at Biomed, I also became engaged in another activity that appears to be common among industrial workers—"counting time." In order to get through a day of gelling, I would count the minutes until each break, lunch, and the end of the day. I also counted off the days of the week. Pfeffer reports that, as the plant's trashman, he would count off the days of the week until his day off although other coworkers were engaged in counting minutes, counting days, and even counting months (until vacation).[12]

Cavendish also engaged in "counting time," although she utilized a different strategy. She would look at the clock and divide each work segment of the day (the time until the first break, from the first break until lunch, and so on) into ten-minute, twenty-minute, and thirty-minute periods and keep track of her production so that she was aware that time was passing.[13]

Many workers are also counting time until they can retire. According to Pfeffer, a coworker, who had worked for more than twenty years at the factory was doing just that: "In talking about it, he said, each day he looked forward to the 12:30 whistle, signaling the end of his lunch half-hour and his return to work, because that meant the date he would retire, in 1982, was one day closer."[14]

Finally, the dependence on overtime work for the Latino, Indian, and older workers was quite striking. Many of these employees worked seven days a week at Biomed when work was offered because they had families to support. Since Biomed's wage of $3.50 per hour was only fifteen cents above the minimum wage, as Pfeffer states, "economic compulsion" requires that these workers "voluntarily" work additional hours of overtime.[15] From my discussions with these particular workers, it appeared that only extreme fatigue would result in these workers turning down any overtime.

In conclusion, adapting to high-tech factory work did not appear to be much different from adapting to other types of lower-tech industrial work. The working conditions in the high tech factory were not informal, relaxed, or better than those of other types of industrial work, as its proponents claim.[16]

5.

The High-Tech Labor Process

AS MENTIONED IN THE FIRST CHAPTER, COLCLOUGH AND TOLBERT AND
Mohseni discovered that high-tech production work is organized according to the principles of scientific management, where planning and execution of the work tasks are separated by both time and space, and the
production process is both fragmented and routinized. Consistent with
the use of scientific management, Hodson found that time and motion
studies were prevalent in high-tech factories as a method for measuring
the workers' individual productivity levels.[1]

Although there has been a continuing debate in the 1980s and the
1990s concerning the ongoing transformation of work from the Taylorist/
Fordist model of production to one of post-Fordism, there is no evidence
of the emergence of a post-Fordist production regime for unskilled and
semi-skilled production workers in high-tech industries.[2] Specifically, post-
Fordism can be characterized by a reduction of the "traditional reliance
on centralized bureaucracy and standardized tasks" and an increase in
flexible specialization.[3] Although theorists disagree on whether there is a
real substantive difference between Fordist and post-Fordist production
regimes, however, based on a substantial amount of evidence, it has been
argued that flexible specialization inherent in post-Fordist regimes often
leads to an intensification of the workers' effort through the deploying of
labor in a more sophisticated way and, thus is merely a variant of neo-
Fordism.[4] As will be shown in this chapter, Colclough and Tolbert's,
Mohseni's, and Hodson's findings[5] are consistent with the nature of the

labor process at Biomed; in addition, there was no evidence of the emergence of a post-Fordist production regime characterized by an increasing unity of conception and execution of work tasks among the production workers at the firm.

As will become apparent through my discussion of the performance of a wide range of work tasks at Biomed, the assembly process was highly segmented. Each worker performed a limited number of movements, over and over. Much of the work at Biomed, and all of the unskilled work, required little, if any, use of one's mental faculties. The only obligation at Biomed was that one "learn" the proper technique of one's assigned job and then "learn" to perform it quickly. At Biomed, mental fatigue occurred much sooner than physical fatigue, due to the repetitive nature of the infinitesimal actions performed.

Unlike most of the other factory workers, I was quite fortunate to have had the opportunity to perform a wide variety of tasks in all the production departments except one—the disc anterior pad assembly department. This was due to a set of special circumstances, but mostly because I was "promoted" to the position of janitor/utility man after approximately three months of work at Biomed. I spent about half the day performing my janitorial duties and the other half of the day doing production work in whatever department to which I was assigned by Steve or Debbie.

Although the individual motions of the different production operations appeared to be radically different, the underlying labor process was essentially the same, no matter what job you did in the factory. This resulted in the workers holding extremely similar attitudes toward their work.

ATTITUDES TOWARD WORK

After about two weeks of work at Biomed, Sam showed me the jobs that he had been working on that day. One job involved placing metal clips on small plastic parts. The other job was punching out the circular tin elements for the disc anterior pads. Performing such jobs prompted Sam to say, "I don't think there is one happy employee at Biomed. All the jobs in this place are miserable. There are no good jobs."

When Pedro, a young Latino worker who was short and happy-go-lucky, was temporarily transferred from gelling to a new job requiring that he stamp dates on disc anterior and electrode bags and boxes, I thought that he would at least be happy to leave the miserable job of gelling behind. I asked him how he liked his new job and he replied without much enthusiasm, "It's alright but it's boring. I'd like to be able to move around rather than sit in one place all day." His message was clear—it does not matter what meaningless job I do if I have to do it all day; one meaningless job is the same as another.

The labor process was not viewed more positively by Kay, the line foreman of the snap-type electrode department and a young woman in her early thirties. Although the line foremen were supervisors and had much more autonomy than the average production worker "on the line," they were still required to do a certain amount of production work. After being fired from a relatively high-paying job as a warehouse manager, she worked a series of part-time jobs before working one day at Biomed a few years ago.

"I spent the day cleaning glue off of plastic connectors with a razor blade but I found the work to be so miserable that I quit," she said. Economic necessity forced her back to Biomed a few months later. "This is a terrible place to work," Kay said. "Who would work here if they didn't have to? Look at the people who work here. They work here because they need the money."

Matt, the cocky and arrogant son of the president of Biomed, who worked in the factory only during his vacations from college, made comments similar to those of the other workers, "I hate what I'm doing, counting the racks of elements while standing. I'd never do gelling or assembly. I know that I have an easy job, but I'd just like to drive all day—the longer the better." Because of Matt's father, Matt was never assigned to perform either gelling or assembly work. He spent a good part of each day driving for Biomed to pick up supplies, to make deliveries, and so on.

There was only one occasion in which I had the opportunity to discuss the labor process with a higher level management representative. Lou was the supervisor of the subassemblers and the electronic technicians, a graduate of DeVry Institute of Technology, and a young man in his mid-twenties. Lou had long hair, and an earring and often dressed in punkish styles. I had once heard him refer to the unskilled factory workers in a derogatory manner when he said to the plant manager, while laughing, "Why don't you get one of your vegetables to do it?"

I had discovered that Lou periodically gave his workers written quizzes and tests so I asked him about them. "I give all my workers tests to see if they know what they are supposed to know," he said. "One worker took offensive [*sic*] to the tests. I asked him why he didn't answer one question, and he told me that he didn't know the answer. I said, 'Fine, that's what these tests are for—to see what you don't know.'"

The conversation drifted to the unskilled production workers. Lou said, "Nothing against the workers in the main area of the factory, but they don't use their minds." I defended them. "They don't have a chance to use their minds because of the way the production process is structured," I replied. "The workers should try to come up with better ways for doing things," he continued. "Most of the new ideas I suggest to Robin (the vice president of the company) were figured out by my workers."

"The supervisors control the production process at the factory," I countered. "They don't give the workers a chance to figure things out on their own." "Well, that's wrong, " Lou said, finally concluding the discussion.

I was not sure that Lou believed me. He might have felt differently if he had performed some of the unskilled production work himself. Lou would have seen that management wanted the workers only to follow orders, not "to come up with better ways for doing things."

WORKER INGENUITY

Lou's appraisal of the workers' levels of intelligence might have been different if he had been aware of the occurrence of two events. Once Kay asked me to cut plastic strips of foam rings. Each strip had ten rings and the procedure was to cut one ring off at a time, using a pair of scissors. This process was quite slow and laborious.

I had been using a paper cutter to perform another task so I used the paper cutter to cut three strips of foam rings at one time. I had assumed that this was the proper procedure for the job. Kay, the line foreman of the snap-type electrodes department came by, observed me working and said, "You're using the paper cutter to cut the rings?" "Isn't this how you are supposed to do it?," I replied. Kay examined the cut rings and saw that they had been cut more neatly and more quickly than by hand. From that moment on, using the paper cutter to cut the strips of foam rings became standard procedure.

The second event concerned the cutting out of oval-shaped tin backings for an experimental product. I had spent a few hours one afternoon performing this task, as well as a couple of hours the following morning. I was working with Chris, a young African American man who was the line foreman of the disc anterior pad assembly department. He told me that we needed 160 pieces by noon, and judging from how long it had taken me that afternoon to cut out thirty pieces, I knew that it would be hard to finish this task on time. I was working faster than before although the process was still quite time consuming.

After the morning break, Chuck, an African American punch press operator in his late twenties, came by to help us out. He showed us how to cut five pieces at once, a technique he had learned from a young Indian woman worker, Sonita. Even Steve was not aware of this technique, because he would have demonstrated it to me the day before when he had shown me "a fast way" to cut out the tin backings. Chris was happy that Chuck had shown us this method. We finished the project more than an hour before the deadline.

I had mixed feelings. Chuck realized what he had done, so he said, "I should have let you continue the way you were working before to stretch the work out the whole day." I told him that I would not have minded doing just that.

Such labor-saving processes raise some important fundamental issues concerning the relationship between labor and capital. If a number of workers spend their days cutting tin and one of them discovers a way to do it faster, it does not pay for the worker to inform management of the discovery because this may result in the dismissal of several workers who would normally perform this task. It is much better for the workers to keep the discovery to themselves and use it to work at a more comfortable pace while still "beating the rates." If Sonita had this plan in mind, she is much smarter and more creative than Lou believed unskilled production workers could be.

GELLING AND RUNNING

Except for a brief period doing subassembly work, I spent the first two months at Biomed gelling disc anterior pads. Gelling was the toughest and most miserable job at Biomed. At one time I heard Debbie say, "We should start everybody out in gelling, so when they're moved to a new job, they will appreciate getting out of gelling. I feel sorry for the people in gelling."

During his second day of work, Roy, a young African American geller who was studying to be an insurance agent, asked me, "How long do you have to spend in gelling?" "It depends on a lot of things," I answered. Roy was already sick of gelling. "I am going to apply for a job at a warehouse tomorrow," he continued. I never saw Roy again after the end of that day.

Although workers from all the racial and ethnic groups (white, African American, East Indian, Latino, Assyrian) began work in the gelling department, the white and African American workers were eventually "promoted" to the "better" production jobs. Thus, the gelling department remained a virtual ghetto of Latino workers with a sprinkling of East Indians and Assyrians.

Throughout my first few weeks of work, my gelling steadily improved. Occasionally several TR60s were sent back to me for regelling but usually I was not concerned about this.

After about a month of gelling, I was introduced to TR3s. This model was used exclusively for infants, so the TR3s looked very similar to the TR60s except that the two circular pads were the same size in addition to being quite small. A gold-colored wire took the place of the cable attached to each pad on the TR60. A thin sheet of transparent plastic was used as a covering for the TR3 pads instead of the heavier lids, which were reserved for the larger models. Because this model was very small, it had to be delicately gelled. At first, I had trouble adjusting to the TR3s after working with the other models. I constantly overgelled them.

One day in early February, Art examined some of the gelled TR60s at my table. He told me that I had improved quite a bit. I was happy that he had noticed because I thought that my gelling skill had increased. I attributed this improvement to a new technique that I had developed while gelling ZB3s. I transferred this technique to the TR60s and had a similar degree of success. My new method involved using a greater portion of the spatula to squeeze gel into the pad.

That same day, after I had gelled twelve TR60s, Art came by and told me not to gel any more of them. It appeared that the wrong connectors had been attached to the cables. Art said to me, "Somebody is going to catch hell for this!" If the line foremen had pointed out which were the correct connectors for each model, then the workers would have been able to identify problems before it was too late. Maybe the line foremen thought that the workers were not smart enough to perform such tasks.

My back, which initially hurt only while I was gelling, began to ache constantly. I felt pain in my back while I rode the bus home after work. At times, my back hurt so much that I did not feel comfortable sitting in a normal position. I continued to experience this pain into the evening hours. I was certain that this ache would remain with me as long as I was a geller.

In the middle of February, I became the "runner" for the gellers because Art became increasingly busy with both his inspecting and packing duties. The runner was the worker who picked up the gellers' completed disc anterior pads and delivered them to the inspecting tables, provided the gellers with more pieces to gel by taking boxes of ungelled disc anterior pads off of the large storage shelves, gave the gellers more napkins and plastic lids, and cleaned and refilled the gel containers. The runner had to gel only when he was not performing his running duties, so the runner never had to gel for an extended period of time.

Whenever the gellers needed anything, they called out "Vic!" and I arrived immediately to see what that individual geller wanted. Through my duties as a runner, I became quite friendly with the other gellers who I previously had not had a chance to get to know.

I enjoyed running because it gave me the opportunity to walk around and to get out of sitting all day long. The day went by much faster when I was running because I performed a variety of activities. It was also much easier to gel for only a portion of the day and to do a good job of gelling.

As a runner, I was able to see who the fast and slow gellers were. Ophelia, a pleasant, slightly overweight, Latino woman, really was able to knock off the disc anterior pads. When she had to leave early one day, I saw her completed production work report and it stated that she had gelled one-hundred-eighty ZB3s in five and a half hours, a fantastic total! I was not too surprised because it seemed that I was constantly getting new materials for Ophelia. On the other hand, a young Latino woman right out of high school, Irma, was the slowest geller that I had ever seen. She took nearly six hours to gel twenty TR3s, a job that should have been done in one-and-a-half hours even if one worked slowly. She left the factory to go into the hospital for a kidney ailment before Biomed had a chance to fire her.

After I had been a runner for a couple of weeks, Debbie told me that she was thinking of having two runners—one runner for each row of tables. She revealed that the purpose of this plan would be "to get more gelling work out of the runners." The new runner system was never instituted.

I was eventually relieved of most of my running and gelling duties when I became the factory janitor. Andy, an African American geller in his late twenties, became the new runner after my brief tenure. After only two days of running, Andy told me, "Running sure beats gelling."

A job that was nearly as miserable as gelling was pounding tin. This job was constantly rotated among several male workers. I had the opportunity to pound tin for a couple of hours one afternoon in early January. I was gelling TR60s when Debbie told me to report to Liz after I completed my next set. When I went to see Liz after the afternoon break, she smiled and said, "Oh, yes. I have something fun for you to do."

We walked to the back of the factory and entered a small room off to the side of the main area. Liz showed me how to pound tin, which was the punching out of tin bottoms for the disc anterior pads. She placed a metal tin puncher on a sheet of tin and hit it with a hammer three times. Then, she separated the circular tin bottom from the tin sheet with her fingers. This process was to be continued until the tin sheet was used up. I asked Liz for some cotton for my ears because the hammering made such a dreadful noise. She went to look for some but could not find any.

When I began to pound tin, I had trouble with the puncher because I was not hitting it hard enough. Eventually I began to hit it harder and more than three times. This new method proved to be much more effective.

It was hard to believe that Biomed had one of its workers perform this inhumane job. My back began to hurt, I developed blisters on my hands, and the noise left a tremendous ringing in my ears as well as giving me a headache. Time passed slowly. I longed to return to gelling. I was glad that this was only going to be a temporary job.

The following day Bob told me that he had pounded tin for his first two days at Biomed. He was thinking of quitting but the plastic fabricating machine was repaired so he was transferred to operate that machine instead.

Early one morning in the middle of January, Steve motioned for me to come over to him. I was certain that I was in some kind of trouble. "How would you like to get out of gelling?" he asked. "How would you like to solder?"

"I don't know how to solder," I truthfully replied. "Well, how would you like to learn?" "Sure," I answered.

"Do you have a good memory?" Steve inquired. "Yes." "I'll have to ask Debbie to see if I can get you out of gelling. I know that Debbie will hate to lose a good geller." As I walked back to my workplace, Steve added, "If you don't work out, you'll be back to gelling."

Steve conferred with Debbie and my transfer to the subassembly room was arranged. At approximately 9:07, I gelled my last ZB3.

I reported to John, the new supervisor of the subassembly workers. He was tall, broad-shouldered and with his long hair and beard he looked like a rugged outdoorsman. The defibrillator testers, the equipment that serves as an interface between the defibrillators and the disc anterior pads, were assembled in this special room. After helping John count, unpack, and store some equipment, I cleaned the oil and grease off of metal plates. I cleaned over six-hundred plates in under three hours. Compared to gelling, this job was easy. It was great to have escaped from Debbie and the gelling "assembly line."

After lunch, John taught me how to strip, cut, and crimp pieces of wire, the first steps in making a molex connector unit. Up to this point, nothing seemed too hard. I was shown how to do some simple soldering at the end of the day and after a little practice, I was able to master this skill.

I was quite happy with my transfer to the subassembly room. The atmosphere was a bit more friendly and personal than the one found in the main production area of the factory. Work did not seem as oppressive under these conditions. At times, John acted more like a fellow worker than like a supervisor.

The day seemed to go by faster working among this small group of seven workers. The subassemblers performed a wider variety of tasks than the unskilled factory workers. They often completed a unit from start to finish. Although I still had to fill out a production work report at the end of the day, it seemed somehow different under these conditions.

I also was happy that I was receiving some elementary training in electronics. I felt that possessing some knowledge in electronics was valuable, since one of the few industrial sectors experiencing growth was the electronics industry (statistics backing up this claim have been presented in chapter 1). I learned that John obtained his training in electronics during his stint in the army. The other subassemblers either had some kind of electronics background from school or from on-the-job training at Biomed.

At the start of my second day in the subassembly room, John showed me how to use the voltage meter to test the resistance of each unit. Once each unit passed this test, John demonstrated the method for placing the blue and white wires in the molex connector with a small screwdriver. Upon completing this step, the molex connector unit was finished. I felt that I was learning quite a lot in a short period of time.

Right before lunch, I began to make another batch of molex connector units. All of the steps of the assembly process went much smoother this time. Manuel watched me solder some wires and said, "You're doing a good job but you'll have to work much faster in the future." He also told me, "I like this job because you are working with the guts of the thing."

Everything was proceeding smoothly until John showed me how to cut the plastic clips off of the connectors. When John had given me the connectors the last time, he had already removed the clips himself. It took some time for me to master this procedure; I struggled but I finally was able to remove the required parts.

When I finished the batch, John saw on my production work report the time that it had taken me to complete these units and said, "You've taken a long time for making this batch but don't worry, you'll become faster in the future." I was surprised by this comment because I thought that I had been working fairly quickly!

I was beginning to like my new position. I was much more mobile as a subassembler than as a geller. I spent most of the day working in the subassembly room but I also spent some time in the main production area of the factory. My new job was also much more challenging than my former job. Although I was doing "semi-skilled" work, I was still making only $3.50 per hour, as were the rest of the subassemblers. Because of the job content, I felt that I was in the "aristocracy of minimum wage labor" at Biomed.

However, I noticed that there was one major similarity between my work as a subassembler and that as a geller: the emphasis on working fast. John and Manuel kept stressing how important it was to work quickly. I saw Lou pushing Isaac, a Polish-born subassembler in his early twenties, to quicken his pace.

Before the start of work on my third day as a subassembler, Sharon said, "It's good you're out of gelling. Work you do now—easier." By the end of the day, I was sitting next to Sharon gelling ZB3s. The day began when John told me to cut one hundred pieces of wire for the "duals" that he was going to show me how to make. I was about halfway done when John asked to speak to me outside the subassembly room.

"I have some bad news for you," he said. "You're going to have to go back to gelling. Making forty-five molex connector units in 2 hours and 40 minutes is just too slow. Look, you gave it a good try. It just didn't work out."

"But you said I would become faster with more experience," I replied. "I know," John said. "It wasn't my decision. We're not getting anything done with me being the new supervisor and having to teach you everything. We're probably going to get somebody with some electronics experience from DeVry. I guess Debbie is expecting you now."

I walked out of the lunchroom. I was crushed. I was going back to the gelling department where each minute of the day was counted and had to be waded through. It was hard for me to believe that I was being sent back so soon. I had been working in the subassembly room for less than two days. I could not really blame John, although I did feel some hostility toward him. He was only doing what Lou had told him to do.

Manuel said that when people were sent back to do unskilled work in the factory after working in the subassembly room, they often quit. I could understand that. After experiencing somewhat better working conditions in the subassembly room, I could see how hard it would be to readjust to more boring work and tighter discipline. I should have been thankful that my transfer came before I had become too comfortable with the improved working conditions. I knew that it would have been much tougher to handle such a change after several weeks of work in the subassembly room.

Nevertheless, I felt like a failure. I was worried about being able to handle gelling again after I thought that I had made a clean break with it. But there was no choice to be made. If I wanted to remain in the factory, I would have to handle being a geller. I was determined not to follow the route of the other unsuccessful subassemblers.

I felt very embarrassed during the morning break. I was sure that everyone in the factory would soon know of my transfer back to gelling. I talked with Alvor, a young Latino subassembler, and told him what had happened. I could tell by his reaction that he had not known about my transfer. "That's too bad," he said. "But you have to work very fast in the subassembly room."

After the break, I saw John showing a young Latino woman how to use the crimping machine. I wondered if she was my replacement. During lunch, I found out that she was.

I had been talking to Bob, explaining to him that I had been sent back to gelling. I told him that John had mentioned that Biomed would be getting someone with some electronics experience from DeVry. Isaac, who was sitting at our table, listened to what I had said and laughed, "She doesn't have any electronics experience either. They hired her to take your place." He continued, "She has never soldered before either. John said, 'Oh, no. Not this again!' The other subassemblers started to laugh." I felt a bit uncomfortable while Isaac was telling this story.

During the afternoon, I noticed that Kay was running a time study on one of the women workers in her department. I also heard her tell another worker—a young Indian woman who was obviously new—that she would have to work faster in the future. Nothing had changed.

CUTTING TR3 PLASTIC COVERINGS

The most relaxing job that I performed at Biomed was cutting plastic coverings for the TR3 disc anterior pads. Although the job was boring (as was the rest of the factory work), cutting TR3 plastic coverings did not make your muscles ache.

I became the "official" plastic cutter in early March when I mentioned to Art that our supply of TR3 plastic was almost depleted. Since the worker who had been regularly cutting the plastic had taken an extended leave of absence, Art asked me if I knew how to cut the TR3 plastic. When I did not respond affirmatively, Art went to find a worker who could teach me. He found Billie, a middle-aged white woman from the cable department, to demonstrate this process.

Cutting the TR3 plastic coverings was easy. First, five strips were marked off with a metal marker and a standard-size piece of cardboard. Next, the strips were cut with a pair of scissors and separated. Finally, the five strips were placed one on top of another and cut into twenty squares using a paper cutter.

Once I had some practice, I began to enjoy cutting the TR3 plastic coverings. It was an activity that I was able to do without exerting either much physical or mental effort. My mind often wandered during the afternoons that I spent cutting plastic. It was nice, sitting in the back of the factory, cutting strips from the large roll of plastic mounted on a wooden pole above my head. I cannot remember being bothered by any of the supervisors while cutting TR3 plastic coverings.

WORK IN THE PACKING DEPARTMENT

Ever since I had started to work at Biomed, I had wanted to work in the packing department because I thought that these were the best jobs in the factory. At the beginning of May, I got my chance to work in this department.

Late one afternoon, Sam showed me how to pack TR3s after Art instructed him to demonstrate the fundamentals of packing to me. The wires had to be folded twice around the TR3 without them touching either the pads or the plastic coverings. It took a little time for me to learn the correct procedure, but after that I did not experience any problems. The only disadvantage of spending the whole day packing was that one had to stand in the same place the entire day.

After Jack, a young stamper and box maker who was shy and quiet, quit in the middle of May, I spent a good portion of each workday stamping disc anterior pad bags and making boxes. I had always thought that stamping was an easy job until I actually tried it. I had watched Jack stamp bags in the past. His motions looked effortless once he established his normal rhythm. I envied him and secretly wished that I could have his job.

Stamping required more effort and concentration than I had previously imagined. One must place the large rubber stamp in just the right position on the ink pad so that it picks up the required amount of ink. Then, the stamp must make contact with the bag at just the right angle so that the stamp is not too light and all of it is visible.

My first few stamps were only partially visible. This activity was requiring a lot of concentration, and I experimented with various techniques to see which one provided me with the most favorable outcome. After I had stamped the first hundred bags, I became much more proficient at stamping.

I also discovered another drawback to stamping. One had to exert a considerable amount of pressure to obtain a good impression, so consequently the stamp pressed into the stamper's hand, making stamping quite a painful activity. The area directly below my index finger became quite sore while stamping, considerably detracting from the little pleasure I was able to derive from the activity. I wondered how Jack could have put up with this pain day in and day out. I knew that it would be hard for me to handle this kind of daily pain. After my first day, I did not want to stamp bags again.

The stamping went much better on my second day. I was able to work fairly quickly and my hand did not hurt from the pressure of the stamp. However, I had trouble making the boxes that are used for shipping Biomed's products. The flaps of the boxes refused to stick into the inserts. Debbie saw that I was having trouble so she came over and showed me an easier way to make the boxes.

After stamping bags and making boxes for several days, my arms and hands became quite sore. I reasoned that the soreness was due to using muscles in a repetitive manner that I had not used in a long time, if ever. During a break, Art even asked me if I had developed a callous on my hand from stamping. Because my hand had been getting sore from this procedure, I tried to hold the rubber stamp in different positions for different sets of bags. Sometimes it helped, sometimes it did not.

Making the boxes was better than stamping the bags. After about a week of constructing boxes, I reached a point where I was able to feel when I had made a box correctly. I constructed boxes without thinking. My hands glided over the bends and folds instinctively until I arrived at the finished product.

The last job that I performed in the packing department was unraveling TR5s. Groups of TR5s were put in bunches after they were made, so subsequently the wires of the TR5s became entangled. Unraveling TR5s consisted of simply separating the individual electrodes and placing them in a bin box. There was no specific technique for unraveling TR5s, so each individual worker adopted the method that best suited him.

While unraveling my first bunch of TR5s, I experienced some trouble. I seemed to make matters worse rather than better when I tried to untangle the wires. I began to sweat profusely from my frustration although it was already extremely warm in the factory, being late in June. After the first bunch, I developed my own technique and things went much smoother. This job seemed no worse and no better than the other jobs in the factory.

CABLE WORK AND REWORK

The work that I "enjoyed" the most at Biomed was the rework that I performed in the cable department. If products were defective for some reason, customers returned them. These products were then reworked so that the cable could be used again in the future.

The first product that I reworked was the TR3. The inventor of all of Biomed's products, as well as the chairman of the board, Robert Herman, determined that the optimal length for the TR3 cable should be eleven inches rather than the thirty-inch length that was currently in use. Therefore, all the TR3 cables in the factory, whether they had been returned or recently assembled, had to be cut down. I spent several hours cutting off the last eleven inches of cable on each TR3.

Not all rework in the cable department was as simple as this. Reworking the TR60, TR80, TW82 and TW92 cables required us to cut off the defective foam pads and the plastic connectors before proceeding to split and strip the cable. The TR60 cables were tougher to cut and strip than any of the other cables because of their thickness. A lot of force had to be used to perform these actions.

The only other "skill" that I performed in the cable department was the attaching of the molex connectors to the crimped cables. The crimped cables were inserted into the middle two holes of the connector and then a small screwdriver was used to snap the cables into place. Then the connector was turned over and a small amount of pressure was applied on the crimps until another snap was heard. Sometimes a snap could not be heard, so one had to learn the correct feel of the action. It was hard working with such small parts and I was clumsy at first. I became more adept at this task although I found it tedious and hard to concentrate.

SNAP-TYPE ELECTRODE ASSEMBLY WORK

Of my seven months of work at Biomed, I spent only three hours working in the snap-type electrode assembly department. Steve sent me over to work in Kay's department late one morning when he could not find anything else for me to do. Kay taught me how to assemble microtrodes, which were the electrodes manufactured exclusively for infant use.

First, a small amount of blue gel was squirted out of a syringe and placed on the clear plastic backing in the center of the attached small, white foam ring. Next, a chlorided element was placed in the center of the foam ring and turned a number of times in order to distribute the gel evenly against the plastic backing. After checking to make sure that the gel was satisfactorily distributed, a second foam ring was placed on top of the element and the original foam ring.

The process was fairly easy and straight forward. At first I squirted out too much gel which caused some problems. After assembling about a dozen microtrodes, I got the hang of this job. The toughest part of this procedure was making sure that not too many air bubbles were trapped in the gel between the element and the plastic backing.

Steve came by to observe the assembly process. Turning to me, he said derisively, "I hope you can make these faster than you make TR60s. Eight to ten minutes for a TR60, geez!"

I was surprised and shocked when I heard this comment. I realized that all of my production averages, as well as those of the other workers, were being calculated. I now realized that "padding" was the correct and only strategy to pursue when filling out production work reports. I would continue to use it in the future without hesitation.

The assemblers received a new batch of chlorided elements right before noon, so Steve told us to postpone lunch until we had used up these elements. By 12:30, part of the batch still remained but we took our lunch break anyway. At about 12:50, Steve walked into the lunchroom and began to harass Kay. "When are you going to get back to work?" he bellowed at her.

After lunch, Steve toured the area once more and he asked an assembler how many microtrodes he had made. "About 200," he replied. "What do you mean about 200?," Steve asked rather indignantly. "Debbie came by and took some," he answered. "I didn't keep count."

Turning to me, he queried, "How many have you made?" I lied. "220," I said, not knowing the actual number I had assembled.

A short while later, Steve dispatched me to the back parking lot to pick up garbage. I was glad to go because it meant no more assembly work for the day. My back was beginning to hurt while assembling the microtrodes. I also found that it took a lot of concentration and effort to work on objects that small. Fortunately, I never returned to this department.

CHLORIDING ELEMENTS WITH VINOD

Another activity at which I worked for only a few hours at Biomed was chloriding the elements for the snap-type electrodes. Debbie sent me over to help Vinod, a jovial, middle-aged, Indian man who spoke English with a thick accent. Vinod prepared a chloride solution each day, which was analyzed by Robin, Biomed's vice-president, before it was used on the electrodes.

The first thing that Vinod had me do was to place the elements on a large screen after they had been soaked in the solution. I placed about two-hundred of them on the screen. The solution stung my fingers.

In the afternoon, I prepared the chloride solution with some help from Vinod. First, I shook the solution in a big bottle for seven minutes. My arms became quite tired from doing this. Next, I poured the solution into a blender and blended it on a low speed for two minutes, followed immediately by a third of a minute of high-speed mixing. Finally, I poured the mixed solution into a container with the elements, letting them soak for five minutes.

JANITORIAL WORK

In the middle of March, I became the permanent janitor at the factory. Once I had acquired this job, I was responsible for keeping the offices, the toilets, the lunchroom, the loading dock, the parking lots, and the entire factory clean. I also performed a variety of miscellaneous activities that cropped up now and then—shoveling snow, laundering work rags, scraping tape off of the floor, and so on.

I liked working as a janitor because it freed me from the incessant grind of the "assembly lines." I also felt that I had more control over my own time and labor when I performed my janitorial duties. Being the janitor, in addition, allowed me to perform a variety of tasks, in all the different sections of the factory, which put me in closer contact with many more of the factory workers.

TECHNOLOGICAL CHANGE AND THE LABOR PROCESS

I first heard talk of automation at Biomed during my first week of work. Debbie told me that certain parts of the factory were supposed to have been automated by June 1982. She also stated that the last operation to be automated would be the gelling process. As of December 1982, the only job that had been automated was the manufacturing of the plastic lids, and there were still problems with this crude level of automation.

Early one morning in late December, Mr. Williams, the president and the chief executive officer of the company, was showing a potential customer or investor around the factory when I overheard the two of them talking. When they arrived at the gelling department, Mr. Williams said to his companion, "As you can see, this process is still done by hand. They have to force the gel into the pads with their spatulas. This is what makes them so heavy. We are working on automating this process but it is hard to do this because of the pressure needed to force the gel into the pads." About two months later, I heard Mr. Williams give the same brief talk on another factory tour.

Biomed was serious about automating the gelling process. With a large increase in sales projected for the near future, the company decided that this was the only way to proceed. By the middle of March, Bob, under the guidance of Biomed's engineer, was experimenting with a gel dispenser that would dispense a regulated amount of gel onto the disc anterior pad.

"With this device, gellers will just have to rub the gel in. It will save time, money, and gel," Bob said. "Biomed is also working on a machine that will rub the gel into the foam pad as well as dispense it. Such a machine will eventually cut down the number of gellers needed for the production of the disc anterior pads."

Billie, the woman who showed me how to cut the plastic coverings, also informed me of the technological changes that had occurred at Biomed over the past year. She mentioned that Biomed had previously purchased a lot of their finished materials but now that they were made in the factory. I asked her about the possibility of automation and how it would affect the factory's workforce.

"They have just recently automated the production of the plastic lids. This took a long time," she said. "When I was hired, Biomed told me that automation would upgrade the skill levels of the workers." She continued, "Biomed will eventually outgrow this place and move. I don't know if it will happen this year, but it will eventually occur."

In late March, Biomed acquired a new punch press, which when set up was about thirty feet long. The acquisition of this press resulted in the automation of pounding tin. Automating this job was a most positive step for all workers who have ever had to pound tin at Biomed.

Plans for technological change were also made for the snap-type electrode department. In the middle of May, Robin, the company vice president, and Kay talked of mechanization, including gel dispensers, as well as making major changes in the labor process. By the end of May, a new snap-type electrode assembly line had been instituted at Biomed. Instead of having each individual worker manufacture the whole electrode, the labor process was broken up into its component parts, with each worker performing only one step of that process.

The new assembly line required that the workers sit around two tables instead of having each worker occupy his own table. When one worker finished performing his own operation on the string of plastic foam rings, the string was passed on to the next worker so that he could perform his particular step in the assembly sequence. Each worker performed one specific task for the entire day, such as squirting gel onto the plastic of the foam ring, placing the element inside the foam ring, and so on.

About a month later, the new assembly line was refined. Ben, an industrial engineer hired in May who was given the position of production manager, built a new snap-type electrode assembly line. The line, made out of wood, needed nine workers to operate it at its highest level of efficiency. One long string of the foam rings moved down the center of the line while the workers, situated on both sides of the line, performed their individual operations.

Ophelia told me that she liked working on the new line. It is quite possible that many of the workers on the line "enjoyed" or "liked" their work at first because it was something different from the other work in the factory. Whether they enjoyed this work after a few months is another issue.

Technological changes also occurred in the subassembly department. The work of the subassemblers became more "assembly-line" in nature after my brief period of work in the department in January. Lou devised a series of timetables for many of the production processes, resulting in a "Taylorization" of much of the work in the department. One of these representative timetables follows:

S/Dual

Set Up—*2:10*
1. Strip and tin 1 inch off straight cable *1:16*
2. Cut strain relief in half and put lubricant inside *:57*
3. Slide cable in housing nice-n-slow *:45*
4. Solder RA (white) to RA (yellow) and hot melt in corner of housing *1:05*
5. Solder LL (blue) to LL (red) and hot melt in corner of housing *:56*
6. Cut and solder ECG wires together and hot melt in place *2:51*
7. Strip other end of cable so when sparking, wires will not touch *:52*

8. Spark cable *:42*

9. Get clamps and pads *:21*

10. Glue housing together and clamp *1:51*

Total min. sec.—*12:48*

Another technological change that had far more serious consequences for the subassemblers than the Taylorization of the work process was the adoption of the PC (printed circuit) board by Biomed in April. John, the supervisor of the subassemblers, told me that the PC board resulted in a simplification of the labor process in the construction of the defibrillator testers and that a number of subassemblers who were on a short, temporary layoff might not be called back to work.

A couple of weeks later, Afrem, a middle-aged subassembler originally from Iraq, told me that the subassemblers were no longer needed because the PC board eliminated the need for gluing in parts, and so on. I received what I believed to be the most accurate information concerning this issue from Willie, a young electronic technician, a few days later. He told me that several subassemblers were on an indefinite layoff but if Biomed constructed another PC board, it might lead to the total elimination of the subassemblers.

ANALYZING THE HIGH-TECH LABOR PROCESS

The labor process at Biomed contained the major features of the capitalist labor process as described by a noted labor process theoretician— "deskilling, fragmentation of tasks, hierarchical organization, the division between manual and mental work, and the struggle to establish the most effective means to control labour."[6] Since several labor process issues are intimately connected with management control, a discussion of "hierarchical organization" as well as methods for controlling labor will be addressed in the next chapter. The remaining issues will be discussed below.

Before "deskilling" and "fragmentation of tasks" can be discussed, it is necessary to define what is meant by "skill." Although the concept of "skill" in the labor process may be difficult to adequately define, Thompson provides a general definition of "skill" by stating that it is "largely based on knowledge, the unity of conception and execution, and the exercise of control by the workforce."[7]

Based on this definition, all of the production jobs at Biomed, with the exception of those of the subassemblers and the technicians, would be considered to be "unskilled." However, this does not mean that these jobs did not require certain kinds of competencies. Thompson points out that deskilled jobs still require the utilization of "specific dexterities" or "tricks of the trade" to successfully perform them, an analysis extremely similar to that of Kusterer.[8] In addition, a number of researchers have pointed out that precision and speed are the most important production skills found in high-tech industries.[9] This was definitely the case for the vast majority of production work at Biomed.

Although the jobs that the production workers performed were initially organized as "deskilled" jobs, and not "deskilled" in the sense that skilled craftsmen jobs have become "deskilled" in terms of Braverman's analysis, there was a significant trend at Biomed for even these "job-specific skills" to be fragmented along Taylorist lines.[10] This was evidenced by the introduction of the new snap-type electrode assembly line as well as through the work reorganization of the semi-skilled subassemblers. Shapiro-Perl, who worked in a costume jewelry factory in 1978, reports of a similar Tayloristic fragmentation of job-specific skills among semi-skilled production workers in the costume jewelry industry.[11]

Although all of the jobs that I performed at Biomed were deskilled, this does not mean that all jobs at which I worked were equally unpleasant. For example, I "enjoyed" the work in the cable department (as much as one can enjoy factory work) and I felt very relaxed while cutting the plastic coverings, with respect to the other work in the factory. In fact, when cutting the plastic coverings, I experienced a feeling that Baldamus refers to as "traction," which he defines as "a feeling of being pulled along by the inertia inherent in a particular activity." In addition, when discussing "traction," Baldamus adds:

> The experience is pleasant and may therefore function as a relief from te-
> dium. It usually appears to be associated, though not always, with a feel-
> ing of reduced effort, relative to actual or imagined situations where it is
> difficult to maintain continuity of performance.[12]

New automation was also introduced at the factory during the time I worked there and it continued to be added in the months following my firing. Because Biomed was a growing company, increasing factory automation did not mean an immediate loss of jobs for the majority of the plant's workers as in other situations where automation has been introduced.

Although there is an ongoing debate on whether workplace automation increases or decreases the skill levels of workers,[13] the adoption of automation did not upgrade the skill levels of the workers at Biomed, contrary to the company's claims and promises. However, not much deskilling took place because, as has already been discussed, most of the jobs already lack any requisite skills, with the exception of precision and speed. This last observation is supported by Hodson and Parker's finding, obtained through their review of the empirical literature on work in high technology, that "assembly jobs in the electronics industry" are probably the most deskilled jobs found in the high-technology sector.[14]

However, the introduction of assembly lines also contributed to a minimal loss of skill in the manufacturing process. Another technological change, the utilization of PC boards, resulted in the deskilling of subassembly work and a more drastic consequence, the elimination of several subassembler positions.

Although there was a separation between manual and mental work at Biomed, with the different fractions of management planning the labor process, this does not mean that the workers did not ever use their ingenuity in the labor process. As was discussed earlier in the chapter, I devised a more efficient way for cutting strips of foam rings and another worker developed a faster way to cut out oval-shaped tin backings. These types of discoveries are not unique to Biomed, but have been found in many industrial settings dating back to the nineteenth century. In order to take advantage of worker ingenuity, companies have utilized various programs ranging from suggestion programs and Scanlon Plans to employee involvement programs. In a more recent industrial ethnography from the late twentieth century, Juravich discusses how a "deskilled" production worker in a wire factory devised her own method for blocking terminals at the ends of wire.[15]

All of these unskilled production jobs at Biomed were typical of those found in the secondary labor market. Jobs found in this sector command low pay, provide little job security or rewards for seniority, offer few chances for promotion, possess low skill and educational requirements, and have high turnover rates. To put it succinctly, secondary labor market jobs are "casual 'dead-end' jobs."[16] Therefore, the only route open for improving one's position at Biomed, and only by a little bit, was to become a line foreman, although that option was not available to the majority of the plant's workers.

Even a transfer to the subassembly department was not necessarily a step up. Although performing this "semiskilled" work might be viewed as better than doing unskilled production work, this departmental transfer did not mean an increase in one's wages. A subassembler was only able to become an electronic technician if she or he had had training in electronics from a professional school. This requirement was not unique to Biomed, but is a requirement that is consistent with the electronics industry as a whole.[17] Thus, to escape these dead-end jobs, the only realistic alternative was to find another job that offered more opportunities and higher wages.

To summarize, the high-tech labor process at Biomed was based on the fragmentation of tasks as well as the principles of scientific management. In addition, the trend in Biomed's labor process was *not* moving toward a greater unity of conception and execution of tasks as represented by post-Fordist production regimes, as has been occurring to a degree within at least some jobs within the more traditional industrial sectors such as the clothing and the pulp/paper industries,[18] but rather toward an increased fragmentation of the already largely deskilled jobs. Thus, to put it simply: deskilled, high-tech production jobs were becoming even more deskilled.

6.

The Dictatorship of High-Tech Management

COLCLOUGH AND TOLBERT HAVE POINTED OUT THAT STRONG MANAGERIAL control in high-tech firms is displayed through a top-down hierarchy of managerial authority, where management determines policies and the workers are responsible for carrying them out. Consistent with this approach is Hodson's finding that management practices in high-tech firms are built on a set of bureaucratic rules and procedures connected with the close monitoring of production workers and their individual productivity.[1]

Besides the presence of close managerial control at the point of production, Hodson found high levels of managerial incompetence in high-tech firms. He discovered that high-tech managers often do not possess human relations skills and that they have managerial styles that are more authoritarian and less professional than those of managers in other industries. As will become apparent in this chapter, management control at Biomed was not only consistent with the above cited research findings, but was its quintessential representation.[2]

Control of the production process rested entirely in the hands of Biomed's management. Furthermore, management's control was directed toward one aim—maximizing the workers' productivity, no matter what the physical, psychological, or social costs to the workers. Management would often institute policies and plans to increase the workers' efficiency if they thought that such tactics would lead to higher output levels. Such schemes rarely resulted in the desired outcome, but often led to a deeper manifestation of resentment on the part of the workers.

Contrary to what Lou, the supervisor of the technicians, believed, management had no intention of letting "the workers use their minds," unless it was to aid management in getting more work out of the workers. An example of this occurred during a company–imposed speedup in April. Robin and Steve asked Pedro, a young Latino geller, for tips on how the gellers could gel the disc anterior pads faster so that they would be able to complete more in a day. Such strategies only deepened the antagonistic feelings that the workers often expressed about management amongst themselves.

FACTORY DISCIPLINE

The management of Biomed attempted to engage the workers in production for every single minute that was designated as "work time." To do this, management believed that it had to impose certain rules and clamp down on worker behavior that detracted from this ultimate goal, even if such arbitrary decrees had no grounding in reality.

When I first started working at Biomed, the workers were allowed to talk while performing their repetitive, monotonous jobs. In addition, there were two radios turned on; one at the front of the factory and one at the back. These helped to alleviate the boredom inherent in such an atmosphere. Two weeks after I started, however, an event occurred that resulted in the factory becoming a more oppressive place than it already was.

It was a Tuesday in late December, and I was beginning to get into a rhythm for another day of lethargic gelling. Late in the morning, Lori approached Vern, a young white geller, and said, while smiling, "A little tired today, Vern?" "No, I'm alright," he replied while still looking down at the pad he was gelling. I thought that Lori's comment was a rather strange one to make to Vern. A few minutes later, Debbie came up to Vern and said rather sternly, "Read this piece of paper, sign it, and punch out."

My first thought was that Vern had been fired. I could not figure out what his offense might have been. Vern slowly read the piece of paper and signed it. I was shaken a bit, thinking that something like this could happen to any worker in the factory.

Shortly thereafter, Debbie, standing by one of the inspecting tables,

82

announced, "I want to see all of the gellers up here right now." When we were gathered together by the table, she continued, "From now on, there will be no radio playing or talking when gelling. If you talk, you will be issued a warning. Three warnings and you're out of here. You have one week after you start to get up to the average. If you don't make the average, you will get a warning. Is that clear?" No one replied. "OK, punch out for lunch."

I felt rather uncomfortable. I thought that Vern had received a warning because his production level was too low. The content and tone of Debbie's talk appeared to be an attempt to bully the workers into producing more. If Vern had received a warning, I figured that I could get one too. As we punched out for lunch, I heard Vern tell Sam, "I shouldn't have any trouble hitting the average. I'm already doing about fifty-five a day."

I nervously gulped down my lunch in the lunchroom. I heard Debbie discussing the situation with Kay, but I could not really follow the conversation. Kay had her own problems. She complained to Debbie about her own lack of authority and her low wages. Debbie seemed rather unsympathetic.

Toward the end of the lunch period, I asked Sam why Vern had received a warning. Sam was unaware of this but he did mention that Vern had been sleeping while he was supposed to be gelling. Sam added, "I hope that they don't set an average for me. How many I do depends on how many times I have to get up to do other things."

I learned more about Vern's warning from Art during the afternoon break. Art told me that this was Vern's second warning for the same offense—falling asleep while gelling. He had received his first warning at the end of November and his punishment had been a three week suspension. "They can make it pretty miserable for you between warnings," Art said. "They'll give you the worst jobs but they won't fire you. They'll make you want to quit."

Because Robin saw Vern sleeping, Biomed, consistent with its past tradition of egalitarianism, decided that the whole workforce would be punished for Vern's misdemeanor. When Joe, my ex-tutor, asked Debbie how long our punishment—no talking or radio playing—would last, she replied, "I don't know, but prepare for the worst." One would think that Biomed would encourage talking and radio playing if one problem at the factory was keeping the workers alert, attentive, and awake. Common sense would dictate that. But Biomed was more interested in instituting a system that they hoped would lead to the desired results than in basing their decisions on reason.

After "martial law" was instituted at Biomed, the situation only became worse. When John, a subassembler, found out about the new factory conditions, he told me, "This place is becoming more like a prison camp everyday."

There were periods of time when the "no talking" rule was strictly enforced. Steve would walk around the factory, often lurking behind the large storage shelves, in order to catch workers in the act of holding a brief conversation. The Latino women gellers reacted to this rule by passing paper towels back and forth with lengthy messages written on them in Spanish. I do not know where they found the time to both gel and write. At other times the rule was relaxed a bit and you could say a few words to the worker next to you as long as you whispered and did not talk for longer than two minutes.

During one of these "lenient" periods, Andy, a young African American geller, and I held a brief conversation, lasting only a couple of minutes. Approximately ten minutes after we had concluded our discussion, Art approached the two of us while we were gelling and said, "I know you guys are busting your asses but please don't talk when Steve is around. It's no big deal but don't do it in the future. I'm telling you guys for your own good."

Andy thanked him while I remained silent. Art then told Andy that he could not sit next to me, but rather that he would have to sit kitty-corner from now on. Apparently, this was done so that we would no longer be able to talk.

Art emphasized that he was only carrying out Steve's orders, which I had realized before he had pointed this out to us. I remained outwardly calm although inside I was furious for this pettiness. I viewed this as another attempt by management to break down each worker into a docile, unthinking creature robbed of dignity. Andy and I were being treated as if we were children talking in class, caught in the act by the teacher. These infringements on the workers' self-respect contributed to the total brutalization of factory work at Biomed. A few minutes later, Art returned and reiterated that "it was no big deal."

Later in the day, I told Bob, the young, bearded punch-press operator, about this incident. Bob told me that Steve had threatened to fire Greg, the thirty-year-old eccentric utility man, and him for talking to each other. Since Bob worked at the back of the factory and Steve's desk was at the front, Steve asked Bob to spy on the workers in his area and to write down the names of those who talked while working. Bob refused. He told Steve that he was not paid to perform this function. A few weeks later, Steve asked me to squeal on two female workers who were talking, but I refused to comply with his request.

Although talking seldom interfered with working, it appeared that management wanted the work to be performed in as *painful* a manner as possible. Two specific incidents illustrate this point.

Late one afternoon, Debbie sent me over to rework electrode bags with Jack and Mark. As soon as I arrived at their worktable, I joined in on their conversation. Debbie obviously heard us talking, joking around, and laughing because she shouted in an admonitory tone, "You guys seem to be having a good time over there!" Under his breath Mark said, "Wench!" I could not understand it. Besides having to put up with hard, boring, and low–paying work, the workers were not even allowed to enjoy the camaraderie which made these working conditions more bearable.

The second incident involved Mick and Kevin, two disc anterior pad assemblers, who were telling jokes and laughing while performing their assembly jobs. Lori did not approve of such behavior so she sternly told them, "There should be no laughing while you are working." Mick was upset by her statement. "Who does she think she is?" Mick asked. "No laughing, shit. I'll laugh when I want to laugh."

In order to further reduce the talking among the gellers, Debbie decided to rearrange the gelling tables, because she said that the old arrangement was "not working out." Instead of having two rows of seven tables where the rows of tables faced each other, the new arrangement consisted of seven rows of two tables with all of the tables facing the front wall of the factory. The new arrangement contributed to the unpleasantness of the working conditions in addition to providing the line foremen with more control over the gellers. (I am sure that this setup was instituted for both of these reasons.)

Debbie said that she had arranged the tables this way "in order to discourage talking." Previously, it had been fairly easy to talk with any of a number of gellers working nearby without it being noticed. With the new arrangement, a geller had to turn to his or her side or completely around to talk to a fellow worker. Debbie's desk was now situated directly behind the last row of gelling tables, which made it easier for her to keep an eye on the gellers' behavior. The new setup also discouraged the elaborate system of writing notes on paper towels that had been adopted by the Latino women gellers.

I mentioned to Debbie that this new pattern reminded me of a classroom situation. She responded, "That's right. This new system means no talking." Actually, my observation was quite accurate. Debbie, as a line foreman, occupied the role of a "teacher," instructing the gellers in what to do and how to act. The gellers filled the role of "students." Every one of their movements was controlled and regulated so that they would become "educated"—that is, they would learn obedience and discipline so that the production process would proceed smoothly.

A few days after this change was instituted, I asked Pedro how he liked the new arrangement of gelling tables. He replied, "I don't like the new arrangement. It's discrimination against the Latino workers. In the back of the factory, the other workers always get to talk but we don't." He continued, "But what can you do? I don't even like to come to work in the morning. I'll stay here until something better opens up."

Talking while working was not the only offense for which workers were hassled by management. If a worker did not reach the designated production standard for a job, reprisals against the "guilty" worker often occurred in the form of verbal harassment, written warnings, layoffs, or even firings.

One example of this verbal harassment occurred when Steve approached Andy late one afternoon while he was engaged in some soldering work. "How many have you made today?" Steve asked. Andy pointed to his pile of completed electrodes on the table. "That's all you've done today?," Steve exclaimed. "What's the average time for completing one of them?" Andy did not know, so Steve went to find out the average time from Liz. When Steve returned, he counted Andy's finished electrodes and said to him, "That's only two hours and ten minutes worth of work!"

Steve continued to give Andy a hard time and I could see that Andy was beginning to feel bad. Although Andy had spent most of the day on this activity, this was only his second or third day of soldering work so I thought that Steve was being unfairly harsh with him. Steve went to get Liz to help Andy finish his soldering work. She came and helped Andy, in addition to providing him with tips for working faster and more efficiently.

Besides verbal harassment, written warnings, layoffs, and firings, workers who committed a transgression were often punished by being sent to work in the gelling department for a period of time. Mark, an inspector/packer with a crew cut, was sent one morning to "do time" in gelling for refusing to follow Debbie's and Art's orders. Mark left at noon, claiming that he had a doctor's appointment in the afternoon. I was sure that he had left, though, because he did not want to spend the afternoon gelling. He had often told me, "I'll quit if they make me gell for any length of time."

After the break one morning, Debbie told me to set up John, the supervisor of the subassemblers, for gelling. After lunch, I asked John why he was working in the gelling department. He replied, "I've been a bad boy because I've missed work. This is my punishment." Biomed's reasoning led one to believe that being a permanent geller was equivalent to a life sentence in solitary confinement.

The pettiness of Biomed's discipline permeated the entire working life of all of the factory's production workers. Lori continually threatened to dock the workers if their times cards were not placed in their properly designated slots. Early one morning, she even made threats about washroom use to the gathered workers. "If you don't keep the bathroom clean, you will only be able to use it during breaks. We will have to lock it at all other times," she threatened. Although such a threat is morally repugnant, there are no written federal, state or city regulations or ordinances that make it illegal for a company to lock bathrooms during nonbreak times. However, according to the Occupational Safety and Health Administration, employers are expected to make "reasonable accommodations" for their employees in terms of bathroom use.[3]

Biomed's disciplinary procedures became even more extreme when I was not allowed to sit while performing a job that I had performed while seated for months. One morning in late spring, I was sent by Debbie to clean and fill the dirty gel containers. I pulled up a chair, as I usually did, sat down, and began to empty out the bad gel from the containers into a large plastic drum. A short time later, Art came over and said, "I have just received orders from the top management. You will not be allowed to sit while filling gel buckets and you must work as fast as you can."

I immediately stood up but I did not say anything to Art. I felt like telling him, "If I'm sitting, they might think I'm taking a break, huh?" Apparently management thought that cleaning and filling gel buckets was too pleasurable an activity to do while sitting. If you had to stand, maybe you would work faster because it was not so much fun anymore. I decided that I would stand for hours if I had to, but I vowed that I would not work any faster.

A couple of weeks later, while cleaning the gel buckets, I asked Steve why I could not sit in a chair while performing this task. He could not come up with a good reason, much less any reason at all, so he said that I could sit in a chair as long as I worked quickly.

Getting the workers to work quickly was only one of management's concerns. The other concern was getting the workers to work every minute of their scheduled work time. When the production workers were quitting work a few minutes early and punching out before 4:00, Lori called the line foremen into the lunchroom to discuss ways to eliminate this problem.

With the addition of Ben, the designated "efficiency" expert, and the increasing attention given to worker productivity and "lost" minutes of production time, Biomed modified its policy on breaks. A rule was put into effect which stated that workers would be issued written warnings if they arrived back from a break late—by even as little as one minute. If too many workers made it a habit to arrive late from the breaks, management threatened, the breaks would be reduced from fifteen minutes to only ten minutes. Shortly after this rule was instituted, Sam and Mike received a written warning from Debbie for arriving two minutes late from a morning break.

In my seven months of work at Biomed, I received only one written warning, and that occurred under unusual circumstances. I arrived back from the laundromat (where I had been cleaning the gellers' dirty rags) during the lunch break one Monday in late June. At that time, Sam informed me that I had stamped the wrong date on a set of TR60 boxes the preceding Friday. I had trouble believing that I had actually done this. Then I thought back over that Friday's events. In the afternoon, Debbie had told me to do some cable work after I had finished stamping.

I thought that she had instructed me to stamp only the bags and not the boxes, so I began to work on the cables once I had completed this activity. Before the afternoon break, Debbie asked me if I had stamped the boxes and I replied that she had told me not to make the TR60 boxes. "That's right," Debbie said. "I told you not to make them, but you were supposed to stamp them." She ordered me to stamp the boxes after the 2:00 break.

During the period I was away from the stamping table, another worker must have changed the date so he could use the TR60 stamp to stamp a few bags. When I returned after the break to stamp the boxes, I did not even think of checking the stamp to make sure that it still had the same date on it. Apparently the date had been changed to 16 May 1984 from 18 May 1984.

Sam tried to implicate Matt, the president's son, in this "crime." He did not like Matt and thought that he was an "airhead," so he was sure that it was Matt's fault. I had a hunch that I might receive a warning, which I wanted to avoid at all costs because I was involved in a union organizing campaign (which is discussed and analyzed in detail in chapter 9, "Talking Union"). I knew that the company would eventually find out about my organizing activities so I felt that even one warning would be used against me.

During lunch, I concocted my alibi. I explained to Sam that I was called away from stamping, by Ben, to place a couple of "roach motels" in the lunchroom. (This event actually occurred the preceding Friday morning.) "When I was gone, somebody must have changed the date to stamp a few bags and did not change the rubber stamp back to the previous date," I told Sam. I decided to seek out Debbie to tell her this story.

I found Debbie in the parking lot talking to Liz. "Sam told me about the incorrectly stamped boxes," I said. "Just wait until I get inside," Debbie tartly replied. I could see that she was upset. I was hoping to avoid trouble.

Inside the factory, Sam relayed my story to Debbie. A slight smile of amusement appeared on her face. I repeated the story to Debbie. "Come over to the stamping table with me," she said. "Thirty boxes cost $21.00. I want you to sign this warning," Debbie added. The warning stated that I had stamped the wrong date on the TR60 boxes. The reason for receiving the warning was listed as "failure to follow directions," or something to that effect. I knew that the thirty incorrectly stamped boxes could easily be reworked in ten to fifteen minutes, so that was a false issue.

I argued with Debbie, telling her that I did not deserve the warning because of the extenuating circumstances. "Look, I'm not going to turn the warning over to Ben unless you do something wrong again," she said. "It won't go into your personal records."

"But I was only gone for a few minutes . . . ," I repeated. Debbie would not give in. She continued, "I've got something on everybody in my department." She said this in a manner that made her seem like a cop keeping his stoolies in line.

THE LINE FOREMEN

The line foremen were the lowest level of management and were traditionally the ones who maintained the discipline on the shop floor. They were responsible for hiring the production workers and functioned as a liaison between the workers and top–level management. Although the line foremen helped in the daily planning of production and performed a minimal amount of "brain" work, a good portion of their time was spent doing production work.

These supervisors possessed more workplace autonomy than the production workers and were, more or less, free from the relentless pressure of the clock. They did not fill out production work reports but were, in fact, the ones who reviewed the workers' daily progress.

Interactions between line foremen and the production workers were usually limited to topics concerning the production process. These conversations were usually initiated by the line foremen and focused on problems occurring during production or on an individual worker's current productivity level.

Even though the line foremen were directly responsible for keeping the workers under control and making sure that the factory operated smoothly, their remuneration hardly reflected the demands of the job. The line foremen earned $4.00 an hour when I started working at Biomed in December 1982. In May 1983, they received a 50-cent-an-hour raise, bringing their hourly wage to $4.50, although none of the production workers received a raise at this time. Even though the line foremen were part of the management "team," they did not receive the benefits that the salaried employees (secretaries, salesmen, electronic technicians, and top–level management) obtained such as medical insurance, paid holidays, sick days, and paid vacation. In addition, the line foremen often had to take home paperwork, for which work they were not paid.

Although these supervisors realized that Biomed was not paying them a "fair" wage, they still identified themselves as part of the management team (which they were) rather than as lead workers who also possessed disciplinary power over the unskilled and semiskilled workers. If something went wrong in the factory, the line foremen had to shoulder the responsibility for the problems. Therefore, they were in a unique position. While acting as the main "oppressors" on the shop floor, they were in some sense "oppressed" themselves.

THE USE OF TIME STUDIES

An instrument that contributed to the factory workers' lack of control over the production process was the time study. Time studies at Biomed consisted of having a line foreman, the plant manager or the production manager, time a worker while he produced a certain number of units. During a time study, most workers attempted to work as fast as they could in order to avoid derisive comments from the supervisors, as well as to "impress" them. By doing this, however, a worker's daily quota generally increased because management then expected the workers to produce more once they saw how fast the workers could assemble a small number of units. Thus, management obtained higher daily output totals from workers without any subsequent increase in their pay.

Not all workers, however, reacted this "positively" toward time studies. Billie, the middle-aged woman who worked in the cable department, told me a story about a worker who quit because a time study was done on him after he had been on the job for only two days. While he was soldering electrodes, Robin had stood over him with a stopwatch in her hand. The worker had become quite upset and had immediately quit. Billie said that she did not blame him, and also mentioned that she would probably have done the same thing herself.

Some time studies were performed "secretly" at Biomed, in contrast to Robin's "open" approach. In April, Steve performed "secret" time studies on all of the gellers. He sat at his desk, with an electronic stopwatch, and timed how long it took for each geller to complete a TR60. It appeared that most of the workers did not know that Steve was performing a time study on them, a common industrial engineering procedure. I thought that he should at least inform the gellers of this procedure, rather than using these sneaky tactics. When Steve performed his "secret" time studies on the disc anterior pad assemblers, he lurked behind the huge metallic storage shelves with his stopwatch in hand.

I had a number of time studies performed on me. One day in the middle of May, Art instructed me to fill up the gel buckets. Because many of them were filthy, I asked Art if I should clean them before filling them. He responded that I should just fill them because they were needed in a hurry. I doubted the validity of his statement because there was still an ample supply of filled gel containers. I did as he asked, though, and when I was finished with this task, I saw Debbie talking with Art, holding a stopwatch in her hand. A few days later, a time study was performed on me while I washed the gel buckets. This time Debbie told me that Art was going to perform a time study on me, and she instructed me to notify him when I was ready to begin the activity.

Management knew that time studies motivated at least some of the production workers to increase their output, so, at times, the *threat* of a time study produced the same results as an *actual* time study. One day at the beginning of May, Art approached me while I was taking an inventory on the plastic lids and said, "I just wanted to let you know that Debbie is probably going to do a time study on you. Just a word to the wise." I thanked him and began to work faster.

I started to watch Debbie to see if she was observing me but she was too involved with other things. After I thought about what Art had said to me, I realized how absurd it would be to do a time study on a worker counting lids! Art was most likely set up by Debbie or Steve to tell me this in order to get me to work faster. These tactics initially worked.

One time study performed on me did actually get me to work faster. I was stuffing instruction flyers in TR3 plastic bags one morning when Debbie approached me and said, "I have just timed you for twenty and it took you 4:44. I did twenty myself and it took me 1:57." She showed me the piece of paper with the times written on it. I had seen Debbie come by and take twenty flyers and some bags but I had no idea that she had taken them to perform a time study on herself to see how I was doing. I had thought that I was working at a decent pace, so I was surprised and shocked when she confronted me with this information.

I made up some excuse for why my time was so much slower than hers. I did not know if she believed me but she then demonstrated the technique I should use when stuffing flyers into the bags. I did not know why she had not shown me this procedure before. Debbie's actions made me wonder how many other time studies had been performed on me without my knowledge. I consciously tried to work at a faster pace even after I had adopted Debbie's technique although I do not know if other workers would have reacted in the same manner.

Although Debbie instituted many time studies, Steve once performed a time study on her while she was packaging disc anterior pads. Sometime later, Lori challenged Steve on the relevance of this study, claiming that it was impossible to maintain that pace throughout the whole day. Steve defended the time study in his usual abrasive manner.

By the time I was fired from Biomed, plans were under way to conduct time studies in all of the production departments. Every job was going to be retimed, with at least three workers performing each task, so that new rates could be set.

Another instrument that was used by management to maintain discipline on the shop floor was the production work report. As I have stated before, these reports were filled out daily by each production worker and they indicated how many units each worker produced in a day. Many workers expressed negative feelings to me about having to fill out these reports. Chuck told me, "The production work reports are bullshit because we aren't working piece rate."

Having to keep track of one's production affected the workers' behavior in the factory. I often saw workers produce at a furious pace for fear of not reaching their quota or average for the day. Other times, I have seen workers take shortened breaks so that they would reach an acceptable level of production. Sharon often started to work before 8:00 and she sometimes worked during part of the breaks and the lunch period. Even after she ate her lunch, she often began to work again before 12:30.

Chris, the young African American line foreman for the disc anterior pad assemblers, often walked back and forth behind the assemblers, observing them as they worked. Kevin, a young African American assembler who never made the daily quota of three-hundred disc anterior pads, received words of "encouragement" from Chris. Chris constantly pressured Kevin into working faster so that he would reach the quota. One day, the pressure from Chris became so intense that Kevin worked during the entire afternoon break.

One morning in late March, I talked with Mick about the assembly averages. The conversation centered on the sheet of paper listing the average times for the various disc anterior pad models, taped on each assembler's table. The sheets appeared as follows:

Assembly Averages

MODEL	TIME	QUANTITY PER DAY
TR60	1:15 ea.	300–20
TR80	1:09 ea.	320–40

TW82	:45 ea.	420–40
TW92	:45 ea.	420–40
TR3	1:09 ea.	320–40
ZB3	:40 ea.	455

Set up and clean up time has been figured with these averages.

Mick stated, "Anyone can make one in a minute and fifteen seconds, but you can't keep that pace up all day. I've done a lot of production work before so I know this. Sometimes you're tired, not feeling good, have to get more materials, go to the bathroom. Kevin isn't even making two-hundred a day and he's been here for awhile." Several days later, Mick told me about Juanita, the Latino assembler who sat next to him, "I don't know how she does it but she always hits three-hundred. It's like clockwork, day in and day out. I tried to watch her to imitate her motions, thinking that it could help me but it didn't."

Because Mick wondered if the production standards could be met, he asked Chris about it after our conversation. Chris expressed Mick's doubts to Steve, so a meeting between the three of them was called by Steve early one afternoon in late March. At the meeting, Chris defended Mick by telling Steve that he was a hard worker who was producing more each day. Mick stated that he was interested in knowing if anyone could produce three-hundred disc anterior pads in one day. Steve said that he liked to be challenged and he told Mick that he would show him how to do it if Mick was interested. Mick declined Steve's offer. At the end of the meeting, Steve told Mick that Biomed was a growing company and that he had a future with them.

Mick told me, "Maybe some people can produce three-hundred, but everybody's not the same." Because he had been improving, he added, "I don't know; maybe I'll be able to do three-hundred in another three to four days."

At the beginning of April, I heard Kay call over one of her workers after she figured out this worker's production averages. She told the young Indian woman assembler, who was relatively new, "You are averaging two minutes and five seconds for each electrode, which is one minute over what you should be averaging. If you don't improve, you won't get a raise, and I want all my workers to get a raise."

When the woman volunteered to work during her breaks and lunch, Kay said, "I don't want you to do that. I just want you to work faster while producing at the same quality level. Do you understand?" Even if the woman improved, she would most likely not get the promised raise. If she continued to work at her current rate, Biomed would not hesitate to fire her.

From my observations, it was apparent that the production averages were not "averages" in the true sense of the word, but times that could be achieved only if the workers pushed daily to reach their physiological limits. The time studies were done, not to adjust or set the production averages, but to see how fast the workers really worked or could work.

The production work reports were reviewed periodically, usually every couple of weeks, by the line foremen of each department. The results were then reported to Steve, who kept track of each worker's production averages through a master list on his desk.

Because the workers had to fill out these daily production work reports, many of them kept meticulous track of their production output on scraps of paper. But I am not sure that the workers always honestly reported their daily totals. In mid–April, I examined the work reports of the gellers at the end of one day. All of the Latino gellers had recorded that they had gelled sixty TR60s for the day. (If one worked at the designated "average" pace, a geller should complete fifty-seven TR60s in a day.) This seemed highly unlikely to be merely a coincidence.

It appeared to me that the Latino gellers were "controlling" production by deciding on a figure that they would record that they had produced during the day, no more or no less. Some of the Latino gellers actually may have gelled sixty TR60s (or more), while others most definitely gelled a lesser number. Sixty was a good number to pick. It was a few over the "average," which showed that the gellers "meant well" without being considered "rate busters."

All tasks that the workers performed had to be listed on the production work report. When I reworked the TR60s and the TR80s, I had to record the time it took me to tear open the sealed bags and to remove the disc anterior pads. This seemed to me to be the rationalization of the work process gone wild.

By March, I had to hand in a production work report on my janitorial work. At first, I just had to record the total time that I spent on cleaning each day. Eventually, I had to hand in a detailed work report that accounted for each minute of cleaning and the activities performed during the day (e.g., ten minutes emptying the wastebaskets, and so on). Filling out such a report usually consumed at least ten minutes at the end of the day.

There was an improvement in the method of keeping track of my janitorial duties at the end of April. Debbie presented me with a photocopied worksheet that listed my daily (and weekly) cleaning activities, as well as other jobs that I usually performed. A section was also reserved for the recording of my miscellaneous labor. Each sheet was for one work week and I was supposed to record the amount of time that I spent each day on an activity. For certain jobs, I also had to record the quantity, (e.g., the number of wastebaskets emptied, the number of gel containers cleaned and filled, the number of sheets of TR3 plastic cut, and so on). I had to carry this sheet with me and fill in the required statistics once I had completed each task.

Although this was a definite improvement over filling out the long production work reports, this sheet required more specific information concerning certain of my jobs. I still had to account for every minute of my workday. At the end of each week, Debbie added up the time I spent on each activity during the week. In her justification for the implementation of this procedure, she said, "Harry Williams wants to know where his money is going."

A couple of weeks later, I showed this worksheet to Chuck, explaining to him that I was responsible for keeping track of every minute of my work. "That's scandalous," he said. "There's no way a janitor can keep track of every minute. What if he sees a box of garbage that needs to be emptied just laying around?" "Then you record it," I replied. Chuck, Bob's assistant punch press operator, thought that this sheet was both funny and sad. He told me that he never had to fill out a production work report. Bob performed that job for the two of them.

By the end of May, Ben instituted new production work reports. These reports were similar to the old reports except now there were four production work reports per sheet instead of one. The workers were supposed to fill out one production work report segment for each of the following four periods of the day: from the start of the day until the morning break (8:00–10:00), from the end of the morning break until lunch (10:15–12:00), from the end of lunch until the afternoon break (12:30–2:00) and finally, from the end of the afternoon break until the end of the day (2:15–4:00).

The new work reports enabled management to keep closer tabs on the workers' production output. About a week after these forms were introduced, Debbie told me that Ben wanted me to start using the new form. When I protested, Debbie took the form I had been using and went to see Ben. Before I had finished my cleaning in the morning, Ben told me that he would work out a new form for me to use. The new form turned out to be very similar to the one I had been using all along.

THE SPEEDUP

While I was cleaning the lunchroom one morning in April, I heard Robin tell Lori that Biomed was spending too much for labor. According to Robin, approximately 25 to 27 percent of the cost of making each product was taken up by the cost of labor. She told Lori that for Biomed to make a "suitable" profit the labor cost would have to be reduced to 15.8 percent.

"The punch press will reduce labor costs and so will the gel dispensers that we are going to purchase," Robin remarked to Lori. Besides automation, I knew that there was only one way to reduce labor costs. Each individual worker would be made more productive through a "speedup."

I had a strong feeling that all the production operations would be retimed and the production averages would be raised when I heard Robin tell Lori that they must obtain "standard times" for each process. At the time, I was worried about my own productivity and whether it would come under closer scrutiny.

Two days later the speedup was under way. The line foremen were pressuring their production workers into working at a faster pace. My cleaning activities were also the target of the speedup, even though Biomed classified my janitorial duties as "unproductive labor."

The attempt to speed me up while I performed my janitorial tasks took place over a two-week period. Steve harassed me daily for about a week. Each day at about 8:30 in the morning, he asked me, "Are you done cleaning the offices yet?" When I told him that I still had to do some other things, he looked at his watch in a disgusted manner.

Throughout the days, Steve periodically challenged me. One day he saw me walk to the clean rag container and asked in a rather provocative manner, "What are you doing with a rag and an empty bottle?" I explained that I was going to clean the gel off of the bottle and that I was finishing off yesterday's assigned task.

I finally got tired of Steve constantly challenging me, so one morning I spoke back to him. Art asked me to move the Biomed packing boxes from the packing and inspecting tables to their proper place on the floor by the stamping table. I was surmising where to put all the boxes when Steve approached me and asked, "What are you doing?" I quickly replied in a firm manner, "I'm asking Art a question. Is that OK?" Steve walked away without responding. I was tempted to explode at him but I am glad that I was able to control myself. I felt myself becoming a little nervous for standing up to him. After this incident, Steve greatly reduced his challenges to me.

MANAGEMENT'S TRICKS

When management could not get what they wanted from the workers by using "legitimate" techniques, they often resorted to deception to accomplish their goals. Sometimes the schemes worked; sometimes they did not.

In the middle of February, Steve approached Andy one morning and asked him if he was the best geller yet. They had a short conversation, but I could not hear what they were discussing.

After their brief talk, Andy began to work at an incredible pace. A short while later, he told me that he was completing a dozen ZB3s every half hour. By the end of the day, he had gelled over 175 ZB3s.

At around 3:30, Andy mentioned to me that he was going to try to gell 150 to 200 ZB3s a day for the next two weeks in order to try to get a raise. I wished him luck although I told him that I did not think his plan would work. Andy then told me that Steve had promised him a raise if he gelled more than the "average" number of units per day. I then realized that this was what their morning discussion was about.

Two days later, Andy and I had a brief conversation in the bathroom at the start of the lunch break. Andy told me that he had "worked his ass off." He had gelled an impressive number of pieces the day before in hopes of obtaining a raise. When Steve saw this total on Andy's production work report, he told Andy that he was "too slow." I asked Andy if Steve's talk of a raise was "bullshit." All he said was "yeah."

Andy was extremely upset. He said that he would be lucky if he gelled thirty disc anterior pads for the entire day. Andy also told me that he was taking the following day off to look for another job.

I was not surprised that Steve screwed Andy. I knew that he would find an excuse not to give Andy his promised raise. I thought that he would string Andy along for a couple of weeks, however before telling him that he was not working fast enough. Because of Steve's actions, Andy was less productive than before he was conditionally offered a raise. Steve's trick backfired, causing the opposite of management's desired result.

A month and a half later, Biomed promised Bob a raise, which he also never received. At the end of March, Bob's father got him a job working at a loading dock from 6:00 P.M. to 2:00 A.M. at $9.00 per hour. Bob informed Biomed that he was quitting because of his new job. The company did not want him to leave because of his many skills and talents, so they made him an offer that he could not refuse.

Bob filled me in on the details during one afternoon break, "They offered me $6.50 an hour and the same benefits as the salaried employees— six sick days, a paid two-week vacation, and insurance. They also offered me the job of supervisor of the punch press division. I'll have one worker working under me and maybe two workers."

He continued, "I'll work this job during the day and my other one at night. The company might not make it. They need to load five trucks a night to break even. So far, they're only loading one or two trucks a night. I was guaranteed only eight hours of pay the first night. Who knows what will happen; the company has been in existence only one or two months."

In order for Bob to get his raise, he had to write up a job description, which had to be approved by Mr. Williams. A week after Bob turned in his job description, it was returned to him. Mr. Williams wanted him to rewrite it. I had a feeling that Biomed was stalling on giving Bob his raise.

Biomed kept promising, but the raise never materialized. By the beginning of May, Bob issued the company an ultimatum. He told Biomed that he wanted his raise retroactive to 1 April, and if they did not give it to him, he would quit. Biomed refused to comply with Bob's request, so, true to his word, Bob quit.

Even though Bob had quit, Biomed continued to try to get Bob to return to work at $3.50 per hour. Robin called Bob four times in an attempt to get him to come back. Bob restated his ultimatum but Robin said that they could not give him a retroactive raise because of the precarious financial state of the company. Bob told me that he had decided to quit when Biomed received a six-month shipment of plastic when they already had enough to last them for four months. He figured that if they had enough money to buy this plastic, they had enough money to give him his long overdue raise.

Biomed did not rule out the use of deception for even small and insignificant events. One afternoon in the middle of March, Harry, a young African American worker who worked in the shipping and receiving department, came into the lunchroom steaming mad. "Who punched my time card? Did you do it?" he bellowed to Steve. "No, I didn't do it," Steve replied, smiling. "Maybe one of the brothers did it." "No, they didn't do it. I was here early in the morning shoveling snow," Harry bluntly stated.

It appeared that Harry had been punched in at 8:00 although he should have been punched in at 7:45 because he was shoveling snow at the time. It looked like Steve was not going to change his time card to 7:45. I defended Harry.

"I saw Harry shoveling snow at 7:40 when I was emptying the wastebaskets in the office," I pointed out. Steve was immediately put on the spot. He changed Harry's card and made a joke out of it.

"What were you trying to do?" Debbie asked Steve once Harry had left the room. I did not hear his reply but I knew what Steve had been trying to do. He had attempted to cheat Harry out of fifteen minutes worth of pay. Biomed was so cheap that they resorted to any tactics that saved the company a few pennies.

Biomed's actions included other unsavory tactics. Several times new gellers were hired and started working while others were on short, temporary layoffs. The company's strategy was to train new workers so that they would be able to make the quota once production picked up. This also occasionally happened in the other departments.

The company also concealed important information from the workers. One day in late March, Art told me that Biomed was going to start using a highly toxic blue gel on several new, experimental products. "Don't say anything about this to anybody or people will begin to panic," he told me. Several days later, when Anna was using the blue gel, I wondered if she had been told that this gel can cause red welts if it is left on the skin for a long period of time.

LAYOFFS

Biomed not only controlled the workers when they were in the factory, but they also decided when workers would and when they would not work. Late one afternoon at the beginning of January, a slowdown occurred. The gellers were running out of disc anterior pads to gell. We were receiving the pads as soon as they were being assembled. Sometimes the gellers had to wait awhile until a batch was ready. Because of this situation, Lori told the gellers to come in at 1:00 the following afternoon.

When I arrived at the factory at 1:00 the following day, I thought about how it was hardly worth it to come in for only three hours of work. With the cost of both transportation and taxes, one was left with only a few dollars. However, I was sure that our three hours of labor was quite profitable to the company.

At the end of that week, I saw that another production "crisis" was developing. Once more, the gellers were running out of pads to gell. Debbie was extremely upset by this situation and she began to yell at the line foreman of the assemblers. I had never seen such open conflict on the shop floor between two line foremen.

Shortly after the morning break, I knew that something was "going down" that would affect the gellers. Debbie was collecting the names of various gellers, and I saw her talking with both Steve and Lori. She looked extremely upset, and I was waiting for something to happen.

Debbie read off the names of nine gellers that she wanted to see immediately in the lunchroom. My name was on the list. While waiting in the lunchroom, I wondered what this meeting was about. I thought that maybe we were not producing enough and that Debbie would threaten to fire us if we did not gell faster in the future. I waited nervously for Debbie's speech, fearing the worst.

Since five of the assembled gellers were Latino, Debbie had a young female worker from the cable department deliver her message in Spanish to that group. To the English-speaking workers, Debbie said, "We are having trouble with one of our machines. We are trying to fix it, but because of this problem, assembly is slow. We are also waiting for more materials. Because of these problems, we have to temporarily lay off most of the gellers."

She continued, "We are keeping only four gellers. There will be no work Monday, but call late Monday to see about when to come in. We hope to have everybody back to work by Wednesday."

I was relieved by Debbie's statements. I did not know if what she said was true about the production problems, but I hoped that the layoff would be as short as she said it would be. Debbie told us to go back to work, but stated that we should punch out for the day at 12:00. We had about an hour left to work. When noon came, I punched out, but I decided to eat lunch at the factory.

When I left the factory at 12:30, I saw that five gellers were still working—Anna, Sharon, Sunil (Anna's husband), Ophelia, and Harry. These gellers were selected to continue working, not because they had the most seniority, but because they were the most productive gellers.

This layoff taught me one of the fundamental lessons of factory work, which is no doubt true of many lower-level service jobs as well. The wages are low and one is not even guaranteed these meager wages on a daily basis because of layoffs. It seemed illogical to me that for several weeks the workers had been asked to work a lot of overtime (including Saturdays and Sundays) when now some of the workers were not even working the standard hours for which they had been hired.

On the following Monday, I called Biomed, as Debbie suggested, to inquire about work on Tuesday. Lori told me that the machine was still broken and that I would not be needed on Tuesday. "What about Wednesday?" I asked. "I don't know," she replied. "We'll call you when we need you."

I talked with Debbie on Tuesday. "What about work for tomorrow?" I asked. She said, "Look, we're having more trouble fixing this machine than we thought. Call back on Friday." "Do you have anything else that needs to be done around the factory? I'll do anything," I said. "I'll get back to you tomorrow morning if I need you," Debbie answered.

I was beginning to strongly doubt the story about the broken machine. If this machine was that important for production, it surely would have been fixed within a couple of days. I was also becoming increasingly depressed by my layoff. Working at Biomed was definitely a miserable experience, but not working at all made me feel worse. I occupied my time off from work with reading books and magazines at home and in the library, as well as wondering whether I should begin searching for a new job.

I talked with Lori on Wednesday. She told me that it looked like we would not be needed until the following Wednesday. Once more, I asked her about the possibility of doing other work in the factory. She said that she would get back to me. I began to worry. First, I was told that we would be off for several days. Then it was a week. Now it was a week and a half. Lori did not even mention the problem with the broken machine. It looked like that was merely a cover story.

Debbie told me on Thursday that there was no work for Friday, but if something came up, she would keep me in mind. When I asked her about work for the following week, Debbie said that she did not know when we would be back at work. I became extremely concerned with Debbie's last statement. Earlier I had been told when we would probably be called back. Now, Debbie would not even give a possible date for our return.

I came in on Friday afternoon to pick up my paycheck for the previous week. Lori told me to report back for work the following Wednesday at 8:00. I felt relieved that I was finally going to go back to work.

On my way out of the factory, I waved to Bob. He waved and motioned me to come over to talk to him. We talked briefly, and he told me that the layoffs had occurred because Biomed had a shortage of orders, something that I had already figured out. I thought that we both might get in trouble for talking so I said, "I'll see you Wednesday."

Early Monday morning I received a call from Lori telling me to come in to work that day. My layoff was finally over.

After this "long" layoff, shorter layoffs of one or two days occasionally occurred at Biomed for some production workers. Only a few workers were affected at a time although the gellers were usually the only ones laid off. When production slowed down, the gellers were the workers most vulnerable to layoffs because once the disc anterior pads had been gelled, they were only usable for the following eleven months. Therefore, Biomed did not want to have an excess supply on their shelves if they did not have immediate customers for the gelled pads.

At the end of April, another "long" layoff occurred at Biomed. The company issued a notice to all of the production workers that the factory would be closed for a two-week period. This incident did not surprise me because of events that had occurred earlier in the week.

Before lunch on Tuesday, Debbie announced to the gellers that the entire factory would be working only thirty hours a week for several weeks. The workers were presented with two options. We could either work from 8:00 until 2:00, five days a week, apparently without a lunch break, or work four full days a week with Mondays off. The gellers unanimously chose the four-day workweek. Debbie did not give us any reason for this change. She said only that "the entire factory has to cut back."

Later in the day, I asked Bob about this situation. He informed me that the change was due to a management reorganization, a changeover of cables, and a number of hospitals that were delinquent in the payment of their bills. Bob claimed that a shortage of orders was not the problem this time. "They have more orders than they know what to do with," he told me.

All the production workers were sent home at 3:00 on Wednesday afternoon. No reason was given to the workers for this early dismissal. I cannot remember any of the supervisors making an official announcement. Because of the shortened workday, the afternoon break was cut short by five minutes.

While I was emptying the garbage on Thursday morning, Andy said to me, "Vic, this place is scandalous. They're sending us home at noon." (Andy often used the word "scandalous" to describe things in the factory with which he was upset.) Once more, no reasons were given by management for this action and no announcement was made. The information filtered down to the workers as if it were simply a rumor.

Shortly before the morning break on Friday, a notice was passed out to all of the production workers. The notice said:

> This is to notify you that Biomedical Electronics Corporation will be closed from 4/25/83 through 5/6/83. We will contact you prior to 5/6/83 if any changes occur.
>
> Steve E. Taylor

When Lori handed me the notice she told me that Biomed wanted me to come in for four hours a day to continue my janitorial work. Steve told me that I should not mention this to any of the other workers.

Fortunately Biomed started to call back some of the production workers on 27 April. I began to work full days once more. Every day a few more workers were called back until the factory was again operating at full capacity. By the end of May, production was booming at Biomed.

Afrem, a middle-aged Assyrian subassembler, summed up Biomed's attitude toward their workers when he said "They hire people when they need them and they lay them off when they don't need them." He was right. Biomed treated its workers without any regard.

FIRINGS

Steve always bragged about Biomed's "progressive" policy on firing production workers. "Biomed never fires any of its workers. We don't believe in firing anybody here." Until I was fired late in June 1983 for trying to organize a union at Biomed, there had been no outright firings. If Biomed wanted to "fire" a particular worker they laid that worker off and simply never called him or her back to work.

I thought that this method was unusually cruel, even for Biomed, because it prevented the fired worker from knowing what was going on. A worker who is told that he is on a short temporary lay-off will be less likely to search for another job than a worker who knows that he has been fired.

The first firing that I was aware of while I was working at Biomed was the firing of Vern. Vern was initially suspended for one and a half days for falling asleep while gelling in late December. At the beginning of January Vern was one of the gellers who was laid off. When I returned to work after the layoff Sam told me that Vern had been fired—information he had picked up from Debbie.

Isaac was fired either late in January or early in February. During lunch one day in early February I asked Lou where Isaac (a subassembler) was because I had not seen him around the factory for quite awhile. "Oh, we let him go," Lou explained. "Is that a polite way of saying that he was fired?" I inquired of Lou. "Yes," he replied. It appeared that Isaac was "let go" because he did not work fast enough.

Greg overheard my conversation with Lou. He said to Lou, "I believe everyone here is trying their best. Don't you feel that way?" "I don't believe in trying," Lou replied. "You either make it or you don't. That's all there is to it."

Two more workers were fired for not working fast enough. Both were not called back to work after Biomed issued the plant closing notice. I learned of Tony's firing while working in the cable department at the end of April. Tony had worked in the packing/inspecting department but had been transferred to the cable department. He was tall and moved slowly and appeared to me to be lethargic and somewhat dull.

Just to make conversation, I asked Leopoldo, a young Latino cable department worker, "Is Tony going to be a permanent fixture in the cable department?" Leopoldo then proceeded to tell me that Tony would not be called back to work from his layoff. When I asked him why Tony had been fired he said, "He works too slow; he doesn't follow orders; you have to explain things to him several times before he follows directions; and he doesn't help to clean up at the end of the day."

The second worker fired at this time was Kevin, a young African American disc anterior pad assembler. I saw him come back to Biomed twice—

once to pick up a paycheck and once to find out when he would be called back to work. I do not know what Steve told him when he returned to Biomed the second time. After this appearance at the factory I never saw Kevin again.

A young subassembler that I had become quite friendly with over the span of a few months also was fired from Biomed at the end of April. While I was emptying wastebaskets in the offices one morning in late April I saw a dismissal notice for Herb on Robin's desk. The notice stated that Herb had been on a thirty-day probationary period for careless work. Apparently Lou thought that his work had not sufficiently improved. Herb's dismissal notice was signed by both Lou and Robin.

After I saw this notice I remembered that Herb was on a layoff and probably had not been informed of his firing. I decided to call him that evening to find out if he knew of his dismissal.

I called Herb late in the evening. He told me that he had spent the day smoking grass and drinking beer in the woods with Manuel and John. While he was talking to me he was smoking a joint and watching a W. C. Fields movie on television. Herb did not seem to be in a talking mood, so I did not press him. By the way he talked I knew that he was not aware of his firing.

About a week later I found out that Herb had learned of his firing from Lou. While talking to Lou at the beginning of May I learned that he had fired Herb. Lou said that Herb was not too upset when he was told of his firing. He stated that he was not happy with either the working conditions or the wages and that he had already been looking for another job. I felt like telling Lou that none of the workers were satisfied with either the wages or the working conditions at Biomed.

ANALYZING THE DICTATORSHIP OF HIGH-TECH MANAGEMENT:
THE ISSUE OF CONTROL

The control of the workers and the labor process is not a management *goal* in and of itself, but a *means* for achieving the firm's drive to obtain profitable production. Edwards states that any "system of control" in the workplace involves the coordination of three components—"a mechanism or method by which the employer directs work tasks," a set of procedures for supervising and evaluating production performance and methods for disciplining and rewarding workers.[4]

There is no single strategy that is effective in maintaining control of the workplace in all situations, but a variety of control strategies exist that a firm can use in an attempt to obtain control over labor.[5] These strategies include the use of discipline, industrial engineering, and the power to fire workers.[6] Biomed did not develop any new and sophisticated control strategies that are unique to high-tech firms, but rather successfully utilized all three of the above-mentioned procedures, which will be discussed in greater detail later in the chapter.

The type of control that Biomed instituted in its manufacturing facilities is called "simple control." Simple control is usually administered for jobs found in the secondary labor market, which would include both the vast majority of high-tech production jobs as a whole and those at Biomed. This type of control is characterized by the arbitrary treatment of workers, the presence of supervisors who possess enormous powers that they exercise in a personal manner, the continual bullying and threatening of workers on the shop floor, and supervisors acting like despots.[7] Many incidents discussed earlier in this chapter indicate that Biomed was the quintessential example of a company administered by simple control.

Edwards's conception of simple control is similar to what Burawoy refers to as the "despotic organization of work"/"despotic regime." In this type of factory regime, "coercion prevails over consent," and "[w]orkers have no ways to defend themselves against the arbitrary whims of the manager or overseer who hires and fires at his own discretion."[8]

On a daily basis, the plant manager and the line foremen at Biomed were responsible for enforcing simple control and for organizing the despotic factory regime. Their concern for increased production and for the workers achieving their daily quotas were the issues that led to the expression of simple control and the despotic factory regime at the point of production. Although these line foremen must have realized that they had slim chances for progressing to a higher level of management within the company, in order to succeed at their jobs they were required, in Nichols and Beynon's words, to "act as if they were [employers]. More precisely, they must act like plant-level manager accountants." Quite simply, this meant that the line foremen were required to keep track of both the workers' production time and production levels. Although the line foremen were poorly paid and did not receive the other material benefits of higher-level management, because of the roles they occupied on the shop floor, they were "highly effective agents of capital," conspiring to enslave the working class.[9]

In order to keep control of the workers on a daily basis, the company utilized a combination of strategies, which, as mentioned earlier, involved discipline, industrial engineering, and the firing of workers. The use of discipline was a major part of Biomed's control strategy, which Robinson and McIlwee found was used as a *primary* control strategy adopted by high-tech manufacturing firms. One aspect of this factory discipline that I continually noticed was the treatment of workers as schoolchildren in many situations. This theme appears in other industrial ethnographies as well. Pfeffer notes that "[w]orkers are surrounded by rules and treated and disciplined as if they were schoolchildren." Cavendish states that certain aspects of her work in a British automobile components factory were "like being back in school."[10]

In her short stint as an assembler, Hembree noticed that the supervisors of a small electronics manufacturer in Silicon Valley, treated her and other workers in a similar manner:

> Hilda acted like a nursery school teacher, patting employees on the head with "Good girl!" and "Good boy!" praise. She alternately scolded and cajoled us to work faster, and other supervisors followed suit. Some days the assembly room rang with commands reminiscent of junior high school: "I said quiet"; "Don't slump in your chair", "Wipe that look off your face, young lady."[11]

Much of the factory discipline at Biomed, as well as at other industrial companies, appeared to be counterproductive to the company's goal of maintaining profitable production.[12] This harsh discipline did not appear to help workers maintain their levels of production, or may have actually hurt production levels, but Biomed somehow believed that instituting this type of discipline was the correct strategy to pursue.

According to Hodson, high-tech firms institute control strategies in order to closely monitor the workers. At Biomed, the management utilized industrial engineering, (i.e., the use of both time studies and the production work reports), as a primary method for achieving this goal. Although each production worker was required to keep track of his or her daily production, the employees were not working under any type of piecework system at Biomed. Even though the company never specifically referred to this system by name, we were working under a system called "measured daywork." Under measured daywork, workers are still required to meet production quotas that are established by time study, but rather than earning a bonus for matching or exceeding the rate, employees are paid a "standard day wage" and are disciplined if they fail to achieve the standard rate.[13]

The use of time studies and production work reports was integral for the successful functioning of this system of measured daywork. Time studies were always used at Biomed to increase production quotas or output. However, unlike piecework or incentive systems, which workers can manipulate to their own advantage,[14] the system of measured daywork could not be so manipulated. Under this system, increased production quotas resulted in *intensified* effort, but the *same* wage levels for the production workers.

Another aspect of production that became readily apparent under this system of measured daywork was that the "average production times" for the various models were not, in reality, "averages," but times that could be attained only if one was working to one's physiological limits for the entire shift. This same phenomenon has been noted by other industrial ethnographers.[15]

The time studies and the production work reports at Biomed also served another purpose. In the words of Thompson, such mechanisms are used to obtain the workers' "legitimation and consent in work."[16] The question, then, that needs to be asked is, how does management get the workers to control themselves?

In some industrial settings, that are based on the piecework system, management is able to obtain the workers' consent and compliance to engage in profitable production through their participation in "games" on the shop floor. As a participant observer in a piecework machine shop, Burawoy discovered that these games of "making out" in production are established as informal rules and practices in order to create space and time for the workers, to make the production work more interesting as well as to limit earnings.[17]

At Biomed, however, time studies and production work reports, not production games, were used to gain the workers' consent and compliance to production. This was a much more brutal approach that was based on the company's attempt to create an "industrial panopticon." Foucault viewed the philosopher Jeremy Bentham's panopticon, the model of an architectural design for a circular prison with the cells being positioned around a central control point, as the ultimate mechanism in the "technology of discipline." The idea behind the panopticon was that since the prisoners never knew when they were *actually* being observed, they would modify their behavior under the belief that they were always being watched.[18]

It appears to me that this was the role of the time studies and threatened time studies, as well as of the production work reports at Biomed. The ultimate goal was to get the workers to work *every* scheduled minute of work time and the use of time studies and production work reports were integral to this strategy. Since individual workers were occasionally told that a time study was going to be performed on them, whether or not this was actually the case, workers often worked quickly under the assumption that a supervisor might be performing a time study on them. However, if an actual time study was being performed on a worker and the worker did, in fact, work fast, this only resulted in higher production quotas that all of the department's workers would eventually have to meet. Thus, through this methodology, an important managerial function was to create the perception among the workers that they were constantly under "(s)urveillance (the all-seeing eye of the Panopticon)" while they were at work.[19]

The use of production work reports also encouraged this same type of behavior. Since the workers believed that their output was being closely monitored on a daily basis, some workers directly modified their behavior by working through breaks and parts of the lunch period to achieve their daily quotas. Other workers adopted the strategy of attempting to work faster during work time. Thus, in a sense, through the utilization of the time studies and the production work reports, the workers at Biomed contributed to their own control, or as Foucault stated, they were "caught up in a power situation of which they themselves [were] the bearers."[20]

Although the issue of opposition to managerial control has been largely ignored in Braverman's classic treatise on the labor process, it should be made clear, that there existed amongst Biomed's workers at least some level of persistent shop floor resistance to these forms of industrial engineering, as well as to the other aspects of management control. Although there has been suprisingly little written of a theoretical nature on the role of worker resistance in the labor process, there are many different strategies that workers use, shaped by the specific nature as well as the space and time of the employment relationship.[21] Hodson argues that workers engage in different forms of resistance, ranging from sabotage to withdrawal, under different working conditions. Johnson notes that this resistance, which he terms "collective control," is necessary in order for workers to effectively handle the stress and the pressures of the workplace, while Hodson acknowledges that "(o)ccasional acts of resistance can help to alleviate boredom and create at least a moment of excitement in an otherwise grindingly dull working day." Kimery discusses resistance strategies in terms of the workers' "everyday coping skills" as an effective antimanagement control strategy for carving out a degree of autonomy in the workplace. And in nonunion workplaces, Hodson discovered that "higher minority representation results in greater informal resistance" (or unorganized resistance) to managerial control.[22]

Different types of unorganized resistance did occur at Biomed in the forms of absenteeism, quitting, and (at least some) workers giving themselves "pencil bonuses" on the production work reports, as well as individual workers withholding "production secrets" from management. Devinatz points out that withholding such production knowledge from management is crucial in order for workers to retain a measure of control on the shop floor.[23]

In addition, shop floor resistance at Biomed contained a gendered component. With an increased interest among scholars in the relationship between gender and the labor process, the phenomenon of gendered resistance has been examined by a number of researchers who have found that certain types of antimanagerial strategies, as well as forms of resistance, are gender specific.[24] For example, at Biomed, one specific way in which the Latino women gellers resisted management control was through the secretive writing and exchange of long notes on napkins in Spanish while engaging in the gelling process.

However, a variety of forms of organized resistance were also present at Biomed. Although there did not appear to be any incidents of restriction of output, as have been discovered in other factories,[25] each of the Latino gellers, as mentioned earlier, at least occasionally, recorded on their production work reports that they had gelled exactly sixty TR60s for the day. Two more overt incidents of organized resistance among the workers at Biomed—"the mass walk-out" and "the uprising of the Latino gellers"—are discussed in detail in chapter 8, "Rank and File Discontent."

Finally, as Edwards has pointed out, methods of control are ultimately based on the power of the employer to fire workers, although the ability of the employer to lay off workers should also be placed in this same category.[26] In the United States, this method of control has historically been reinforced through the operation of the "employment at will" doctrine. Although there is some debate on the doctrine's origins in this country, the essence of this doctrine is that "absent a statutory or contractual restriction, an employee or employer can terminate the employment relationship at any time, for any or no reason, with or without notice." While public employees, as well as employees covered by either collective bargaining agreements or written employment contracts, are not considered to be "at will" employees, federal laws exist that prohibit the termination of "at will" employees for certain reasons such as union organizing and reporting employer safety problems.[27] However, even though the "employment at will" doctrine has been attenuated by legislation and court decisions, this doctrine provides employers with tremendous power, and demonstrates the asymmetrical power relationships that exist, with respect to their employees in the nonunionized workplace.

This control mechanism of firings and layoffs was used extensively by Biomed. As I stated earlier in the chapter, workers at Biomed were never fired outright, but were first laid off and then simply never called back to work. Because of this policy, layoffs, for any individual worker, could actually mean that the worker had, in fact, been terminated. However, because the worker had been "laid off" instead of fired, this might be more advantageous in terms of the worker being able to obtain unemployment benefits, if the worker was knowledgeable and motivated enough to pursue this option.

Most layoffs were based not on seniority but on the individual worker's productivity. The most productive employees continued to work while the less productive workers were temporarily laid off. In addition, layoffs always occurred rather suddenly, with the company being extremely secretive with this information, possibly in order to reduce the likelihood of sabotage on the part of the workers. This secretiveness was a control strategy in itself. Pfeffer notes that at the company where he worked, the cancellation of overtime and the notification of layoffs occurred rather suddenly and in a secretive manner. In analyzing the company's behavior, Pfeffer states:

> As indicated, the factory workers' subordination and related vulnerability
> is effected in part by the company's keeping from workers sufficient advance
> information about the factors of production and intentions of the company

to affect their lives. Perhaps the company is simply unconcerned with informing workers. To conceive of it as a lack of concern, however, is to miss the point. . . . Keeping workers ignorant also helps management to control them. Ignorance, particularly in the face of economic instability, makes workers insecure, hanging for hard information upon company handouts that consistently come too late for a meaningful response. Management treats information as part of its private property and uses information to protect its own authoritarian rule.[28]

In summary, the management of Biomed neither developed nor utilized control strategies unique to high-tech firms, but rather implemented strategies that are found in other industrial sectors. However, management's strategies for control at Biomed were based on an extreme distrust of the workers' willingness to successfully carry out their tasks unless the workers believed that they were continually being monitored by management, a finding consistent with that of Colclough and Tolbert for high-tech industries as a whole. In addition, the management style of Biomed's managers was very authoritarian and unprofessional, which Hodson found was typical for managers in high-tech industries. Finally, because high-tech production jobs are, for the most part, secondary labor market jobs, a major control strategy of Biomed's management was to play upon the workers' fear of losing their jobs, a high-tech control strategy discussed by Robinson and McIlwee.[29]

7.

Factory Life

JURAVICH ARGUES THAT "THE "REALITY" OF INDUSTRIAL LIFE LIES IN ITS EV-eryday, mundane details."[1] This is most certainly true. However, while this "reality" includes descriptions and analyses of the labor process, management control strategies, both unorganized and organized worker resistance in opposition to management control as well as trade unionism (or attempts at unionization), it also extends well beyond them. In terms of doing industrial ethnographic work, the "thick description"[2] of everyday industrial life can be enhanced when one examines how what occurs at the workplace affects the person's outside life (separate from the workplace) and vice versa.

However, in this chapter, unlike in Pollert's study,[3] I will not discuss in either theoretical or systematic terms the inseparability of experiences inside and outside of work. Neither will I discuss the prior socialization of these workers, as in Willis's study,[4] or how they ended up as factory workers in what is referred to as the secondary labor market. The best I can do is to provide several "snapshots" of industrial life that provide a glimmer of insight into a number of the workers' lives outside of the factory and how they came to work at Biomed. I do not argue that this information is either complete or necessarily generalizable.

In order to set the stage for presenting the above mentioned information, however I will briefly discuss the factory's racial/ethnic group composition and analyze the pattern of interaction among these various groups. In addition, I will discuss the racial/ethnic and sexual breakdown of the occupational groupings and departments at Biomed. After presenting information on a number of Biomed's workers' past jobs as well as their future plans for obtaining "better" work, brief portraits of individual workers will be presented, as well as a section on politics in the factory that focuses on the 1983 Chicago mayoral campaign. Finally, I will conclude the chapter by discussing a few odd corners of industrial life that are important to mention here in order to better explain the factory experiences of Biomed's workers.

THE RACIAL AND ETHNIC COMPOSITION OF BIOMED'S WORKFORCE

Although Biomed was continually hiring workers during my tenure at the factory and workers constantly were leaving (either voluntarily or involuntarily), I estimate that the ethnic composition of the plant's workforce was approximately as follows: White (45 percent), Latino (30 percent), African American (10 percent), East Indian (10 percent), and Assyrian (5 percent). Thus, a majority of Biomed's workforce (55 percent) was composed of minorities. According to Hodson, who conducted a comprehensive study of industrial ethnographies that involved measuring the relationship between race, solidarity, and resistance in the workplace, "strong minority presence" exists in the workplace when more than 30 percent of the workers are minorities.[5]

The Latino workers, who were the largest minority group in the factory, could essentially be divided into two groups. Three-quarters of this group were first-generation Latino workers; some may have been undocumented workers. Although a few of these workers were bilingual (Spanish and English), many from this group spoke only Spanish or spoke very little English. Most of these workers appeared to range in age from their early thirties to early forties. The remaining portion of this ethnic group appeared to be second-generation Latino workers. They were all fluent in both English and Spanish and did not speak English with any noticeable accent. These workers had attended high school in the United States (most in Chicago) and were younger than the other group of Latino workers, being in either their late teens or early twenties.

The daily interaction among these various ethnic groups occurred in a specific pattern. The first-generation Latino workers, as well as the East Indian and Assyrian workers, socialized only within their own ethnic groups during the break and lunch periods. However, the white, African

American, and the second-generation Latino workers often socialized together during these periods. Although there were times when the second-generation Latino workers interacted with the first-generation Latino workers, this did not occur on a daily basis. On the other hand, there was hardly any interaction between the white and African American workers and the first-generation Latino, East Indian, and Assyrian workers. In addition, there was little or no contact between the groups of Latino, East Indian, and Assyrian workers.

There were also specific socialization patterns that occurred based on occupational grouping. During the breaks and lunch period, the line foremen usually socialized among themselves, although Steve often socialized with the unskilled white, African American, and second-generation Latino workers. I viewed Steve's socializing as a way to gauge the discontent among these workers as well as a method for preventing this discontent from emerging into any collective action. In addition, the skilled electronic technicians usually socialized among themselves. The semiskilled subassemblers and the unskilled factory workers socialized with one another based on their membership in the ethnic groups discussed above.

There was an interesting pattern in terms of the racial/ethnic/sexual composition of the occupational groupings at Biomed. All of the electronic technicians were young white men, while the subassemblers (who worked closely with the electronic technicians) were composed of white, Latino, and Assyrian men, although one young Latino woman worked briefly as a subassembler. The remainder of the factory workers, with the exception of Bob, were unskilled and labored in one or more of the following departments: assembly, cable, snap-type electrode, gelling, punch press, inspecting/packing, or shipping/receiving. The first four departments mentioned were composed of workers of both sexes from all of the ethnic groups present in the plant, while the punch press, inspecting/packing, and shipping/receiving departments were limited to only white and African American men.

Based on the above breakdown, one can conclude that there was ethnic and sexual segregation among the occupational groupings and departments at Biomed. The skilled jobs were limited by both race and gender (to only white males), while the semiskilled jobs were, for the most part, limited by gender (to only males). Finally, there was sexual segregation among the more desirable departments open to the unskilled workers; only males worked in the punch press, inspecting/packing, and shipping/receiving departments. This task assignment of high-tech manufacturing work by ethnicity and gender is consistent with the findings of Scott, who discovered that female, Latino, and Asian electronics production workers in Southern California were more likely to be found in "the basic, largely unskilled central core of assembly work," which included assembly, clipping, and reworking tasks.[6]

THE WORKERS: PAST JOBS, FUTURE PLANS

Almost every worker I talked to at Biomed had a plan or scheme to get out of this factory. Some of the workers simply hoped to find a better factory job—one that offered higher wages and better working conditions. This was not too surprising because most of the workers' previous jobs had been in factories or warehouses.

Juan, a portly Latino geller, had worked for five years at a sheet metal factory and for five years as a punch press operator at A. B. Dick before being laid off in 1982. When I asked him if he could operate Biomed's punch press, he laughed and said, "It's nothing." He had earned $7.35 an hour and told me, "It was a dirty job but I didn't mind it because I got good pay." Juan checked periodically about going back to work at A. B. Dick. The company was not sure if and when he would be called back from his indefinite layoff.

Pedro, another Latino geller, had worked at a gas station and a warehouse before he landed a job at Biomed. He told me that he had made $5.20 an hour at his warehouse job before he was laid off after working there only three months. "You could do anything in that place," he said. "Sing, dance, talk. It was great." Ten days after he lost his warehousing job, he was hired as a geller at Biomed.

Pedro applied for a job at a notebook factory where some of his relatives worked. The company said that they would call him, although he was not sure when they would contact him. "The starting pay is $4.50 per hour, which is good pay," Pedro told me.

Afrem, the Assyrian subassembler, had been an accountant for more than twenty years in his native country of Iraq. He had tried to obtain an accounting position in this country but had been unsuccessful. "It's too competitive here," he said. "They wouldn't give me a chance." Since he was not able to find a job as an accountant, he went to work as an electromechanical assembler in a factory located in a Chicago suburb. "The work was a little more complicated than the work I do here," he told me. At the time he was laid off, he was making a little more than $6.00 an hour. Afrem was unemployed for a year before he was hired as a subassembler at Biomed. During the lunch periods, Afrem always looked through the "Help Wanted" section of the *Chicago Tribune* in hopes of finding a better assembly job.

Some workers realized that their only escape from factory work would be through attending school. Sam, who was taking a few courses at a local junior college, planned to attend a four-year university by the fall of 1984. Because Clark, a young African American worker in the cable department, could not find a decent industrial production job, he told me that he was going to apply for a grant so that he could take a six-week computer technician course at the University of Illinois-Chicago. "Nothing's happening with this job," he said.

Sometimes workers were able to "escape" from Biomed. At the end of May, Juanita, an extremely productive Latino woman geller, obtained an assembly job at a lamp factory that paid $7.00 an hour. After taking a thirty-six-week course to become a certified ECG technician, Lenny, the head of the shipping and receiving department found employment at a hospital for $5.25 an hour. Although he had spent $1,700 on the course, he felt that it was a good investment. Before he left, in the middle of March, I asked him if he would miss Biomed.

"I won't miss this place at all," he replied. "I will miss some of the people here but I won't miss anybody who works in the front office."

Even the workers who were at Biomed for only a very short time made future plans for leaving the plant. Sundan, an Indian worker in the cable department who had a thick British accent, had owned an auto parts store in India, but came to the United States in hopes of finding a better life. He found the work at Biomed to be very boring. "I find America to be a very lonely place," he said. "I miss my family and friends." Even though Sundan was living with his sister and her husband and had been in the United States only two months, he still wanted to return to India. The only thing that prevented him from making the trip was a lack of money.

Francisco, a young worker originally from Puerto Rico, began to work in the cable department in late June. Although he was only one credit short of graduating from high school, he had had to leave school because he needed the money. Before working at Biomed, Francisco had worked at a power plant for $3.50 per hour but had lost his job when the company brought in undocumented Mexican workers. "I called the immigration service but it didn't do any good," he said. After losing his job at the power plant, Francisco obtained a job at a foodstand. When he learned of Biomed's policy of limited wage raises, he told me that he planned to continue looking for another job.

PORTRAITS OF INDIVIDUAL WORKERS

Of the workers I got to know fairly well at the factory, each had a unique background prior to working at Biomed. Short portraits of six of these workers—backgrounds, personalities, attitudes—follow.

Mark

When I first saw Mark at Biomed, he seemed much different than the other factory workers. He had a crew cut and appeared to be much more serious than anyone else in the plant. Mark began to work in the packing department at the end of February.

When I first talked to Mark, I learned that he had spent the last three years in the "Special Forces"—more commonly known as the "Green Berets"—branch of the army. Mark informed me that this particular branch of the military was involved with insurgency against foreign governments. According to Mark, early in December 1982, he broke his tailbone when he parachuted into North Korea on a "secret" mission. Because of this accident, Mark had to temporarily leave the Special Forces until his tailbone completely healed. He hoped to re-enter the Special Forces within four months.

Mark spoke with pride of having been in the Special Forces. His army training was evident by the way that he immediately barked out answers to my questions. He told me in a rather straightforward manner, "You can look at the things that the Special Forces do as being either good or bad. I happen to think the things they do are good."

A few days later, Mark told me that he was also shot in the shoulder by a North Korean on his last mission. "You only hear of the mission when we mess up," he said. "And you want to go back and do this again?" I asked, rather stunned. "Yep," Mark replied.

I could tell that the Special Forces provided Mark's life with excitement. This job was a challenge for Mark and that was why he enjoyed it. It had nothing to do with ideology. This became apparent, one day, when I talked to Mark about communists.

During the lunch break one day in early April, Sam was reading an article in the *Chicago Tribune* about a Vietnamese history professor teaching in the United States who gave "critical support" to the current Communist government in Vietnam. Mark was reading the article, too, and said, "He's a communist. Get him out of this country." "So you hate communists?" I asked. Mark shrugged his shoulders and replied, "No, it doesn't matter to me. I don't really care."

His comments led me to believe that he was not a member of the Special Forces for political reasons. Mark was not a professional anticommunist, in fact, it seemed that he had not even thoroughly considered many political issues or the true nature and function of this job. I knew that he was joking when he said, "The only good communist is a dead communist."

Mark quit his job early one afternoon in late April. His tailbone and shoulder had sufficiently healed for him to return to the Special Forces in early May. He was a nice guy and I hated to see him go. I wished Mark luck in the future before he left the plant.

Herb

Another worker who had spent some time in the military was Herb. After flunking out of Officers Candidate School, Herb was sent to Vietnam. He told me that he had been in Vietnam during the last three months of 1973 to help in the evacuation of the American troops. Since Herb was involved in communications, he was fairly mobile, never remaining in any one place too long. Herb did not see any shooting and he told me that the time flew by while he was in "Nam."

I asked Herb if he had seen any of the commercial films about the Vietnam War. He smiled and in a twangy, Southern accent said, "You know I could really identify with *Apocalypse Now*. We'd be having parties on the beaches and there would be shooting, which we could hear, only six miles away."

"I wasn't really affected by Vietnam," Herb continued. "I sometimes saw dead bodies on the road, but that's about it." He told me a number of stories; the most interesting one was of Vietnamese mothers giving their children explosives, which they brought up to American jeeps in order to blow them up. Although Herb had already spent a total of six years in the service, he mentioned that he had reenlisted for a world cruise in two to three years.

When I first met Herb, his long hair, full beard, and glasses made his smile disarming. He told me that he was really enjoying working in the subassembly room and that he found the work to be very interesting. Herb complained that his back hurt from leaning over all day and I mentioned that I experienced the same affliction from gelling all day.

Herb's opinion of the work changed once the speedup was instituted. He no longer found the work either interesting or enjoyable. Toward the end of April, Herb received a written warning for incorrectly assembling a cable. He told me that it had not been his fault because the cable had been given to him already incorrectly assembled.

Herb also told me that a new subassembler had received a warning for incorrectly performing a task for which he had not even been trained! "This is the most childish place I have ever worked," he said. Herb was also upset that some of the subassemblers had been promised raises that they did not ever receive.

James

The only other Biomed worker who had spent some time in Vietnam was James. He was a large, physically imposing, African American man in his early thirties. "Man, I was scared those first four months. I never lifted my head. After that, I was OK," James said. He told me many stories about Vietnam, in such great detail that it almost seemed that the incidents had happened yesterday.

Although Herb claimed that he had not been affected by his Vietnam experience, James had been left with physical scars due to his exposure to Agent Orange during his eleven months in Vietnam. He had filed a claim with the Veteran's Administration because his exposure to the chemical caused his hands and arms to swell periodically, which made it hard for him to work.

James's physical problem had been the reason for his termination as a security guard, the last job that he had held before coming to work at Biomed. Because of his swelling arms and hands, James had had to leave work several times before the end of the day. The firm that he had worked for had asked him to sign a statement saying that he would not miss any more days of work due to his medical problems. When James refused to sign this document and went home sick one day, he was fired.

James had attempted to file a claim with the Department of Human Rights but he had exceeded the six-month deadline by four months. Since he did not have the money to pay a private lawyer, James had had to drop the claim. If he had filed in time, the Department of Human Rights told him that he would have had a good chance of getting his $9.00 per hour job back.

After James lost his security guard job, he remained unemployed for a year and a half. Because he was extremely dissatisfied with his job at Biomed, he continued to apply for jobs whenever he could. During the lunch break, James visited other factories and plants in the area in search of a higher paying job. Only a handful of factories were even taking applications.

James had another plan for escaping from Biomed, and possibly factory life, forever—"hitting it big" in the lottery. James told me that he regularly played the state lottery. One morning in late March, he told me, "I ought to win something this week because I had four numbers. It might only be $40, though." He continued, "If I win $40,000, I'll quit my job here. I'd probably quit if I won even $4,000. If I won $100, I'd just buy some more lottery tickets."

James tried to make work at Biomed as enjoyable as possible. He whistled and sang while he worked, much to the amusement of the other gellers. He thought that this behavior—not his swelling hands and arms—might eventually lead to his being fired from Biomed. (James had to leave work at Biomed only once because of his physical problems.) Although James first worked as a geller, he was soon transferred to the cable department to do soldering work.

At the end of April, James received a letter from the post office saying that he had been hired as an elevator operator with a starting salary of $19,000 a year. He had taken a civil service examination in October 1982, reserved exclusively for disabled veterans and recently discharged military personnel, and had scored extremely well on all sections of the test. James had been waiting to hear from the post office and was pleased that the job had finally come through. He was extremely happy that he would not have to return to work at Biomed. When James showed me the letter, he exaggerated, "Man, I can make more off unemployment than from working here."

Mick

Mick became a factory worker almost by accident. Although he was almost six and a half feet tall and looked like a construction worker, Mick began working part-time for a florist while in high school. After graduation, he worked full-time for the florist and was going to be trained to be a floral designer, but after a couple of years, business went bad so he was laid off. A friend told him that Duro Metal Products was hiring workers, so he went down to the factory one morning to fill out an application. He was given a physical examination and started working there the next day. Mick worked as a metal polisher at Duro for more than eleven years before being laid off because of the economic recession of 1981–82.

"I didn't want to work at that factory the rest of my life. Now I wish I had that job back," Mick said. After he was laid off, he applied at more than one-hundred factories but still could not find a job. At a party, Billie, who was Mick's friend, told him that she probably could get him a job at Biomed if he did not mind working for $3.50 an hour. Since Mick had not been able to find another job in almost a year, he took Billie up on her offer. Even though Mick had been making much more money at Duro than he made at Biomed, he told me, "Having this job is better than nothing."

Mick continued to look for a better job. He had checked out the entire industrial area but had found nothing. "Some places won't even take applications," he said. "It's as bad as the 1930s," I told him. "It's worse than the 1930s," Mick replied.

At the end of April, Mick received a job offer from a small packaging plant for $4.00 per hour. He told me that he had turned down the offer because Steve had promised to make him an assistant line foreman of the disc anterior pad assembly department in the future because of Biomed's planned growth.

At times, Mick spoke of going to school to get a two-year degree. "I'd go back to school if I was guaranteed a job. But even people with degrees aren't getting jobs and it costs money to go to school. I don't know," he said. Mick told me of a friend who had gone back to school, earned a four-year business degree, and still ended up working at his old factory job, although he was eventually promoted to foreman.

Still, Mick was not sure that school was the answer for him. "I took a data processing course but I didn't enjoy it and I wasn't very good at it," he said. "It just wasn't my bag. I wish I could find a job where I could use my bulk. That's the kind of job that I'd be good at." Mick was still counting on finding a decent paying factory job.

Greg

I first noticed Greg at the beginning of my second day of work. I saw him walk into the plant carrying a book on Eastern philosophy. During the lunch break that day, I overheard Greg telling Bob about "symbolism, the self, and the social psychologist George Herbert Mead." I thought that this was a strange discussion to hear in a factory lunchroom. As I listened to Greg talk during the following weeks, I got the impression that Greg thought a lot of his own intelligence. I was sure that he viewed himself as an intellectual, and, in fact, one day he told me that he was "a member of the intelligentsia."

Even though Greg thought of himself as an intellectual, he was not one. He was a pseudointellectual. Although he knew of the topics that intellectuals discuss and had a superficial knowledge of them, he was able to speak in an authoritative manner on these subjects only because the other workers had no familiarity with them. Greg told me that he had attended the University of Chicago for one year before transferring to another university. Although Greg did not graduate from college, he claimed that he was involved in doing research with a number of professors at the University of Chicago.

Since Greg attended school to become a chef, his previous jobs had been chef positions at a variety of hotels and restaurants. When he had lost his last job, his brother, Steve, the plant manager, had gottn him a job at Biomed. Greg felt that luck had dealt him a losing hand by forcing him to work in a factory. He felt that he was too smart to perform such menial work.

"You can see I don't have the temperament to be a factory worker. Last week, I was grumpy. I need to utilize the three brain cells I have," Greg once told me. "I hope I find a chef's job soon because I am not a typical factory worker."

"What's a typical factory worker?" I asked. Greg pointed to Sam sitting next to him and said, "He's a typical factory worker. He has just graduated from high school, is green behind the ears, is attending school, and needs a few bucks." Sam smiled.

"Am I a typical factory worker?" I inquired of Greg. "How old are you?" he asked. "I'm twenty-five," I replied.

"Yes," he continued. "You are a typical factory worker. I know things are tough now and people have to take any job they can get. Don't worry, though. You'll grow out of it and find something else to get into."

I thought that Greg's attitude toward factory workers was rather condescending. Who has the temperament to enjoy the grinding, brutal work of the factory? What did Greg mean by his comment, "you'll grow out of it?" His attitude made me quite angry.

In the middle of February, Greg told Debbie that it looked like he was going to be offered a full-time job as a sous-chef at $350 per week. He told her that he would be quitting his job at Biomed in a week to accept this position.

A week later, Greg had Debbie fill out a "leave of absence" form for him. He told Steve that he had to fill in for another chef who was going on vacation for a week. Greg planned to tell Steve the following week that he was not coming back to work at Biomed. He felt that he had to lie to him because Steve would become enraged if he found out the truth.

Five days later, Greg was back at work at Biomed. He gave me a long-winded explanation of the situation and how they wanted him to work the swing shift. Greg said that he was not sure of the status of his new chef's job, although he hoped that something would be worked out soon.

Although Steve and Greg were brothers, there was much tension between the two of them. When Greg came back after his short absence, Steve told me that both Greg and I should perform the plant's janitorial work. "Just make sure you split the work evenly," he said. "I don't favor Greg because he's my brother." In fact, Steve was harder on Greg because he was his brother.

One day at the end of February, at about 3:00, Steve told me to get Greg and to come into the lunchroom. When both of us were there, Steve mentioned that Mr. Williams had given him a hard time because the employees' bathroom and the lunchroom were so dirty. He then began to chide us for our irresponsibility in this matter. Greg explained that the mop was missing and Bob, who came in to talk to Steve, backed up Greg's story. Steve and Greg argued and then Steve said to Greg, "Don't play your psychology games on me." I sensed a real antagonism between the two brothers, a tension deeper than the normal workplace stresses and strains.

One morning at the beginning of March, Steve told me that I would have to do all the cleaning because Greg would not be in that day. "He got drunk and went berserk last night," Steve said. "He had to be taken away." While I was washing the walls of the employees' bathroom a couple of hours later, Steve came in and told me, "Greg will not be in tomorrow. He has been committed to Elgin Community Hospital." That afternoon, I heard Steve talking on the phone about Greg's condition. He was laughing and making jokes about it.

Greg never returned to work at Biomed. I do not know what happened to him after he was committed to the hospital.

Bob

The most skilled worker at Biomed, excluding the electronic technicians, was Bob. Bob had an associate of arts degree and had worked at a number of different jobs over the years. Before working at Biomed, Bob had worked on a loading dock for $4.00 per hour but he had quit when he had had to work fourteen straight hours, in the bitter cold, without any breaks. Besides being able to operate all the machines at Biomed, Bob knew how to fix them when they broke down.

Bob was thinking of going back to school to get a bachelor's degree in mechanical engineering. He had taken some drafting courses and had tried to get a job as a draftsman before coming to Biomed. The company paid Bob $5.00 an hour to do some drafting work for them during his free time.

Bob did not plan to work at Biomed for any length of time. His father was using his connections to get Bob a job as a truck driver, starting at $8.50 per hour. In fact, I thought that Bob looked like a truck driver with his bushy beard and a stocky frame. Three or four times, Bob told me that the job had come through only to tell me later that things had not been worked out yet.

Early in March, Greg said to me, "Bob's got something going on the outside. You know his dad is a powerful man. Do you know about it? Oh, well you should ask him." When I asked Bob about this, he said that his father was trying to get him a job driving a Continental bus. The pay was good—$11.40 per hour. Bob said that his father was waiting for an opening. Some jobs were supposed to open in the near future. I wondered what had happened to Bob's truck driving job.

At the end of March, Bob's father got him a job working on a loading dock. The company that Bob worked for guaranteed package delivery from Chicago to New York or vice versa as quick as delivery by air. Bob worked seven days a week, receiving time-and-a-half pay for Saturday and double-time pay for Sunday. "The company will eventually be union," Bob told me, "because they are hiring only members of BRAC." Bob also mentioned that he would get the next truck driving position that opened up.

Although Biomed thought quite highly of Bob's skills and trusted him quite a bit (he once displayed Mr. Williams' Texaco credit card, which he was carrying in his wallet) he was not able to do everything that Biomed wanted him to do. In the middle of April, the company asked Bob to build a "fake" fire wall for an upcoming fire inspection. Bob said that it would be impossible to do this but he was told "to do the best you can." Bob did not even attempt to build the requested wall.

I was surprised to learn that Bob was a virulent racist and anti-Semite. Bob had made a number of comments that I first thought he had stated out of ignorance rather than racism. After a couple weeks of work, though, there was no doubt in my mind about Bob's true feelings toward African Americans and Jews.

At the end of the lunch period one day in late December, Bob sat down at the table where I was sitting and told me about an incident that had just happened to him in the supermarket. He told me that "a Jewish woman" had instructed her son to push his way in front of Bob. Bob pushed him out of the way and said to her, "You're such a nice woman. Too bad you were too young for Auschwitz!" I stated that that had been a terrible comment for him to make. Bob looked at the newspaper and continued, "I am happy that the niggers are getting their heads beaten in down in Miami. I wish I could join in the fun."

I confronted Bob. I did not want such a comment to go unchallenged, especially with a number of young white workers sitting at our table. "Come on, they are human beings, just like we are, trying to make a living," I said. Bob kept telling me that they were "uncivilized" and "animals." We discussed the issue for about ten minutes and I tried to reason with Bob but I had no success in changing his mind.

After this talk, Bob's racist comments decreased in frequency but he still occasionally made such remarks as the following, "It's called a pipe wrench but it can also be called a monkey wrench. We better not call it that here, though, because it would offend certain people." He was obviously referring to the African American workers.

POLITICS AT THE FACTORY

The Chicago Democratic Party Mayoral Primary, as well as the subsequent mayoral election held six weeks later, were two political events that generated a small amount of interest among the factory's workers. For the first time in recent memory in Chicago politics, a mayoral candidate, Congressman Harold Washington, expressed both pro-worker and left-liberal views. Because of these characteristics, he should have been the enthusiastic choice of the trade unions. In addition, Washington should have garnered a considerable amount of support from rank-and-file workers.

In the Democratic Party primary, many of the factory's white workers supported State's Attorney General Richard Daley, as opposed to the incumbent mayor, Jane Byrne. Bob, as well as Greg, who once told me that he was not a capitalist but a "Jeffersonian" molded in a "democratic, Christian tradition," supported Daley as the "reform" candidate. Although most of the plant's African American workers supported Washington in the primary, Andy was a strong supporter and campaign worker for Richard Daley. Andy stated, "I think that Washington is a good man but it is dangerous when a black man acquires power."

His dislike for Washington stemmed from the fact that Washington reminded him of a former boss whom Andy hated. This boss was an African American man who, Andy felt, was dishonest and abused his position of power. Andy was sure that Washington would act the same way if he were elected mayor.

The day after the primary everybody in the factory was talking about Washington's stunning victory. Steve said to me, "If a black is elected mayor of Chicago, I will move out of the city." Andy and Chuck talked about the primary during the morning break and I talked with Billie about it during lunch. Even Bob had something positive to say about Washington. He told Debbie, "I think Washington will be a better mayor than Byrne." Later in the day, Bob told me, "I am going to support Washington because I hate Republicans more than I hate niggers."

After the primary, Andy became a Washington supporter. He began to wear a "Washington for Mayor" button in the factory. I thought that this was a pretty gutsy move on his part, considering the nature of this particular factory, but I realized that he was able to get away with it because he was an African American. If any of the white workers had worn such a button, I am sure that there would have been derogatory comments made to them by management, as well as by some white workers.

When I first saw Andy sporting a Washington button, I said to him, "I see you've jumped on the Washington bandwagon." He replied, "Yep, I want to do it before it's too late. If you want to back a winner, you should, too."

A few days before the election, I talked with Chuck about the mayoral campaign. He was convinced that Epton, the Republican candidate, was running a racist campaign and that he was doing so well because of the racism of many of the white voters. I agreed with Chuck's analysis of the situation.

At about the same time that I had this discussion with Chuck, I noticed that Ophelia was wearing an Epton button. I approached her and said, "Epton?" She replied, "Yes. You like Epton?" "No," I countered. "What about Washington?" "I don't like him," she said. At the end of June, I discovered that Ophelia did not like Washington because she did not "trust those black people."

I continued to talk about the upcoming election with the plant's workers. During one discussion, I mentioned to Bob that there was another party on the ballot in the mayoral election—the (Trotskyist) Socialist Workers Party. Bob said, "They're the Nazis. They always run for election to various offices." I informed Bob that they were not the Nazis but a left-wing party, but Bob insisted, with a deep conviction, that they were the Nazis. Finally, I told him that they could not be the Nazis because they were running an African American candidate for mayor. My comment put a quick end to the discussion.

Even though the white electronic technicians did not wear any campaign buttons before the primary, they began to wear Epton buttons as election day approached. On the day of the election, Steve gave some white workers a typewritten slander sheet on Harold Washington to photocopy on the company's copying machine. This is what appeared on the sheet:

Harold Washington
Alias: "Brother Mayor"
"Campaign Promises"

1. Raise Whitey's Taxes!
2. Ban Democratic machine—replace with El Rukins and Black Disciples!

3. Move City Hall to 63rd & Cottage Grove!
4. Change donation bureau to "Leon's Rib Basket."
5. Move to "Bridgeport"—3500 S. Lowe.
6. Change City Flag Emblem to "Black Fist."
7. Replace Supt. of Police with "Shaft!"
8. Replace CTA Buses with Eldorados!
9. Change State St. to Amos & Andy Drive!
10. New campaign headquarters to "Cabrini Green."
11. Issue more riot permits.
12. Pay gas bill with city funds.
13. New song for city—"We Are Family."
14. Dedicate my campaign to "All My Chillins."
15. Campaign funds paid by "Mastuh Charge!" Special thanks to the Master Puppeteer—The Rev. Jesse Jackson.
16. Make Richard Pryor "Fire Superintendent!"

Harold Washington was elected Mayor of Chicago with 52 percent of the vote. It was the closest election in recent Chicago history. After the election, Steve began to wear a button with a dark black slanted line through a picture of Washington. I do not know if Steve ever moved out of Chicago.

NATIONAL AND INTERNATIONAL PROBLEMS

Although the condition of the country's economy was dismal, few workers ever discussed the nation's domestic economic problems. Roy once told me, "Only a war will save us from this economic crisis. But a war isn't a good thing to have." While discussing Reaganomics one day, Sam said, "I think this trickle-down theory is full of shit."

Occasionally the workers discussed the civil war raging in El Salvador. At the end of March, during an afternoon break, Art read a newspaper article on El Salvador. Since Art was in the army reserves, he said, "It looks like I might be going to El Salvador." He expressed some sympathy for the rebels when he stated, "All they want to do is to get that right-wing dictator out of power." I mentioned that I had read that D'Aubuisson had stated that all he wanted from the United States was napalm. Art, Sam, and Mark then began discussing napalm and how to make it.

BREAKS IN THE MONOTONY

Working in a factory is, at best, a boring, monotonous experience. At worst, it is a brutal, degrading, and physically exhausting experience. Work at Biomed was more often similar to the latter description than to the former. As one workday merged into another, events occasionally occurred that relieved the tedium and monotony of factory life for short periods of time.

It was an average Tuesday afternoon in the middle of February. The day was proceeding quietly until Art came by to pick up some gelled disc anterior pads at approximately 1:45. Art stopped at my table and asked, "Why are you underground?" I was shocked by his question and I did not know what he was trying to find out. With adrenaline pumping through my body, I thought that he must have discovered my intentions to organize Biomed—but how?

I replied, "What do you mean?" Art continued, "You seem to be underground, hiding from somebody." Probably because of my long hair and beard, he added, "You remind me of Abbie Hoffman. Who are you hiding from?" I told Art that I was not hiding from anyone. He pressed on, "Do you dabble in political science?" "No," I lied as I continued to gel.

I remained agitated for quite some time after this conversation. I tried to figure out why Art thought these things about me. It was probably because of my appearance, but my actions and speech patterns may have had some effect, too. Art seemed so close, yet he was still off the mark. I did not want to question Art about his thoughts. If I did, I was afraid that I would appear too concerned, which would most definitely arouse suspicion. Art's comments put me on my guard, although I was fairly sure that he did not really know anything about me. I let the matter drop, but I still felt a little uneasy.

Occasionally, some of the young workers smoked a joint during the breaks in the employee parking lot when someone had some grass. Although Biomed's "General Production Area Rules" stated, "The use of alcoholic beverages and drugs is not allowed in *any* production area, lunch room, hallway, loading dock or parking lot. *ANYONE NOT COMPLYING WILL BE TERMINATED!*" the line foremen, as well as Steve, constantly violated this rule.

During one morning break, Art took out the last remains of a joint and passed it around. He offered me a hit even though he knew that I did not smoke grass. Nevertheless he asked, "You smoke grass, don't you, Vic?" I asked him why he did not use a roach clip for his joint.

"It's in my car," he answered. "Anyway, how do you know about roach clips? Hey, that was good acid in the '60s, right, Vic?" Art saw Robin drive by so he quickly finished the joint.

Art did not limit himself to smoking grass. At the end of one morning break in February, I saw Art and Debbie take some speed while I was cleaning the lunchroom. Art swallowed the speed while Debbie snorted it—an action that surprised even Art. They were concerned that I might say something to someone about this but I assured them that I would not mention it to anybody. Although Art had earlier referred to the speed as "a vitamin," when Debbie left, he told me that the drug they had just taken was speed.

Besides using drugs, Art sold grass to some of the factory workers in order to make a little extra money. He once showed me a half-ounce bag of grass he was planning to sell to a worker. While standing in the parking lot during the morning break, Art saw a man drive by in a car who looked very straight. He said, "Now that guy looks like a narc." I replied, "A narc wouldn't look like that guy. He'd look like me." Art shot me a surprised glance and said, "I know you're not a narc."

Because of the economic situation, unemployed workers regularly walked into Biomed and asked to fill out job applications. Sometimes applications were distributed to them; sometimes Biomed claimed that they were not accepting any applications. On rare occasions, a few of these unemployed workers were hired.

While cleaning the offices early one March morning, I noticed a young African American man wearing a UAW (United Auto Workers) Local 711 jacket sitting in the waiting room. A short time later, I saw him fill out a job application.

As I was emptying garbage into the dumpster, I saw him walk across the parking lot. I called to him, "Are they going to hire you? So when do you start?" He walked over to me and replied, "They said they would file it."

"So you're an autoworker," I said. "Used to be," he replied. "I worked at Electro-Motive on 103rd. I was laid off a year and four months ago. Man, I thought that I'd always have that job, that the place would never go under. We used to make diesels there. People who worked there twenty years got laid off."

He continued, "I really need a job. It's bad out here. My wife is expecting another kid. It's really bad out here." I told him that I hoped he was hired at Biomed or found another job. I shook his hand before he left.

It was at this time that I realized that American capitalism had, in effect, promised workers a job for life. The work might be hard, boring, and tedious but at least one would be able to support one's family. Meaningful work was never promised, only forty hours or more of backbreaking, soul-killing work. Now, American capitalism was breaking its own sacred contract with the American working class.

Although Biomed's management often gave its own workers a hard time, it was seldom that a worker—any worker—was able to reciprocate. One afternoon late in May, the management team got the treatment they so rightfully deserved from another company's worker. Robin's (the Biomed vice president) fancy sports car was parked in the loading dock area, which meant that the United Parcel Service driver could not pull his truck in to make the deliveries and to pick up the outgoing shipments.

Harry and I were ready to carry the boxes out to the truck when the driver called out, "If I can't get into the loading dock, I won't make any deliveries or pickups!" Robin was immediately notified of this policy, and she came running out of the building to move her car. She apologized profusely to the driver, explaining that she had been out of town and had just recently returned.

The driver, who had had the same problem before with Robin, said, "Bullshit! These guys were ready to carry the packages out to the truck." Robin promised that such an incident would not occur again in the future. The driver grudgingly accepted her apology. I appreciated his actions because I felt that they were in defense of the workers. However, an alternative explanation is that the driver simply did not want to make the pickup because in the early 1980s UPS drivers were on tight time schedules.

Another event that greatly disturbed Biomed occurred early one morning in April. One of Biomed's customers found a cockroach hanging from a disc anterior pad when a nurse opened the sealed bag. Robin was extremely upset by this and thought that a worker might have placed the cockroach in the bag as a joke. Robin told Steve, Debbie, and Art that all bags should be checked after they were opened and before a disc anterior pad was placed inside. Obviously, she did not want to see such an event happen again. In the afternoon, I noticed that a large plastic covering had been placed over the boxes containing the opened bags in order to prevent the occurrence of another similar incident.

NO EXIT

It was not hard to find at least one unhappy worker at Biomed every day of the year. There was not a single day that passed in which one or more of the workers did not express strong dissatisfaction over the plant's wages and working conditions. I became depressed quite often over the situation at Biomed. Some of the hours that I spent there were the most depressing in my life. The system kept wearing me down, attempting to force me to submit and to give up the struggle.

Although I came into daily contact with the secretaries because of my janitorial duties, they were rarely friendly toward me. Mick explained the reason for this: "That's because they're office workers and you're a factory worker. They think that they shouldn't socialize with you. At my other job, we used to have management-worker softball teams that were supposed to bring us together. But after the games, the workers would be standing together at one side of the bar and the bosses would be standing on the other side."

At the end of February, I learned that Biomed was planning to set up another plant at the beginning of March. The company had obtained another manufacturing facility two miles away in a small industrial park. Because of Biomed's intended plans for expansion, the electronic technicians and the subassemblers were moved from the main plant to the new one on March 1. Every few weeks I spent a few hours cleaning up the new plant. While I was there, I often talked with a few of the subassemblers. Afrem asked the same question on each of my visits: "How's production going at the other place?"

8.

Rank and File Discontent

CONSIDERING THE WAGE LEVELS AND THE WORKING CONDITIONS AT BIOMED, it may appear to be surprising that there was not more visible worker discontent expressed both on and off the shop floor. The major reason for the low level of rank and file discontent rested with the high state unemployment rate, which hovered between 11 and 14 percent during the time I worked at Biomed. Most of the production workers realized that if they lost their jobs at Biomed they would have little or no chance of finding others. Therefore, many workers attempted to stoically accept these conditions, while hoping that a better job would eventually come along.

"Biomed is taking advantage of the unemployment situation," Bob once told me. Another time, Kay, the line foreman, said, "They know they can get people to work here because of the unemployment situation." Because of the objective economic conditions, Biomed had the upper hand in dealing with rank and file discontent, although the workers challenged the company on a number of occasions.

As Storey points out, organized worker resistance can occur in the absence of unionization, although Hossfeld states that there is "little incidence" of organized worker resistance (defined as collective mass actions or strikes) found in the high-tech factories of Silicon Valley.[1] In fact, in spite of the objective economic conditions and the low rate of labor militancy historically found in high-tech industries, the production workers collectively stood up to Biomed on two occasions—in "the mass walkout" and "the shop floor revolt of the Latino gellers"—and in the second situation, Biomed was forced to give in to their demands.

This last situation—"the shop floor revolt of the Latino gellers"—appears to be strikingly similar in some respects to the October 1992 unorganized high-tech workers' strike at Versatronex, a $3.5-million-a-year circuit-board manufacturer located in Sunnyvale, California.[2] In both situations, the job actions were conducted by Latino workers who felt that they were being seriously mistreated in the workplace. However, at Biomed, the job action was fairly short and ended in victory, while at Versatronex, the job action was relatively long and ended in defeat.

THE STRIKE AT VERSATRONEX

What is unique about the job action at Versatronex is that it was the first strike in more than fifty years in a nonunionized, high-tech plant in Silicon Valley. The roots of the strike can be traced to an employee meeting at Versatronex in October 1992, when Joselito Munoz stated that the wages of the production workers seemed extremely low, given the fact that many workers were long-time company employees who could perform the jobs of the engineers. In addition, the workers did not receive health insurance and were continually subjected to the verbal abuse of a supervisor, whom they had nicknamed *la lagartija* (the lizard).[3]

The workers also complained that they did not receive proper training and had inadequate safety equipment for working with dangerous chemicals. Maria Henriquez, a striker with seven years of seniority at the company, stated, "I worked in an area with a special kind of glue. They provided us with very thin paper masks. We get all the fumes." At times, the "unidentified toxins" that the employees worked with resulted in nosebleeds.[4]

The day after this employee meeting, Munoz was fired. In response to this discharge, one week later, the largely Latino workforce of eighty-five employees at the plant contacted the United Electrical, Radio and Machine Workers Union (UE) and walked out. In order to support the strike, the UE sent bilingual organizers and attempted to organize support within the immigrant community.[5]

The strikers remained united and stayed out for six weeks. There was good news in January 1993 when the National Labor Relations Board (NLRB) ruled that Versatronex was required to recognize the UE and to take back seven militant workers that it had illegally fired. However, later that same day, the company announced that it was filing for bankruptcy and that it would close the plant in early February.[6]

According to Margarita Aguilera, an assembler who made $6.30 an hour at the company, "When they said they were going to close we were all angry that we hadn't won. We went on strike and we won nothing. But now we can see there's more to it, because someone has to fight, or nothing will ever get better."[7] These were the same sentiments held by the Latino gellers when they stood up to Biomed. This incident will be discussed in more detail later in the chapter.

BACK TO BIOMED: MILITANT TALK BUT NO ACTION

The first incident of rank and file discontent that occurred at Biomed while I was working there happened immediately after the entire workforce was punished for Vern's misdemeanor of falling asleep while gelling. During the afternoon break, emotions ran high among many of the young, male workers. Some of these workers talked of staging a strike and although I believed that they considered this to be a serious proposal, I knew that they would not act on it. Sam even suggested a sit-down strike, although I was not sure that he knew what that meant. Talk spread to how much money Biomed was making on the products that we assembled. Sam summed up the feelings of most of this group of workers when he said, "What a scam they got going here."

Tensions remained at a fevered pitch for a few days, but gradually all of the production workers began to accept the new conditions without any resistance. It was not until late in May that Biomed decided to let the factory workers again listen to radios while they worked.

THE STRUGGLE OVER RAISES AND WAGES

The issue that continually inflamed the production workers was that of raises. Since Biomed did not try to maintain wage secrecy between employees, it was easy to find out the wages of every worker in the plant. In a similar vein, it was easy to learn of the difficulty in actually obtaining a raise from the company. Chuck commented to me, "It's harder to get a raise here than squeezing blood out of a turnip." Much of the verbal discontent among the workers focused on the topic of raises.

In the middle of February, Leopoldo applied to a special management committee for a raise. The committee rejected his application at the beginning of March. At the end of the workday, one day, I overheard Steve and Leopoldo arguing about his rejected application. Steve was giving him a hard time even though Leopoldo was a good worker, had recently taken on more responsibilities, and was still making only $3.50 an hour.

After their argument, Art asked Leopoldo if he had quit. "No," he replied. "I am going to wait another week to see if I get a raise on my next paycheck." I asked Leopoldo, "Can you find another job?" "No, but I don't care," he replied. "I've got other responsibilities to take care of." Although Leopoldo never received his raise, he never told me why he decided to remain at Biomed.

In the middle of March, Harry became head of shipping and receiving when Lenny left Biomed to work at a hospital. When I asked him how he liked his new job, he said, "The new job's OK but I always thought that when you got a new job you got a new salary. $3.50 an hour is too little. We should be making at least $4.50 an hour."

As head of the shipping and receiving department, Harry obtained information to defend his position that all of the production workers deserved raises. "I know the cost of materials," said Harry. "And even with this small number of workers, the company is making loads of money off us. It just isn't right."

Harry was very vocal with Steve concerning wages and raises. He constantly complained to him about not making enough money. During an afternoon break while Harry was lying on his old, beat-up Cadillac, he said to Steve, "Man, I can't even make enough money to support myself." Steve, as he often did, tried to make a joke out of his comment. "Why don't you get a smaller car instead of that gas guzzler?" he asked with a sinister smile on his face. Harry just gave him one of his icy stares.

During a morning break in the middle of May, a group of workers were examining Robin's new sports car, which had been paid for by the company. Sam took one look at the car and said, "Everybody gets a new car here but I don't even get a raise!" Steve was with the group of workers and tried to lighten up the tense situation. It did not work. The workers felt bitter about not getting raises while management got everything that they wanted.

The electronic technicians also were unhappy with their wages. The only time that I heard a group of them discuss Biomed in the lunchroom, they did not discuss the company in a positive light. Ernie, a young, enthusiastic technician, stated that Biomed was growing rapidly and that in several years the technicians would be making "big money." "Yeah, we'll be making $1.35 instead of $1.15," replied another technician. The other technicians laughed. Ernie stated that he would leave Biomed after he finished school and go to work for either Texas Instruments or Hewlett-Packard.

Steve perpetuated the myth that Biomed was interested in giving its workers raises. At the beginning of March, he told me, "You know I have to find ways to save money and increase productivity so I can get you guys raises." Steve then mentioned that each worker was reviewed after three months and then once a year thereafter to determine who deserved a raise. Another time, Steve tried to convince Chris, an African American line foreman, that if the workers' productivity increased, Biomed would sell more of its products and thus would have more money to give raises to the workers. I do not think that he convinced Chris.

Because the line foremen's wages also were relatively low, they too expressed displeasure over a lack of raises. In the middle of February, Art missed a couple of days of work. When he returned to work, I asked him how he was doing.

"To be honest," he said, "not too well." "Are you still sick?" I inquired. He replied, "Have you ever heard of the blue flu?" "Sure," I answered.

"Well, that's what I had, the last two days. I am supposed to get a raise but Biomed won't give it to me so I didn't come to work as a protest," he continued. "Good luck in getting your raise," I said. "I'll need it to get a raise from this place," Art replied.

In the middle of May, Biomed gave all of its line foremen raises of 50 cents an hour, bringing their wages up to $4.50 an hour. This seemed like quite a generous raise from a very stingy company.

One week after the uprising of the Latino gellers, Biomed gave a small number of long-time production employees raises of 25 cents an hour. Anna, Sharon, Vinod, and Billie were the recipients of these raises, bringing their wage levels up to $3.75 an hour. It appeared that Biomed wanted to demonstrate "good faith" to the workers—raises were given and more raises would be forthcoming in the future (although no more raises were ever obtained by the other workers during the time I was working at the company).

When the workers found out that Biomed had given a few workers a raise, a number of workers gathered in the lunchroom after work to talk about the issue. Andy said, "You mean I'm going to have to wait another 3 months for a raise?" Debbie was in the room, heard Andy's comment, and replied, "Don't listen to people who don't know what they are talking about. They're working on raises in the front office. The gellers will get the most, since it's the hardest job. If I have anything to say about it, I will urge them to give the packers a nice raise because they work hard too."

That evening, I called Herb. He told me that he was going to ask for a $1.00 per hour raise the following week so that he would be making $4.50 per hour. "I've never worked at a job where I've made so little," he said. "I can make almost as much by going on unemployment." Herb led me to believe that he might quit if he did not get this raise.

As far as I know, Biomed had not given any of these workers raises by the time I was fired by the company in late June. Biomed kept pretending that more workers would get raises, but no one actually received one.

INDIVIDUAL WORKERS' DISCONTENT

Much of the time, there was a sense of despair in the factory. Workers made comments daily about the miserableness of having to work at Biomed. Clark, a young African American cable department worker, made a comment representative of the feelings of many of the workers when he told me, "Man, this place is the pits. You do the same job over and over." Another characteristic comment about the work at Biomed was expressed by Mick when he said, "There must be an easier way to make a living."

When workers were no longer able to deal with working at Biomed, they quit their jobs. Vicki, a young African American in the disc anterior pad assembly department, quit after working only one week at Biomed. When Lori arrived late one morning and the workers had to wait outside in the cold, a number of workers complained vociferously. One of the most vocal was Vicki. She was upset about the working conditions and the pay, not to mention having to stand out in the cold for a lengthy period of time. Two days later, she quit after Steve hassled her about going to the bathroom during work.

Sylvia, a young attractive Latina worker in the cable department, quit her job because she became "frustrated" with the work. She had not found another job before she left Biomed. She just could not stay at Biomed one moment longer.

THE MASS WALKOUT

One of the two situations in which the workers collectively acted against Biomed was the mass walkout of the production workers when the company issued the plant closing notice at the end of April. Many of the workers were very angry with the company's actions. Andy punched out at 10:00 and told Steve that he was leaving. Andy's exit triggered a response in the other workers. A few minutes later, Clark and Kevin informed Steve that they were leaving too. After the morning break, the Latino gellers left en masse and they visited the other departments in order to convince the other Latino workers to leave with them. By 10:30, there was not one Latino worker left in the factory. They exhibited a mood of defiance as they walked out the back door.

Neither Steve nor any of the line foremen did anything to stop the walkout. They appeared stunned by the workers' resolve. Management could not have fired all the workers involved in the walkout because it would have crippled production at Biomed for a significant period of time.

The workers were understandably upset with Biomed's tactics that week—the "institution" of the four day workweek, the shortened workdays and finally the plant closing notice. When the workers walked out it was as if they were telling the company, "You screwed us over this week so we're going to screw you over today." Even Sharon, the one remaining geller, left by 11:00. I left shortly after I finished cleaning the factory at 11:30.

As I departed from the factory, I noticed that there were only a handful of workers still working. All of the African American and Latino workers had already walked out. There were only a few East Indian and white workers who stayed, concentrated in the snap-type electrode and the disc anterior pad assembly departments. "Take it easy, Vic," Mick said as I walked out the door. The employees who continued working probably felt that they could not sacrifice a few hours of pay with the impending layoff.

THE SHOP FLOOR REVOLT OF THE LATINO GELLERS

The most militant collective action taken by any group of workers while I was at Biomed was the uprising of the Latino gellers on Friday, 25 March. Before I describe this revolt in detail, some background information will be reviewed.

Latinos had become the majority in the gelling department over the preceding few months. All the white and African American gellers had either quit, been fired, or moved to "better" jobs in the factory. As I have stated before, gelling was the hardest and most miserable job in the factory and the one most subject to temporary layoffs. Except for one Indian woman and one Assyrian woman, all of the established gellers were Latino.

The week before this insurrection, some gellers had been laid off because of a tin shortage, created by poor planning on the part of Biomed management. On Monday of the week of the revolt, many of the gellers were not able to come to work because of a snowstorm. In addition, some of the gellers were laid off on Wednesday or Thursday while new workers in both the gelling and assembly departments started work on Wednesday! When a number of the gellers were told by Debbie and Lori to go home after the morning break on Friday, the shop floor revolt was ignited.

Shortly after the morning break, Roberto, a tall, broadly built Latino geller with short, curly hair and a mustache, sat at his worktable staring at Steve while he exercised his finger. A short time later, Roberto got up from his table, walked over to Steve's desk, and began to shout at him in Spanish. A young Latino woman from the cable department was immediately brought in to translate into English what Roberto was shouting at Steve in Spanish. When I saw this situation beginning to develop, I abruptly dropped my cleaning activities and arrived on the scene to begin emptying the gellers' wastebaskets.

Ophelia was talking to Debbie about the present layoff. She charged Biomed with discrimination against the "Spanish-speaking" workers. I asked Juan to fill me in on the details of the confrontation.

Juan, who spoke English quite well, stated, "We're charging Biomed with discrimination against the Spanish-speaking workers. We're the only ones who get laid off, never the black or the white workers. We come back to work and we see new gellers and assemblers but when these positions open up, they only move the black or white workers to fill these positions but never the Spanish-speaking workers. We want to be trained so that we can perform these jobs when they open up. We like the work here but we don't like being laid off. We need the money to support our families. We don't want to cause trouble but we'll take legal action against the company if we have to."

By this time, Lori was also on the scene, confronting the militant gellers. Several of the Latino women gellers were arguing with Lori and

Debbie. Lori tried to calm them down. "We're a growing company and we'll have a lot more work in the future," she said. "We know that gelling is the toughest job and when Biomed can afford to give raises, the gellers will be making top dollar. They'll get the highest wages in the factory."

The gellers did not seem happy with this explanation. They wanted action now and they demanded that they be trained for the other assembly jobs. The Latino gellers had filled out their production work reports and were starting to hand them in. The situation appeared to be highly explosive.

I knew that something was about to happen. I sensed that the line foremen were worried about a mass walkout of all the Latino gellers, which would severely damage production for at least a couple of weeks. Realizing that they had no choice, the line foremen acquiesced to the gellers' demands. Juan and some of the other gellers continued to work in the gelling department while four of the Latino women gellers were temporarily transferred to the snap-type electrode assembly department for training on two different models of electrodes. None of the gellers were laid off! The struggle had ended in a grand victory for the Latino gellers.

Meanwhile, Roberto, the leader of the revolt, had quit. He was upset about the layoffs of the Latino gellers while the African American and white workers were never laid off. I went outside to talk to him under the pretext of emptying garbage into a dumpster. Roberto was sitting in his car and he still appeared to be quite angry. I tried to talk to him but I had trouble understanding him because he was speaking rapidly, more in Spanish than in English. I shook his hand and wished him luck in finding a new job. He smiled and said, "Thank you."

Inside the factory, the atmosphere was still electrified. I heard Art tell Debbie, "This has been coming for a long time. It was only a matter of time before it occurred." The gellers' militance inspired Art and he was talking about "telling Harry Williams a thing or two." Debbie claimed that she was sympathetic with the gellers, stating that "they are absolutely right."

Lori and Kay "informed" the gellers, "We were going to train you in these other jobs. We just needed more time. We can't train everybody at once." This lame excuse did not explain why new workers were hired when assembly positions opened up in these departments instead of training the Latino gellers.

I was very excited with what I had just witnessed. This was the kind of action that I had been waiting to see—workers standing united while taking the situation into their own hands. In certain situations when workers are backed against a wall and believe that they have no alternative, they will fight and organize in order to protect their livelihoods. The Latino gellers had organized themselves, stood together, made their demands, and won.

After things had cooled off a bit, I told Juan that I was glad that they had fought for their rights and stuck together. I gave him the "thumbs up" sign. I repeated my comments to Ophelia and told her that she was "one tough lady." She smiled and said, "Thank you." I received the same warm response from another Latino woman geller when I told her the same things that I had said to Juan and Ophelia.

I talked with Bob a little while after the revolt. He seemed pretty excited, too, about the events that had just occurred. "Imagine that," he exclaimed to me, "a wildcat at Biomed!"

I was sure that there would be reprisals against these workers by the management of Biomed. After lunch, the line foremen, Lori and Steve, had a closed-door meeting with the top-level management in the conference room. Robin must have informed Mr. Williams about the morning's events because she had been on the shop floor when they occurred. I feared that the present "industrial peace" would not last.

I waited for the boom to be lowered once the meeting had ended. The supervisors returned to the shop floor but there were no retaliations made against the defiant gellers. In fact, another concession was made to this group of workers. At the end of the day, I learned that the gellers who had missed work that week due to the layoff could come in to work on Saturday for the purpose of filling an order of snap-type electrodes that had to be sent out immediately. It appeared to me that management was afraid of further inciting the workers and was bending over backward to placate them.

In addition, Biomed told the Latino gellers that Roberto could come back to work on Monday if he wanted his job back. Roberto did come back to work on Monday. Later in the day, Steve said "Hi" to Roberto. When this happened, Roberto made a face at me indicating that he still hated Steve.

During the lunch period, I asked Sam what he thought of the morning's revolt. He had some very chauvinistic feelings toward the Latino workers. "If they can't speak English, they shouldn't be allowed to have jobs in this country. Anyway, they take jobs away from white workers," he said. I attempted to counter his statements but I did not have time because the lunch period was over. Mark, however, was much more sympathetic to the Latino workers' grievances.

The following Monday morning, Chuck told me that there were rumors going around that Biomed was considering firing "unproductive workers." Chris, an African American line foreman, had provided him with this information. I asked Chuck if Chris had told him what had been discussed at the previous Friday's meeting. Chuck said that Chris had mentioned that they had discussed the issue of raises. As I have stated before, a few raises were given on the Friday after the uprising.

News of the confrontation reached the other manufacturing facility. When I cleaned this plant the following week, Herb and another sub-assembler were interested in finding out more about the revolt. I provided them with some details but I gave it to them in a highly simplified form because I had a lot of cleaning to do at the plant that day. Both of them were very sympathetic to the workers and indicated that they would probably have reacted in a similar manner under the same circumstances.

UNDERSTANDING RANK AND FILE DISCONTENT

It is not surprising that the successful shop floor revolt occurred among the Latino gellers. Of all the different racial and ethnic groups in the factory, the Latino workers were the ones who were the most discriminated against by management. In addition, of all the ethnic groups in the plant, the Latino workers possessed the most group solidarity, which includes such aspects as friendship, shared meanings, and shared norms, as well as mutual protection.[8] As Hodson has demonstrated in a comprehensive study of industrial ethnographies, the presence of workplace "solidarity significantly increases organized resistance to management."[9]

Hodson has also identified another factor that appears to be related to the frequency of organized resistance in the workplace. He found that workers "with the most insecure jobs" are more likely to participate in acts of organized resistance than are other workers.[10] As has been mentioned earlier in the book, of all the occupational groupings in the plant, the gellers' jobs were the most insecure due to the fact that factory layoffs were most likely to occur in this department when product sales temporarily declined. Therefore, it is not surprising that the gellers served as the foundation of the two major collective actions that occurred in the factory during my period of employment with Biomed.

Since a majority of the Latino workers were concentrated in the gelling department and they seemed to have developed a true spirit of community at the factory, it is hardly surprising that a powerful primary work group developed in this section. Although primary work groups have been found to be crucial to the success of organized resistance in unionized settings,[11] such groups are also important for nurturing acts of resistance in workplaces where unions are absent. Davis elaborates on the importance of the primary work group in such settings:

> Managers have always known that even in the absence of trade union recognition the primary work group (defined by common tasks, skills, or departments) is a natural counterpole to management authority and the basis for collective counteraction. The daily work group constitutes a social unit for the individual worker almost as intimate and primal as the family. It is the atom of class organization and the seed from which great cooperative actions of the working class have always developed.[12]

It was obvious that *individual* worker discontent was not effective in bringing about change or in challenging management authority. Without collective bargaining rights, it was nearly impossible for the workers to obtain raises from Biomed. Individual or even collective begging was an insufficient strategy for dealing with this corporation. The only time that a few raises were wrestled away from management was after the Latino gellers attacked the illegitimate authority of management. It took a threat to the company's economic power to obtain a handful of meager raises for only a few of the workers.

Although the open expression of militancy is likely to be muted in an unequal power situation, as at Biomed, there were direct manifestations of militancy on two separate occasions, as has been discussed in this chapter. Based on these two militant outcomes, a question that arises is: what were the limits and possibilities of collective action at Biomed? After the successful Latino gellers' revolt, one might have expected to see a more structured and coordinated militancy emerge at Biomed. Even though the mass walkout occurred approximately one month after the uprising of the

Latino gellers, the action was, nevertheless, spontaneous and uncoordinated. Why was this the case?

While militant collective actions are more likely to occur in unionized firms, where workers feel that they have more protection and support, this does not mean that such actions will automatically occur in such settings. For example, after my stint at Biomed, during the early to mid-1980s I worked at two unionized firms in the Chicago metropolitan area: a textile factory organized by the Toyworkers Union and a food processing plant organized by the Teamsters Union. Although I worked at each place for a significant period of time, and at times workers at each plant expressed dissatisfaction over various aspects of their work situations, neither were there *any* incidents of shop floor collective action at these plants during the time I worked there nor did I hear any reports that such actions had occurred in the past.

Since "spontaneous" strikes that occur among nonunion workers can be considered "wildcat strikes,"[13] the collective actions that occurred at Biomed could technically be defined as wildcat strikes. However, the term is usually reserved for describing strikes among unionized workers that are not sanctioned by either the national or international union.[14] Wildcat strikes often occur as a worker response to managerial actions that are perceived as unjust. Although some wildcat strikes are relatively spontaneous and uncoordinated, others are just the opposite; they are well planned and organized in advance.

So, why were the collective actions at Biomed so uncoordinated? The answer, I believe, lies in the fact that a "culture of solidarity"[15] was lacking throughout the entire workforce. As in some of the wildcat strikes that have occurred in unionized settings, the militancy that occurred at Biomed was a direct and immediate response to managerial actions that were perceived as unjust by Biomed's workers. Since the revolt of the Latino gellers was limited to sectional demands directly relating to only the Latino gellers, I believe that many of the factory's other workers did not generalize this experience to understand how militant collective actions could also potentially improve their own immediate situations.

In addition, as was discussed in chapter 7, there was very little social interaction between a number of the ethnic groups in the plant. This made it extremely difficult not only to nourish and coordinate shop floor militancy, but even to discuss its possibility or the ramifications of the two militant collective actions among a wider audience of workers. Finally, the racism inherent among at least some of the workers of the different ethnic groups provided another obstacle to a structured and coordinated shop floor militancy at Biomed. This racism was expressed not only among some of the white workers toward minority workers, but was also apparent in the Latino workers' attitudes toward the African American workers. (This has been touched on in chapter 7 and will be discussed in more detail in chapter 9, which deals with the union organizing drive.)

9.

Talking Union

BECAUSE OF THE TYPE OF SHOP FLOOR MANAGERIAL CONTROL PRACTICED IN high-tech industries, combined with a fear that collective bargaining agreements and strikes will undermine this control, it is hardly surprising to discover that high-tech industries are one of the most union-resistant sectors of the U.S. economy. Although many firms in all economic sectors actively oppose unionization, high-tech firms have opposed unionization *even more vigorously* than have other industries. This vehement anti-union sentiment has resulted in high-tech companies, including Biomed, resorting to a variety of insidious tactics to prevent the unionization of their firms. Case studies of organizing attempts at two high-tech firms during 1982–83, specifically the Glaziers Union's attempt to organize Atari (Silicon Valley) and the attempt by the Communication Workers of America (CWA) to unionize Wavetek (Indianapolis), support these conclusions.[1] (For a discussion of these various tactics, see chapter 1.)

This chapter examines a number of topics connected with unionization. It briefly discusses how the workers at Biomed felt about unions as well as provide information on former trade unionists who worked for the company. However, the bulk of the chapter is devoted to a discussion of the attempt to organize Biomed. The chapter concludes with an analysis of the union organizing campaign at Biomed.

Since there was no union at Biomed and the unemployment rate was quite high, the company was able to impose low wage levels, no benefits, poor working conditions, and arbitrary work rules and discipline. Most of the production workers realized that a union would make their life at work better although few had the inclination or were prepared to take on the company in a sustained struggle such as an organizing drive. One morning before work, Chuck said to me, "Things wouldn't happen like this if we had a union."

The worker at Biomed who knew the most about unions was Bob. As I mentioned in an earlier chapter, Bob's father was a member of the executive board of one of the large railway unions. Although Bob was never involved in any organizing drives himself, he knew much about this topic in addition to general information about unions.

Bob's views of unions were quite class collaborationist. In late December he told me, "Management should never fear unions because the unions and management can work together in harmony." Although he mentioned that he thought Biomed could be organized, he felt that a union would not be able to do much to improve the wages and the working conditions there. He never explained to me why he felt that a union would be ineffective in improving wages and working conditions for the company's workers.

Bob's feelings about the possibility of organizing Biomed seemed to shift nearly every week. A few days before the shop floor revolt of the Latino gellers, I told Bob of the organizing drive at Atari in Silicon Valley. I mentioned that Atari planned to ship much of their production to factories in Hong Kong or Taiwan, most likely because of an organizing drive by the Glaziers and Glassworkers Union. Bob said, "The same thing would happen if there was an organizing drive here. They would shut down and move south."

At other times Bob appeared to be very much in favor of organizing a trade union at Biomed. Even when he got his new job at the loading dock and was planning to leave Biomed, he still considered trying to organize the workers after he saw the power of the Latino gellers at the point of production. Almost immediately after the revolt he said, "I can organize this place now. I should have a BRAC organizer here on Monday morning." Later in the day, he repeated the comment.

Although Bob's father got him a decent-paying job at a loading dock, which Bob told me "will eventually be union because they are hiring only members of BRAC," Bob once lost a nonunion job at a local hospital because of his father. When the hospital found out that Bob's father held an important position with a trade union, Bob was fired even though he was not trying to organize the hospital's workers. After Bob was fired, organizers from several unions converged on the hospital, eventually organizing several sectors of the hospital staff.

Since Bob came from a trade union background, it was surprising that he did not show much labor solidarity. In February, during the middle of the independent truck drivers' strike, I asked Bob for his opinion of the strike. "Independent truck drivers are the scum of the earth," he said. "They all average $140,000 a year. I don't know why they went out on strike."

I responded by telling him that I had read that many of them claimed that they could no longer make a living from truck driving. "They're lying," Bob argued. "You have to be very lazy not to make at least $25,000 a year from driving a truck."

Another worker who expressed interest in organizing Biomed was Greg. Bob informed me of Greg's plans to have Biomed unionized within a year, although he thought that this was just one of Greg's "real wild schemes." Greg may have been sincere, but he was more of a talker than a doer. He also thought that he was very knowledgeable about the American labor movement, while in reality he knew very little about it. For instance, Greg did not even know that the Teamsters Union had been expelled from the AFL-CIO in 1957 and was no longer an affiliate union in 1983.

One of the line foremen, Kay, surprised me when she told me that she was interested in trying to organize a union at Biomed. "Everybody would have to stick together," she said. "Biomed could fire all of us and then pick up and move. There is also a good possibility that they would lock us out." Although Kay may have been fairly serious about organizing a union, she would not have been able to join the bargaining unit because she was part of the "management team."

FORMER TRADE UNIONISTS

I knew of only three workers who had been members of trade unions before coming to work at Biomed. When I met Clark, a young African American cable department worker, the first comment that he made to me was, "Man, what this place needs is a union." He told me that he had worked for four years at a plastic injection mold factory in Lake Bluff, Illinois. Clark said that the plant was unionized and that he had been making $6.85 per hour at the time of his layoff. Although he could not remember the name of his union, he felt very positive about unions and realized that there was a strong positive correlation between unionization and higher wages, benefits, and better working conditions.

The second worker that I knew who had been a former trade unionist was Mick. While he worked as a metal polisher, for more than eleven years, at Duro Metal Products, Mick was a member of Industrial Workers Local 44. He seemed fairly positive about the union but he told me that he did not like the fact that there was a strike every three years around contract time. "We'd be out eight weeks and get a nickel raise," Mick said.

While talking of strikes one day, Mick said to me in a serious tone of voice, "We'll never have a strike here because we don't have a union. We'll never get a union in here because these people don't know about unions. If we tried to get a union in here, management wouldn't let us."

"What could they do?" I asked. "Things couldn't be worse than they are now." "They would raise the production rates," Mick said, ending the conversation.

The third former trade union member at Biomed was Roy, a young African American geller who worked only briefly for the company. Roy had worked on a dock at Chicago Specialty Manufacturing Company, a plumbing fixture factory, but had been fired after he had an argument with his boss. Even though Roy could not remember the name of the union that represented him at the factory, I knew that the Metal Processor's Union Local 16 had organized the factory where he had worked.

"What's the name of the union you've got here?" Roy asked me. When I told him that we did not have a union at Biomed, he looked surprised and exclaimed, "There's no union here!" I could not believe that he thought that we had a union, considering that he knew of our low wages and lack of benefits. "I forgot to ask if there was a union here when I started working," Roy said. I encouraged him not to bring up this issue with the supervisors.

TRYING TO ORGANIZE BIOMED

After working at Biomed for only a few days, there was no doubt in my mind that a union was desperately needed at the plant. I had been in contact with a number of different union organizers for several months preceding my being hired at Biomed and I was particularly impressed with one from the United Electrical, Radio and Machine Workers of America (UE). Lois Valdez seemed very interested in what I was doing and gave me a lot of helpful advice. I was also very familiar with the UE and I liked their aggressive organizing tactics, their fight against the current trend of concessions, and their militant history and traditions, which were still very much alive in the union.

I called Lois after working only four days at Biomed, to see if the UE might be interested in organizing the factory. When I described the plant and the products that were manufactured there, she became enthusiastic about the organizing possibilities. Lois told me that she would try to check out Biomed at the international office in New York, although she advised me to try to find out as much as I could about the company without appearing to be too nosy. "Keep your eyes and ears open but keep your nose clean," she told me. "They might suspect you of being an industrial spy who is trying to get their production secrets to give to another company. Be careful what you do."

Every few weeks I called Lois with more pertinent information about the company. The more I told her, the more enthusiastic she became about organizing the company. In early January, Lois enthusiastically discussed the possibility of organizing Biomed at a District 11 UE staff meeting.

I called Lois on the evening of the Latino geller shop floor revolt. As I retold the day's events, she became quite animated. "I know how you feel," she said. "You think that you will work years in the factory, nothing will ever happen, you'll die and go to heaven."

When I informed her that Bob had mentioned that he was thinking of having a BRAC organizer come to the factory the following Monday morning, Lois became concerned. She wondered what his motivation was since he was planning to leave the factory in a few weeks. She was worried about him ruining our organizing campaign although I told her that I did not think he was serious.

"If a BRAC organizer is there on Monday morning, give me a call Monday evening and we can have an organizer there on Tuesday morning to pass out leaflets and union cards. We don't like to do it this way but if we're against a wall, we will. We'd rather work from the inside and go slowly. This guy doesn't seem willing to do serious work the same way you do," Lois said.

"Anyway, I think it's time that I put you in contact with Louie, the head organizer. I think he should be aware of what's going on. I'll call him to tell him about it. I have given him the clippings to read and told him that the company was growing. I have also mentioned Biomed in my reports as a place to watch in the future. I'll be arriving back in town Saturday evening and I'll give you a call. We can set up a meeting at your place for Sunday evening and you can tell Louie everything you know."

I also told Lois that Biomed wanted Roberto to come back to work on Monday. She was ecstatic about that. "They want the leader of the revolt to come back to work? That's great!" she exclaimed. She told me that the UE had a good reputation in the Latino community because of the neighborhood organizing work they did there. Fortunately, there was no union organizer from BRAC in the factory parking lot to greet the workers on the following Monday morning.

The meeting with Lois and Louie was arranged for a Tuesday evening in early April. At the meeting, I told Louie all about Biomed. After I presented him with all the facts, he said, "This information here shows me that the company is viable. It could have five-hundred workers in a few years. We should definitely try to organize it while it's still small." Later he added, "This company actually makes a socially useful product. I bet that they save quite a few lives."

Both Lois and Louie seemed to be interested in focusing future organizing campaigns in the field of medical electronics. "We are losing a lot of our industrial base and we're not doing much organizing work now," Louie said. "This could be the field of the future."

Louie was convinced that we should launch the organizing drive while Biomed was concerned with their future growth and their plan to go "public" with their stock. He felt that it might be hard for Biomed to counter a campaign under such circumstances.

As Lois and Louie were leaving, Louie said, "We'll have to figure out a way to get all of these workers together. What I need now from you are names, addresses, and a list of telephone numbers." They also gave me some UE newspapers and literature. "We don't believe in concessions. They won't save industry," Louie added. "We're one of the few unions who still believes this and fights against concessions. You might say we're an old-fashioned union." As they walked out the door, I replied, "I hope 1930s style." Louie laughed. The campaign was under way.

Louie called the following week. I asked him, "So, are you interested in organizing Biomed?" He replied, "I am very interested in organizing Biomed but I'd like to check out the employee situation a little closer." I told Louie that the supervisor of the electronic technicians had told me that he could see Biomed employing between 150 and 200 workers within several years. He did not find that at all surprising. We talked for awhile and Louie said that he would call me after the Chicago mayoral election was held on 12 April.

During this conversation, Louie mentioned that he wanted me to set up a meeting with Herb so that we would have a contact at the other plant. Because of a variety of circumstances, I was never able to meet with Herb. As I stated before, Herb was fired at the end of April.

Louie called again in the middle of April. I told him of a consummated deal with a large pharmaceutical company so he asked if that meant that more workers would be hired. I told him that I did not know. "If more workers are going to be hired, we might want to wait several weeks before starting the campaign to get them involved," he said.

I also reported on my progress in obtaining workers' addresses and phone numbers. "You should also be thinking about who you want on the organizing committee," Louie said. "I've been thinking about that," I replied. "I'm sure you have," he said in a confident manner.

The day after the plant closing notice was distributed to the workers, I called Louie to inform him of the latest events. After mentioning the mass walkout, I asked him if he thought that we should begin the campaign now because of worker resentment. "Many workers will be looking for jobs during these next two weeks," Louie said. "Most of them won't find anything because there is nothing out there. Don't worry; they'll still remember this layoff, especially since they won't get a check one of those weeks. They might forget the layoff a month later, though." Louie suggested that we wait to launch the campaign until the workers came back to work.

Louie and I continued to talk on the telephone once a week about what was happening at Biomed. We decided to launch the campaign at the end of May, once Louie came back from a trip to Philadelphia.

Louie called me on 1 June. Production was booming so after talking about the recent events that had occurred at Biomed, Louie asked, "OK, whom do you think we should contact first?" I mentioned both Pedro, the Latino geller, and Andy, the African American inspector/packer. I told Louie that I knew Pedro fairly well and that he was a good friend of Roberto, the militant geller who had sparked the March shop floor revolt.

Louie told me to talk with Pedro the following Tuesday, 7 June, to try to arrange a meeting between Louie, Pedro, Roberto, and myself at a nearby restaurant after work on Thursday, 9 June.

I asked Louie for a strategy for approaching Pedro. "What if he tells me that he doesn't want to get involved because he is afraid that he will be fired?" I asked. "Tell him that he mustn't tell anyone now because if the company finds out, they can fire him because we can't prove that we had an organizing attempt going on. If the company finds out later, we can prove that we had an organizing attempt in progress and get workers reinstated."

"What if he says that he is afraid that they will close the factory if we try to get a union in?" I asked. "Tell him that they won't close this factory because it's a gold mine." Louie continued, "When you approach him, tell him that we've got to do something about the wages in this place. Don't say, 'What have you got to lose?' because he has something to lose if he is working in this factory. Also stress that he mustn't tell anyone about this, except Roberto."

I assured Louie that I felt that both Pedro and Roberto were trustworthy. I told him that I was sure that neither of them would tell management. "In fact, Roberto hates management," I told Louie. "The afternoon break was called one minute late today. Roberto pointed to the clock and raised one finger to indicate that we were cheated out of one minute of our break. He was angry."

"Good," Louie continued. "If Pedro asks the name of the union, just tell him that it's a union for factory workers. At the meeting, I will ask them questions to which you already know the answer. I will also ask them to do certain things, such as to count the workers in the factory and their department. I will also give them literature, but not enough to give to the other workers."

"Well, good, we're under way," Louie concluded enthusiastically. "Give me a call on Tuesday evening."

I was able to get Pedro alone during Tuesday's afternoon break. As I began to talk to Pedro, I felt a surge of nervousness course through my body. We were watching some of the workers play softball in the parking lot when I said to Pedro, "You know, we need a union in this place." He replied, "We need a lot of things in this place." I continued, "I know this guy who is a union organizer and he's interested in organizing this place. He'd like to talk to you and Roberto."

Pedro seemed very enthusiastic. "Sure, I'll talk to him," he replied. I mentioned that the organizer wanted to ask them about the problems at Biomed. This opened up a Pandora's box for Pedro. He spent about five minutes talking about all the problems in the place and he did not even cover them all. I asked Pedro to talk to Roberto and I reiterated that we should not tell anyone else about this just yet. Pedro said that he would talk to Roberto.

I called Louie in the evening to tell him that the meeting was on. He was happy about that and confident that things were progressing well.

Pedro did not show up for work on Thursday. After work, I hurried over to Sylvia's Restaurant to meet Louie. I told him that Pedro was not at work and I also mentioned that I thought that he had not talked to Roberto. We talked of the recent developments at Biomed and then we took a ride in Louie's car so that I could show him the two plants. Louie and I decided that I should attempt to set up another meeting for the following Tuesday, 14 June.

As Louie was driving me home, he told me of his background and how he got involved in the labor movement. Louie grew up in a tough, working-class area of Philadelphia. His father was a chauffeur and his mother was unemployed much more often than she was employed. Louie dropped out of high school because he felt that he was not learning anything. The high school that he attended only operated for a few hours a day. The school did not have a lunch period because the administration feared that somebody would be killed.

When Louie dropped out of school, he linked up with a radical priest and became involved with community organizing work. Through this contact, he began to do boycott work for the United Farm Workers of America (UFWA). Shortly thereafter, he headed to Georgia to do more work for the UFWA because he had heard that that "was where the action was."

After leaving Georgia, Louie came back to Philadelphia and took a minimum-wage job in a factory started by a White Russian. He had hopes of organizing this five-hundred-worker plant but his plans fell through when he discovered that the factory was very close to being a sheltered workshop. Upon learning this, Louie went down to Florida to work, once more, for the UFWA.

"I helped to organize Minute Maid," Louie said proudly. "I was shot at, beat up, and thrown in jail down there." After this stint, Louie entered a UE shop that was weak in order to strengthen the union local. "So you and I have similar backgrounds in the labor movement," Louie told me. Although Louie was not tall, and had thick glasses, his enthusiasm and commitment to the labor movement indicated to me that he had fire in his soul and was a fighter who would not give up until the job was completed.

Pedro was back at work on Friday morning. At 9:00, I approached him under the guise of picking up some garbage near his gelling table. "How's it going, Pedro?" I asked. "We have to talk during the break." He apologized for missing the meeting. "We'll talk during the break," I repeated. "Sure, sure," Pedro responded.

During the morning break, we talked outside while waiting for the snack truck. We arranged a meeting for Tuesday, after work, at the same restaurant. Pedro promised that he would talk to Roberto some time that day.

I saw Pedro talking with Roberto near their cars during the afternoon break. They were talking quite intensely as I talked with other workers. I felt like going over to them to find out what was going on, but I decided against it. When we re-entered the factory after the break, Pedro said, "OK, everything's arranged for Tuesday." Roberto smiled at me. A few minutes later, Pedro told me that Roberto was very receptive to the idea of a union.

When I talked with Pedro during Tuesday's lunch break, he told me that Roberto had left the factory for the day and that he would not return until Wednesday. Roberto had a large boil behind his right ear and had gone to a hospital to have it treated. I told Pedro that the three of us—Louie, Pedro, and I—would still get together.

After work, I talked with Pedro briefly, and I told him that I would meet him at Sylvia's Restaurant in a few minutes. Louie was waiting for us, sitting at the counter, when we both arrived. We took a booth at the back of the restaurant.

Louie talked with us about Biomed, asked Pedro some questions, and told him about the UE. Pedro seemed fairly interested and attentive. When Louie asked us at 4:50 if we had to go, both of us said we could stay longer. Louie also provided information about UE contracts and the wage levels at UE shops, although he did not guarantee us that we would receive a certain wage increase if the union got in.

When Louie asked Pedro about the ethnic composition of the shop, Pedro said, "Steve likes the niggers. He always says 'hi' to them and jokes around with them. He never says 'hi' to the Spanish-speaking workers."

Pedro also complained that the "niggers" had the easier jobs while the "Spanish-speaking workers" were concentrated in the gelling department. Since Pedro had used the word "niggers" again, Louie asked him if he was referring to the African American workers.

Louie then launched into an explanation of how management attempts to divide the workers by making each ethnic group suspicious of the other ethnic groups. I told Pedro that I thought that Steve was actually a racist and that he joked around with the African American workers as part of his "labor relations" policy. It was interesting to learn that Pedro thought that Steve sincerely liked these workers while I viewed his behavior as a way to keep the African American workers under control.

Before the meeting broke up, Louie gave Pedro some UE literature and mentioned that he would like to set up another meeting for the following week, this time with Roberto. Pedro inquired about asking Juan to attend the next meeting. Louie decided against bringing Juan into the organizing committee until later. He gave Pedro his card and asked him for his phone number. Pedro seemed reluctant to provide this information, so Louie did not press him about this. Pedro shook both of our hands before he departed.

While Louie drove me home, we continued to talk. He felt pretty positive about Pedro but was worried about his attendance record at work. "You know, it's hard to get a first contract these days without a strike," Louie said. "What I'd like to do is to provoke the company into an unfair labor practice and then pull off a strike. This way we'd have a good chance of getting a contract."

Louie mentioned that we had a long road ahead of us. He thought that if we won the National Labor Relations Board (NLRB) election it would be by a small amount. "What we do after that depends on how strong the workers are," he said. Louie added that the UE still did not have a contract in a shop where the union had won the representation election more than seven years before!

The following day I talked with Pedro about the meeting with Louie. He thought that it had gone pretty well but he still had some doubts. "They'll promise you anything before the union gets in. We'll just have to wait and see," he told me.

On Monday, 20 June, I arranged another organizing committee meeting with Pedro and Roberto for Wednesday, 22 June. Both workers seemed fairly enthusiastic about the meeting.

When Louie called that evening, I confirmed Wednesday's meeting with him. Earlier we had talked about bringing an African American worker into the organizing committee. We had decided it should be Andy because of his militance in leading the mass walkout. Louie told me to talk to him "first thing tomorrow."

DYING FROM THE INSIDE: THE FINAL WEEK

21 June

I approached Andy during the morning break, in the employees' parking lot, before the arrival of the snack truck. "What's up, man?" he asked. I began to talk to him in his own "language." "You and I know that this place is scandalous and something has to be done about it, right?" I asked. I then proceeded to tell him about the union organizer who wanted to talk to him, about the planned meeting on Wednesday afternoon. However, I did not mention that Pedro and Roberto would also be at the meeting.

Andy seemed interested in the meeting but he was not sure that he would be able to attend. He told me that he had to go home to take care of his sons immediately after work because his wife started her job in the late afternoon. "Look, let's just keep this between us," I said. "Don't mention this to anybody because if the company finds out, we can be fired because we can't prove that we have an organizing campaign going." "Don't worry," Andy said in a sophisticated manner. "I know about these things."

I felt fairly pleased that my discussion with Andy had gone so well. I did not anticipate the problems that I would encounter later in the day.

Andy arrived back from the morning break a few minutes late, which concerned me because I knew that he would receive his second warning. While Debbie waited for Andy, she held a warning form in her hand. When he sauntered toward the inspecting tables, Debbie confronted him. They talked briefly by these tables and then left the factory through the front door. When they came back to the factory, both of them seemed to be in a good mood.

While I was constructing boxes late in the afternoon, Andy came by the stamping table and said, in a low voice, "I was talking to Debbie about the union, I didn't mention no names, and she said that she would like to see some literature on the union." I was taken by surprise. "Debbie can't be in the union because she's a foreman!" I exclaimed. Andy looked shocked. "We'll talk later," he said.

I tried to figure out why Andy had told Debbie about the union, especially when he had agreed not to tell anybody. I was not sure if Debbie thought that she could be in the union or if she was trying to set me up. I knew that it was only a matter of time before the other line foremen, Lori, Steve, and the upper level of Biomed's management would find out about the union. I began to feel extremely uncomfortable. I was sweating profusely, more from my nervousness than from the excessive heat in the factory.

When I went to get some more boxes at about 3:30, I overheard Debbie talking with Liz at the back of the factory. "I don't know about unions," Liz said to Debbie as I passed by. The word was already spreading around from supervisor to supervisor. A short while later, I saw Liz and Steve leave the factory through the back door. I had a strange feeling that Liz was informing Steve about the union.

I considered trying to talk with Andy but I decided against it because I felt that it would give me away. When Debbie asked to see me at 3:40, I was positive that she was going to question me about the union. She did not mention the union, however. She just wanted me to load a pallet with unmade boxes.

I left the factory in a state of extreme agitation. As soon as I arrived home, I called Louie. He was not at his office but on his way home so I left a message on his answering machine.

When Louie called, I told him the whole story. "That dumb shit," he said, referring to Andy. "Well, I don't want to meet with him but I still want to meet with the other guys. This is the first time that something has gone wrong so early in a campaign." I told Louie that I had obtained Andy's phone number although Andy did not know that I had it. I also mentioned to Louie that Andy's number was unpublished but he told me to call him anyway to find out some information. Louie said to call him back after I had talked to Andy.

When I first called Andy at 6:30 in the evening he was not home, so I called him back an hour later. When he answered the phone, he was playing music quite loudly so he had to turn it down to hear me. After he knew it was me, the first thing he asked was, "How'd you get my number, man?" I tried to brush off his question but I eventually told him that I had obtained it from a "sheet."

"What did you say to Debbie?" I asked him. He was very defensive but he finally replied, "I was just asking Debbie some questions, like, how the company would feel about a union." "What did you specifically ask her, so that we can protect ourselves if it gets out," I continued.

"It's out already," Andy answered. "Steve knows about it and asked me about the union. I didn't give him no names but told him that somebody came up to me during a break and told me about a union. Don't worry, everything's cool." He repeated, "Everything's cool."

I informed Andy that our organizing committee meeting scheduled for the following day was cancelled. He misunderstood my comment and thought that I had asked him if we were going to have a meeting at work on Wednesday. "I don't know if we're going to have a meeting tomorrow," he said. When I straightened him out, Andy said, "I'm not going to any meetings."

"Everything's not cool," Louie said when I called him back after talking to Andy. "If Andy didn't tell them that it was you, he will when a little pressure is applied to him. Anyway, they will be able to figure out it was you." He continued, "Your vocabulary, the fact that you're the only one who talks to all the different ethnic groups, will let them know that it's you."

Louie said that Biomed committed an unfair labor practice when they questioned Andy about the union. "It's as illegal as hell," Louie said. I asked him what I should do if management confronted me about the union. He said that I should tell them, "Damn right, I'm for the union. And I'm going to keep talking about the union on my own time. I know my rights, so if you hassle me, you're going to get in trouble with the labor board."

Louie told me that it was not my fault that this had happened. "You just misjudged the guy," he said. "Coming from your background, you've done a good job. You haven't taken the workers on any adventures and you've done everything you were supposed to do."

He continued, "This might work to our advantage. The whole shop might be buzzing tomorrow. If any raises are given, we must take credit for this. Anyway, we are forced to move faster now."

Louie told me that we should still meet on Wednesday with Pedro and Roberto, but at a different place. I suggested Ye Old Pancake Shoppe, which was located near Sylvia's Restaurant. I mentioned that I was very concerned about a possible confrontation with management the following morning. Louie tried to reassure me that if a confrontation occurred, it would not be as bad as I expected it to be.

22 June

I arrived a few minutes late to the factory this morning. I was running toward the back door when Andy confronted me in the parking lot. He was drinking a can of Fanta Orange Soda when he stopped me and said, "I want to talk to you, man." He pulled me aside and said, "Look, I don't know where you got my number, but you better lose it fast." I replied, "Don't worry, I won't call you again." I nervously entered the factory, not knowing what to expect from the company.

I walked over to the time clock. I was relieved to see that my time card was still on the rack. I punched in. It was 7:48. I was still very tense as I took off my windbreaker. I began to vacuum the offices.

A few minutes later, Ben entered through the front door, said "hello" to me, and walked to his office. He reappeared, not more than two minutes later, and told me that he wanted to see me in his office. I was sure that Ben was going to make some kind of comment about the union if he did not ask me directly about it. I was prepared to defend both myself and the union.

When I arrived at Ben's office, Andy was standing there waiting for the two of us. Ben, who was short and looked like an accountant, turned toward me as he addressed me.

Ben: "Andy tells me that you called him last night. Where did you get his phone number?"

I: "That's none of your business."

Ben: "I'm asking you a direct question. Where did you get his phone number?"

I: "I'm not going to tell you. I told Andy that I wouldn't call him again."

Ben (turning to Andy): "Your number is not in the phone book and cannot be obtained from directory assistance."

Andy: "That's right. Last night he said that he got it from a sheet."

Ben: "If you don't tell me where you got his number from, don't bother punching in."

I: "I've already punched in."

Ben: "Well then punch out."

I: "So you're firing me?"

Ben: "If you don't tell me where you got his number."

This scene seemed to be rehearsed too perfectly. Everything happened too quickly for it not to have been planned. Although I did not have any proof, I strongly suspected that Andy had phoned Ben last night, after he had talked with me. The sophistication of these tactics led me to believe that Biomed's attorneys were contacted by the company late Tuesday afternoon. I am positive that they advised Biomed not to mention the union to me under any circumstances.

I punched out at 7:57. I left the factory and walked over to a nearby hotel to call Louie at home. I told him of the events of the past fifteen minutes.

The first thing he said was "That Andy's a real fink." "I couldn't tell him where I got the phone number, right?" I asked Louie. He agreed.

At the time, I was not even sure where I had obtained Andy's phone number. I had been collecting workers' phone numbers and addresses from a variety of different sources—from the workers themselves, from phone books, from other workers, and from a clipboard hanging behind Steve's desk. Since there were no pay phones at Biomed, whenever an employee had to make a personal call, he had to record it on this clipboard. Before making the call, the worker had to sign his name, receive a supervisor's approval, and write down the number called. When I used the phone, I memorized several of the workers' numbers listed on the clipboard, thinking that they might have been the workers' home phone numbers. I recorded these phone numbers for possible future use. Later in the day, I remembered that I had obtained Andy's phone number from this clipboard.

Louie advised me to tell Ben that I had gotten Andy's number from somebody in the plant in confidence. If that did not satisfy him, Louie instructed me to try to provoke Ben into commenting about the union. He said that I should attempt to draw Ben into a big discussion about the union, hopefully with some of the other workers present. Louie told me, "You did the right thing, although you probably left too soon. If he doesn't let you go back to work, call me at home. If you do go back to work, call me at the office at noon."

I was still somewhat rattled but I walked back to the factory rather defiantly. As I walked through the factory, I tried to hide my feelings of intimidation. I saw Ben enter the front offices through the corridor door so I waited for him in front of his office. When he came back to his office after several minutes, he walked up to me and said, "Well?"

"OK, I'll tell you where I got the number from," I replied. "I received the number in confidence from someone." "From someone in the plant?," Ben asked. "Yes," I replied. Ben stared at me for what seemed like an interminably long time although it was actually only a few seconds. "OK, punch in," he said. I could not believe that it had been that easy. I was expecting that I would have to put up a fight. I punched back in at 8:15.

I felt extremely uncomfortable when I went back to work. I was dripping with sweat, more from my nerves than from the heat of the day. I had won the first round yet I knew that I was a marked man. I had been granted a temporary reprieve but that was all. Management knew about the union and was trying to get rid of me. I realized that this would not be their last attempt.

When I went to clean the lunchroom at 8:45, Ben and Robin were standing close together, whispering to each other. I knew that they were talking about the confrontation that had occurred just a half hour before. As soon as I entered the room, the whispering stopped.

Robin started to talk in a rather loud voice to Ben, "So how's the new line coming along?" "Fine, fine," Ben replied. "Good," said Robin. Ben then headed toward the coffee machine to get a cup of coffee. When he tried to insert a few coins into the slot, he dropped them on the floor. He appeared to be a bit agitated. Then he turned to me and mumbled something that I could not understand. I continued to clean the tables.

When I returned to the main production area of the plant after I had finished cleaning, I saw Andy talking to Ben by Steve's desk. Although I had no proof, I thought that Ben was probably telling Andy what I had said in regards to his phone number. I began to feel the pressure mounting although I tried to remain calm on the outside.

At the start of the morning break, Andy began to verbally harass me. He attempted to get me to tell him who had given me his phone number. When I refused to comply with his request, he said, "I'm going to find out where you got my number from and then I'm going to get you." I did not take this threat lightly, remembering that he had told me that he had spent three months in Leavenworth Prison for jumping an army officer in West Germany when he was in the service. I turned to walk away from him but Andy said, "Don't walk away from me, man." I listened to what he had to say and then I walked away.

Although I was extremely tense and excited, I went outside to see what was happening and to talk with the other workers. Art said, "There are some rumors flying around about you." As I walked past him, I replied, "Let them fly." I walked over to Sam and Mike, who were leaning against Sam's car, and asked Sam, "So what's the talk going around?"

At first, he did not reply. Then he said, "Andy says that you want to get a union into this place." "How would you feel about that?" I asked. "Sure, I'd like the factory to be air-conditioned and I'd like to get raises,but this isn't going to be my life's work. Anyway, I don't think that Robin would let us have a union," Sam replied.

I explained the procedure for organizing a union to Sam. "It's for the workers to decide if they want to have a union," I said. "An election is held and if the majority of workers vote for a union, then we get to have a union." Sam's comments did not seem atypical of those of many American workers—reflecting an almost complete lack of a trade union consciousness or any kind of a working-class consciousness.

I felt a little better after the break. I did not feel as nervous as before. As soon as the lunch break began, I rushed over to the hotel to call Louie. I informed Louie of the events of the past few hours. "So things are a bit tense over there," he replied. I asked him if he thought that the company was worried and he said, "The company is a hundred times more nervous than you are." That made me feel a little better.

"We have to move quickly now," he continued. "You should spread the word that Andy is a fink and that the workers should watch out for him. You should also go around and see how the workers feel about organizing a union." I told Louie that some of the African American and white workers were still in the dark about the last two days' events. The shop was not buzzing as we had hoped. Louie told me that I should fill Pedro in on the latest developments and have him talk to the other Latino workers.

I hurried back to the factory and talked to Pedro before the end of the lunch period. After I told him what had happened, Pedro said, "See, I told you that you can't trust the niggers." I also mentioned to Pedro that Louie wanted him to call him at home. Pedro readily agreed to this request.

A few minutes after the end of the lunch break, Andy left the factory, laughing and smiling. I did not know the reason for his early departure but I was sure that it had a lot to do with Biomed's union-busting plans.

At the start of the afternoon break Chuck was talking with a group of workers in the parking lot. "So, Vic, when are we going to get a union in here?" he asked me. I responded bluntly, "Whenever you guys are ready." I knew that Chuck's question was asked in a spirit of only half-seriousness.

"If you get a petition with thirty-four names for a union, I'll be the thirty-fifth person to sign," Chuck laughed.

Clark was sitting next to Chuck, so I tried to appeal to his pro-union sympathies. "Clark, you've worked in a union shop so you know that you had higher wages, paid holidays and a vacation, benefits, and a grievance procedure," I said. Clark did not say anything. He just nodded his head. I went over to talk to Juan.

I told Juan about Andy, the union, and so on. I was surprised that he did not know what was going on in the shop. Juan seemed to be genuinely interested in the union. He asked me how much money the workers in this union made per hour. He became more interested when I told him that the wages in the UE shops ranged from $5 to $10 per hour. Juan thought that bringing in a union was something definitely worth considering.

The last part of the workday was relatively quiet. Louie had called off the meeting that had been scheduled for the afternoon. I relayed this information to Pedro and I told him to inform Roberto of this change.

Not one supervisor mentioned the union to me. Mr. Williams was very friendly toward me and even Debbie seemed uncharacteristically nice.

I was relieved when the day was over. Louie had wanted me to call him when I got home. When I called him for the third time that day, I elaborated on the events that had occurred after lunch. On Andy leaving work early, he said, "I'll bet the company had Andy meet with their lawyers to try to prove that you got his number from company property." "How can they prove that?" I asked. "They can't," Louie replied. "But that won't stop them from scheming."

"You've really been handling this well," he continued. "But don't break your arm patting yourself on the back." Louie told me that I should continue to talk up the union with the workers. He wanted me to call him on Friday to let him know of the prevailing sentiment in the shop.

23 June

I felt much more relaxed at work this day than I had the day before. Whereas a number of the workers had asked me about the union the previous day, none of them approached me about the union on this day. It appeared that "the union" was only important enough to receive limited attention. Too much interest might have indicated a seriousness that the workers were afraid might eventually lead to trouble.

Even if the workers "forgot" about the union, I knew that the company would not forget. Management knew where I stood, and I knew where they stood. There were no longer any secrets between us. Everything was out in the open.

I was still wary of Andy. I wondered how the workers felt about Andy and me. Louie had stated that he thought the workers were much more sympathetic toward me than toward Andy. Although Andy seemed uncomfortable around some of the workers, I was not sure that the feeling was mutual.

I was not even sure that the workers felt betrayed by Andy. By squealing on me, he had not only harmed me but also the hopes of the other workers for improved wages and working conditions. I had a feeling that most of the African American and white workers viewed this betrayal as a personal feud between Andy and me, however, one in which they were hesitant to choose sides.

While there might have been a certain resignation about the maintenance of a nonunion shop in some workers' minds, I continued to get the word out about Andy and the union. During the morning break, I talked with Sunil and Sundan, the two Indian male workers that I knew the best. "How do the Indian workers feel about the work here?" I asked them. Sunil responded, "If there is work to do, they will come and do it." I then proceeded to tell them about Andy and the union.

"How do you think the Indian workers would feel about getting a union into this place?" I asked. Once again, Sunil replied, "I think that they would be for it," he said. "I know that my wife (Anna) and I would be for a union. I don't talk with them much. You should talk to them yourself." Sunil seemed to know a lot about the functions of a union. He explained them to Sundan.

"Has everybody agreed to a union?" Sundan asked me. I told him that I was going around and talking to the workers to see how they felt about unionization. "Nothing is decided yet," I said.

"How do the Spanish-speaking workers feel about a union?" Sunil asked me. "A number of them are very pro-union," I answered. Sundan chimed in, "I think it will be hard to organize a union because of all the different ethnic groups." "It's been done at other factories and we can do it here, too," I said quite matter-of-factly.

Andy and I were actively avoiding each other. Since he had informed the company of my phone call to him, I felt that Andy was working "hand in glove" with the company. I do not think that Andy had originally planned to be a fink but was just stupid to open his mouth about the union to Debbie. When he realized that he was in trouble, he told Steve everything that he knew. Now, to save his own butt, he was working with the company to get rid of me.

I continued to talk to the other workers. Most of the workers seemed to be at least mildly in favor of a union, although some of them seemed to be rather apathetic. Few of the workers appeared to be ready to jump into an organizing campaign although Juan seemed quite willing to become involved. During the afternoon break, I briefly talked with him again. He asked me repeatedly, "When's the meeting?" Juan thought that I had already arranged a meeting between the workers and the union organizer.

"The work isn't bad, just the pay," Juan said. "In 1971, when I started working, I made $3.50 an hour." We talked of inflation and how his wages were barely able to cover the necessities of life.

24 June

I was more than happy that Friday had finally arrived, the last day of the workweek. Louie called late on Thursday evening because he thought that I had called earlier in the day. I told him of the workers' reactions toward the union. He said, "I'm not surprised at their reactions. This is how I thought they would react." Louie said that he would call back on Monday to see what was happening at the factory. At that time, Louie said that we should discuss how to best proceed with the organizing campaign.

I spent the day cleaning, stamping bags and counting and sorting out racks of elements. The work at Biomed seemed much more miserable than in the past, now that I was "exposed" and, in a sense, all alone.

During the morning break, I talked with Ophelia. She was chatting with two Latino women gellers in Spanish when I approached her. I asked her how she was doing and she said, "Fine." When she asked me, "How are you today?" I replied, "Not too well." I then proceeded to tell her about the union and about how Andy had finked on me to the bosses. She said, "I know. Pedro told me all about it. You can't trust those black people. We had the same problem where I used to work. See, that's why I was against Washington for mayor."

Ophelia translated my message about Andy and the union into Spanish for the two other women gellers. Their facial expressions indicated both surprise and shock. When I asked Ophelia what she thought about trying to organize a union at Biomed, she replied, "It would be good to have a union."

At the beginning of the afternoon break, I sought Harry's opinion about trying to unionize Biomed. When I asked him about it, his reply was terse and to the point. "I'd have to answer 'no comment' to that question because anytime you're for a union you put your job in jeopardy." I did not know how to respond to his statement.

27 June

On Monday, Steve was back at work for the first time since the previous Tuesday. While I was vacuuming the carpet in the front offices, I saw Ben and Steve conferring together by Robin's desk. I was sure that they were discussing "my situation." I had a feeling that they had a scheme that they were going to put into action soon.

I felt very uneasy that morning. I could not put my finger on why I felt so uncomfortable. I just had a premonition that something was going to happen that day. When I went to the back of the factory to pick up some cleaning supplies, I saw Andy and Steve talking together near the gelling tables. Now I had another reason to believe that something was up.

This was the day that Mick returned to work after a week's absence. He had spent the past week visiting the Wisconsin Dells for his honeymoon. During the morning break, I asked him about his wedding and honeymoon. After Mick elaborated on the details of these events, I told him about Andy and the union.

"I thought that someone would become fed up with these conditions and try to organize a union," he said. "This is just what we were talking about before." When I asked Mick what he thought of trying to get a union in at Biomed, he replied, "I'd be with you, Vic, if I wasn't planning to leave."

After his wedding, Mick had moved into his wife's place thirty-two miles southwest of Biomed. It took him over an hour and a half to get home during rush hour. He was looking for another job closer to his new home but he'd had no luck so far.

Mick asked if the company had said anything to me about the union. "No," I replied. "I am sure that they talked to their lawyers and their lawyers told them not to. It's an unfair labor practice for them to ask me about the union."

During the afternoon break, Mick asked me if anything was new with the union. I told him that nothing was new. "Maybe the company will forget about it," he said. I knew that Biomed would never forget about such a thing.

Although I had talked to many of the plant's workers and to every worker that I thought might be interested in organizing a union at Biomed, there was no noticeable upsurge in interest about the union. I was disappointed.

Late in the afternoon, there was a torrential downpour, which not only added to the gloom of the day but also seemed to foreshadow a coming confrontation. Twenty minutes after the beginning of the storm, at about 3:50, Debbie called Andy and me into the lunchroom. I knew immediately that this concerned the previous week's events. As I walked into the lunchroom, I was surprised to see all of the African American workers, Chris (an African American line foreman), Lori, Steve, and Ben. Ben did all of the talking. He talked about the occurrence of the "incident" the previous week and then proceeded to address me as if this were the Spanish Inquisition or even the McCarthyite Witch-Hunt.

Ben: "The people in this room are the only ones in the factory who know Andy's phone number. They have all denied giving you the phone number, so we want you to tell us who gave you his phone number."

I: "I'm sorry; I got the phone number in confidence. I can't tell you that."

Ben: "Is the person who gave you the phone number in this room?"

I: "I'm sorry but I can't answer that. I got the phone number in confidence."

Ben: "If you don't tell us who gave you the phone number, we'll have to assume that you got it from the files."

I: "From what files?"

Ben: "From the personnel files, and if that's where you got it from, we don't want you working here anymore."

Ben asked me again about the phone number. I repeated my answer. Sensing that I was going to be fired, I said, "Let me think about it tonight if I'm going to tell you who gave me Andy's phone number." Ben agreed.

He told me that I should see him before punching in for work the following morning. The meeting was over at 3:55.

A few minutes after the meeting had concluded, Debbie approached me and asked, "Why don't you just ask the person who gave you Andy's phone number if you can tell Ben?" I did not answer Debbie. It appeared to me that she believed my story.

The meeting had happened so quickly that I had been taken by surprise. Ben had planned to fire me at the meeting. I had just obtained a minimal extension but I knew that the end was near.

I should have exposed this charade but I was too stunned to react. I opened my mouth at one point and started to say, "What is this really all about?" but Ben told me to let him finish. I stupidly complied even though I do not think that any comments that I could have made would have affected the final outcome.

I called Louie when I got home. I informed him of the confrontation and mentioned that I thought that I would be fired the following morning. "Well, do you think that you can get him to say something about the union?" Louie asked hopefully. I told him that I did not know but that I would try to provoke Ben into talking about the union. Louie said that I should call him at his office early in the morning if I had been fired.

28 June

The day of reckoning had come. I woke up early after a night of light sleep. I tried to steel myself for this final confrontation although I felt much calmer than I had previously imagined. Adrenaline pumped through my body as I got off the bus and walked through the empty parking lot to the back door of the plant. The factory was dark and vacant as I made my way toward the time clock. Lori saw me coming so she pulled my time card. "Ben wants you to talk to him before you punch in," she said. I went into Ben's office to wait for him. It was only 7:40.

I paced back and forth in Ben's office until he arrived at 7:50. After he entered the office, he began to question me in the same manner as the previous afternoon.

Ben: "OK, who gave you Andy's number?"
I: "I'm not going to tell you. I got his phone number in confidence."
Ben: "Everyone who knows Andy's number has denied giving it to you."
I: "That's their right to deny it."

Ben:	"Well, if you don't give us the name of the person who gave you the number then we'll have to assume that you got it from the personnel files."
I:	"Are you accusing me of taking the number out of the personnel files?"
Ben:	"Oh, no. We're not accusing you but if you don't tell us who gave you the number then we'll have to assume that you got it from the files."

Ben walked to the other side of his office, turned around, and after a brief pause began to speak again.

Ben:	"Well, you don't work here anymore."
I:	"Are you firing me?"
Ben:	"Yes."
I: (rather indignantly)	"When did you become interested in Andy's phone number, before or after you found out about the union?"
Ben:	"I don't know about any union. I don't have to make a comment about a union."

After he said this, Ben left his office and walked into the main production area of the factory. About fifteen seconds later, I followed him into this section. Workers had been arriving for the past ten minutes and were beginning to congregate by their workplaces. I shouted at Ben, who was pretending to do some work on the dock.

"I know that I'm being fired for trying to organize a union in this place, for trying to get decent wages for the workers, and more than one washroom for fifty workers, and for trying to change the sweat shop conditions here!"

Ben and Steve tried to shut me up by saying, "That's enough! That's enough!" I was hustled out of the factory. It was all over.

Since it was only 7:55, workers were still arriving at Biomed. I told Mick and several Latino workers what had happened in a firm but excited manner in an attempt to stir them up. It did not work. "So what are you going to do now?" Mick asked me. "I'm going to try to get my job back. I'm going to file an unfair labor practice charge with the National Labor Relations Board," I replied. "Good luck," he said as he shook my hand. "I hope everything works out for you."

Andy walked out of the back door to see what was happening. I am sure that he was pleased with his role in this entire affair. I flagged down Sunil and Anna when they drove into the parking lot. "I've just been fired for trying to organize a union," I told Sunil. "What do you want us to do?" he asked. "I want you to talk it up among the other workers," I firmly stated. "We'll see what we can do," Sunil responded without emotion.

I was hoping that the workers would become outraged by Biomed's latest actions and would attempt to organize to do something about it although I knew that they would not do any such thing. I walked to the hotel and called Louie. We discussed the possibility of filing an unfair labor practice charge with the labor board against Biomed.

FILING AN UNFAIR LABOR PRACTICE CHARGE WITH THE NLRB

Three weeks after I was fired by Biomed, the United Electrical, Radio and Machine Workers of America (UE) filed an unfair labor practice (ULP) charge on my behalf against the company with Region 13 of the National Labor Relations Board (NLRB). On 19 July, accompanied by Louie, I met with a field examiner in the Chicago offices of the NLRB in order to swear out an affidavit against Biomed concerning my dismissal.

The field examiner for my case, Ms. Farrow, was an attractive African American woman appearing to be in her late thirties. Ms. Farrow shook her head in disbelief when I gave her a brief overview of the situation. She could not believe that I had been fired for refusing to tell Biomed where I had obtained Andy's phone number. As I outlined my story, she diligently recorded my comments while she probed for details with occasional questions.

When I mentioned that I had asked a Latino worker (Pedro Alvarez) to attend an organizing committee meeting, Ms. Farrow wanted to know his name so that she could record it in the affidavit. "Why do you need to put his name in the affidavit?" Louie asked Ms. Farrow. "This guy has a family to support and he could lose his job if the company finds out that he has been involved in an organizing campaign."

"I need to know his name so that I can better examine the case," Ms. Farrow replied. "Anyway, if Mr. Alvarez is fired, he can come down here and file an unfair labor practice charge against the company." After a considerable amount of discussion, Louie and Ms. Farrow agreed that certain workers' names would remain confidential and not appear in the affidavit.

Even after she completed writing out my thirteen-page affidavit, I still thought that Ms. Farrow was sympathetic to my case. This illusion did not last much longer. Upon her initial examination of the case, she discovered that I had indeed been involved in union organizing activities although the company still claimed that I had obtained Andy's phone number from their personnel files. Even though Ms. Farrow had not talked with Andy, she was ready to throw out the charge against the company based on what the company had told her!

Louie continued to press her for a more thorough investigation of the case. Although I had informed Ms. Farrow of how I had actually obtained Andy's phone number, she decided not to include it in the affidavit. On 5 August, I talked with Ms. Farrow by phone. She asked me to repeat this story so that she could attach an addendum onto my affidavit. Ms. Farrow also asked me for Andy's phone number so that she could talk to him "cold."

Louie told me on 20 August that my case had been thrown out by Ms. Farrow. She had refused to tell Louie what Andy had said to her. He told me that he was going to appeal the decision to the NLRB in Washington, D.C. and try to get the international union's lawyers to work on the case, if they were not too busy fighting Litton's antiunion activities. With the Washington-based NLRB dominated by a Reaganite majority, I was not too hopeful that the regional decision would be overturned.

As Gagala points out, the key to winning ULP charges filed with the NLRB rests with the field examiner's investigation,[2] and from what I know about how my ULP charge was handled, it appears to me that Ms. Farrow did not thoroughly investigate my charge against the company. However, since I was fired for allegedly stealing Andy's phone number from the company's personnel file and not for engaging in union activity, my ULP charge would be considered a "mixed motive discharge." According to Gagala, these types of discharges are "[t]he most serious and often the most difficult cases to prove to the Board" because "[e]mployers attempt to justify the punishment on grounds other than union support."[3]

In addition, in light of the fact that I feel that I did not obtain justice in front of the NLRB, I view Ms. Farrow's attitude concerning placing Pedro's name on the affidavit as being rather arrogant. When Louie argued that Pedro could also lose his job if the company found out that he was involved in the union organizing campaign, Ms. Farrow's response was that he could also file a ULP against the company! Once he did that then he could expect to receive the same kind of "justice" that I received from the NLRB, a federal agency whose mission is to protect unions and workers from employer harassment.

I believe that the type of campaign strategy that the UE was planning to pursue at Biomed was the correct one: slowly building an underground in-plant organizing committee composed of workers of the different ethnic groups, through the holding of small group meetings among the plant's workers before going "public" with the campaign. The purpose of developing such an organizing structure is to build union commitment and leadership among the workers and to prepare them for the antiunion strategies that the employer will most likely utilize throughout the organizing drive, once the employer learns that a campaign is actually under way. In addition, had the campaign not ended so abruptly, I am aware that the UE had planned to use housecalls, a method that involves the external union organizer, the rank-and-file organizer(s), and prounion workers visiting the homes of bargaining unit members to make personal contact with them during the drive.

Recent empirical research on union organizing strategies has demonstrated that the use of these tactics, referred to as a "rank and file intensive strategy" result in higher success rates in union organizing drives. Specifically, Bronfenbrenner has discovered that "the components of a "rank and file intensive strategy" are associated with union win rates that are 12–26 percent higher than union win rates in campaigns that do not employ that strategy."[4]

In spite of the reported success rates when utilizing a "rank and file intensive strategy," I do not believe that the use of such a strategy would have resulted in a successful organizing campaign at Biomed because of the significant problems that existed in the workplace *before* the campaign was under way. However, I do not believe that an obstacle confronting the organization of Biomed was the workers' attitudes toward unions.

One might argue that the major problem with the brief union campaign at Biomed was that there was not sufficient interest among the plant's workers to make a serious attempt at organizing a union. If one equates the term "sufficient interest" with "commitment" then that statement is most certainly true. However, the statement is untrue if sufficient interest in organizing a union is interpreted to mean the same thing as "in favor of" organizing a union. As has already been discussed, when I was talking with Biomed's workers about how they felt about unions in the week before I was fired, the vast majority of workers stated that they were in favor of unions. A few workers, such as Harry, stated "no comment" or something to that effect, but none of the workers told me that they were opposed to unions. In addition, at least one line foreman was in favor of organizing a union. As was mentioned earlier in this chapter, Kay expressed interest to me in organizing a union even though she did not realize that she would be ineligible to join the bargaining unit.

If this support for unionization is broken down by ethnicity, there was majority support for unionization across each ethnic group in the plant although clearly the strongest support for unionization was among the Latino workers. This is not surprising considering the fact that the group of Latino workers was the catalyst behind the two incidents of collective action at Biomed. What is even more interesting is the Latino workers' strong support for unionism occurred in spite of the fact that some of the Latinos may have been undocumented workers, which would pose a significant additional risk. However, as Delgado demonstrated, in a case study of a successful union organizing campaign among undocumented workers in a Los Angeles waterbed factory, that once these workers found stable work away from the border areas inhabited by INS agents, the fear of deportation did not appear to affect their decisions concerning becoming active in the organizing drive.[5]

Since there was support among the workers for a union, why was there so little interest on the part of the workers in attempting to organize a union at a place like Biomed, which offered low wages, no benefits, and poor working conditions? It appears that the combination of these factors should lead Biomed workers, or other workers experiencing similar conditions, toward actively embracing unionism. However, in order to understand why the presence of such conditions may not lead towards active employee involvement in a union organizing campaign, a model consisting of five variables should be considered.

The first variable concerns the presence or absence of an instigator to initiate a union organizing drive. The instigator can be either a single worker or a group of workers who decide to contact the external union organizer and initiate the campaign. The second variable concerns the presence or absence of a preexisting disposition toward pro-union sentiments. The third variable is the workers' fear or lack of fear of losing their jobs and experiencing unemployment. In order for a successful organizing attempt to occur, the workers must not be afraid of losing their jobs. The fourth variable is that the workers are committed or not committed to remaining at the company over the long term. If workers are committed to remaining at the company over a longer period of time, then they will be more likely to devote their time and energy to becoming involved in a union organizing campaign. Finally, the fifth variable is the presence or absence of cooperation among the workers. If the workers are willing to cooperate with one another, then any union organizing attempt is more likely to be successful.

Thus, in order for a successful union organizing drive to occur, it is a necessary but not a sufficient condition that there is an instigator to initiate the union campaign; the workers possess a preexisting disposition toward pro-union sentiments; the workers are not afraid of losing their jobs; the workers are committed to remaining at their jobs over a relatively long period of time; and there is cooperation among the workers. Although it is obvious that the lack of an instigator or pro-union sentiment will undermine an organizing drive, this model shows that the obverse of any of the above-mentioned conditions for the remaining three variables will produce the same effect, with one apparent exception.

As discussed in chapter 8, the Latino gellers were predisposed to engaging in collective action precisely *because* they felt that their jobs were in jeopardy. Although this would appear to contradict our model, one must be careful to distinguish between two different reasons that might underlie fear of unemployment. The Latino gellers had reason to believe that their jobs were in jeopardy because of factors beyond their control; hence, participation in an organizing drive was not perceived to put them under any additional threat. For the remaining workers, however, such participation was perceived to significantly increase their chances of unemployment. To precisify our model, we might state that workers will be disinclined to engage in union organizing if they perceive that this organizing will significantly increase the likelihood of being without a job.

This model can be used to analyze the union organizing campaign at Biomed. Clearly, there was an instigator for the campaign and the workers had favorable preexisting dispositions toward unions. However, the major problems with the campaign become apparent when we examine the last three variables of the model.

When we consider the third variable of the model, it is apparent that the workers were afraid of losing their jobs by becoming involved in the union organizing campaign. With a high unemployment rate—over 12 percent in the Chicago metropolitan area during 1982–83—the workers had a legitimate fear of losing their jobs, and not being able to find another one, if they became involved in a union organizing drive. However, even though fear might have been the most apparent, it was not the only reason for the workers' lack of commitment to union organizing.

Considering the fourth variable, the majority of workers were not committed to remaining at Biomed; many of the workers did not view employment with Biomed as constituting a long-term option. Ironically, this was due to a combination of the company's low wages, the absence of both benefits and promotional opportunities, and poor working conditions— the very factors that in other situations would stimulate a serious attempt at organizing. Work at the company was seen as something temporary until one could find a "better" job, difficult as that may have been during this time period. Furthermore, finding a "better" job meant different things to different workers. To some, like Lenny and Sam, it meant a "career" with the possibility of advancement; to others, it simply meant other factory work or other similar work that offered both higher wages and better working conditions. Because many workers adopted this strategy of searching for better employment opportunities, and were willing to leave Biomed for as little as a fifty-cents-per-hour wage increase, it is not surprising that Biomed's workers were unwilling to devote time and energy to organizing a union.

Although Hodson discovered that "higher minority representation results in greater informal resistance" to management in nonunion workplaces,[6] which union supporters hope will translate into greater union organizing success, the ethnic composition of Biomed's workforce was extremely problematic in terms of cooperation among the workers during the union organizing drive (the fifth variable of the model). Even before I was fired, it was clear that the Latino workers had negative perceptions of the African American workers and that a number of white workers had racist views of the African American and Latino workers. Furthermore, the Latino workers' feelings toward the African American workers were exacerbated once Andy had finked on me to Biomed management. After this happened, they believed even more strongly than before that African American workers could not be trusted. Such an eth-

nic divide would have been extremely difficult to bridge in the organizing campaign, and the strategy of emphasizing class over ethnicity in this
situation in order to unite the workers probably would not have been successful.

I am not sure if Louie was aware of all of these problems that existed
among the workers at Biomed. Clearly, what attracted the UE to attempt
to organize a union at Biomed was both the financial success and the
potential future employment growth of the company. However, even
though Louie was initially optimistic about the union organizing drive,
he acknowledged that if the UE won the NLRB representation election it
would only be by a small amount. Louie realized that winning the election was only the beginning of the struggle to build an effective union
and that a union would not be successfully organized until the first collective bargaining agreement with the company had been obtained.

Since it was (and is) difficult to get a first contract without a strike,
Louie's plan was to turn an economic strike—that is, a strike that occurs
when the union reaches an impasse with the firm during collective bargaining—into an unfair labor practice strike—that is, a strike that occurs
because the company has committed a violation of U.S. labor law. The
reason why external union organizers desire to turn economic strikes into
unfair labor practice strikes has to do with the employment protection that
unfair labor practice strikers possess in comparison to economic strikers.
Economic strikers can be permanently replaced by the company but if the
NLRB rules that the company has committed an unfair labor practice—
that is, it has violated U.S. labor law—then the strikers cannot be permanently replaced and must be given their jobs back once the union has
unconditionally ended the strike. Thus, by turning an economic strike into
an unfair labor practice strike, the strikers do not risk losing their jobs by
remaining on strike.[7]

These are the obstacles that the union organizing drive faced even *before* there was active opposition on the part of the company. Even if I had
not been fired so early in the campaign, tactics that other companies have
successfully used to defeat union organizing drives, such as the hiring of
consultants who utilize questionable or illegal tactics or the circulation
of rumors concerning job loss or plant closings, not to mention the distribution of anti-union letters as well as the holding of captive audience
speeches (that is anti-union speeches held by the employer during company time that the workers must attend,)[8] most likely would have been

very effective for Biomed in the existing climate of fear and intimidation. As one can see, employers have a tremendous advantage over unions in organizing drives, even when workers are actively supporting a unionization attempt.

Analyzing the campaign from the company's perspective is a much more difficult task because I do not know what went on behind the scenes concerning discussions between various management representatives, or between the management representatives and (most probably) the company's lawyers, although a few points can be made with certainty. Louie was certainly right about one point: the company committed an unfair labor practice when Steve, the plant manager, asked Andy about the union in June 1983. However, by the late 1990s, such employer questioning would no longer necessarily constitute a U.S. labor law violation. In 1984, the NLRB determined that employers questioning employees about their attitudes and involvement in union organizing drives was not always an unfair labor practice; it depended upon the conditions under which the questioning occurred.[9]

The company knew that unionization among the plant's workers would challenge their prerogatives, so they fought tooth and nail to "legally" remove me from the factory. A worker espousing trade unionism in an environment such as Biomed was viewed as an extreme menace by the company. Biomed probably *perceived* that most of the factory workers would be sympathetic to the organizing of a union because of the objectively poor wages and working conditions in the factory, so even one worker circulating such ideas would have to be suppressed. Firing such a worker would also present a clear message to the remaining rank-and-file-workers—If you get any ideas about organizing a union, you will be fired, too!

This analysis is supported by the empirical literature. Holley and Jennings point out that in the last twenty years, the number of unfair labor practice charges for terminating union supporters during union organizing campaigns has increased sixfold. In addition, research shows that employers fire union activists for two primary reasons during organizing campaigns. The first reason is to remove the "key union organizers" from the workplace and the second reason is "to send a chilling message" to the workers remaining in the facility.[10]

In fact, union activists discharged by high-tech employers have found it extremely difficult to even obtain a *hearing* by the NLRB. From 1971 through 1984, in spite of the countless firings of union supporters by high-tech employers, the NLRB held only *two hearings* on behalf of discharged employees. As described by Gagala, the reason for this might be because many of the dismissals were "mixed motive discharges," which was true of my case, as was discussed earlier.[11]

However, even if I had not been fired for my union organizing activities, it would still have been extremely difficult to organize Biomed's workers, for the reasons that I have already discussed. There was a climate of substantial fear among the workers, with many feeling that their jobs were continually at risk, not unlike the conditions at two high-tech factories studied by Robinson and McIlwee. Such a climate prevented some of Biomed's workers from even telling me how they would feel about unionization of the company. As Robinson and McIlwee point out, feelings of job insecurity are "not conducive to workers standing up to management and choosing union representation."[12]

Another obstacle to unionization in high-tech factories is the difficulty of workers maintaining a more intimate relationship with coworkers outside of work. Robinson and McIlwee argue that this intimacy—that is, the opportunity for coworkers to socialize outside of work—is important for building solidarity, an ingredient that is crucial for unionization.[13] This was certainly a problem at Biomed, where the employees lived in many different neighborhoods of Chicago, as well as in a number of suburbs, and so did not hang out together at a nearby bar or restaurant after work. Although I attempted to get to know some of the workers outside of work, I was unsuccessful at establishing more intimate relationships in this manner.

Although I have previously mentioned the ethnic divisions already present inside the plant, Hossfeld points out that these divisions are "major barriers to organizing" high-tech workers that have not been "readily acknowledged" by unions.[14] Management would probably have played up these divisions in the factory during any organizing campaign. Even though the Latino gellers were clearly the core of the vanguard group of the factory's workers, it would still have been difficult for them to become the driving force behind any successful attempt at unionization. Although these gellers were the most militant of the shop's workers and also expressed the most pro-union sentiments of any group in the plant, it would have been extremely difficult for them to have shut down the factory or to have inflicted long-term economic damage to the company. The objective economic conditions that were present during 1983 would have resulted in Biomed being able to hire a sufficient number of replacement workers.

In conclusion, it is clear that a major reason for the low rates of unionization in high-tech industries is due to vigorous employer opposition and to the tactics that these firms adopt to remain union-free. However, the model that I have presented focuses on the employees, not the employers, and attempts to explain why employees do or do not become actively involved in union organizing drives. Such a model may be helpful in explaining the extremely low rates of union organizing drive success in high-tech industries. While the relevant literature has focused on high-tech firms' vigorous opposition to unionization, the characteristics that high-tech workers possess may also partially explain the low rates of unionization in the industry. Future research should center on the variables outlined in this model, to see if they provide additional understanding for the unions' dismal organizing success at high-tech firms.

10.

The Return of the Despotic Factory Regime?

FOUR MONTHS AFTER I WAS FIRED FROM BIOMED, AT THE END OF OCTOBER 1983, I called Mick to see what was happening at the factory. He was surprised to hear from me but he was friendly nonetheless. Although Mick had found another job, closer to his new home, he filled me in on the events of the past summer.

Mick informed me that he had finally been officially transferred to the cable department in July. Because Chris frequently arrived late for work, Steve had asked Mick to become the line foreman for the disc anterior pad assembly department. He declined this offer because he did not want to take another person's job.

"Things seemed to get worse after you left," Mick said. "They watched you like a hawk. There were no raises, which was kind of the pits. There were more new people every day although a few of the old people left. The Hispanic workers were still there, though."

Mick also told me that there was no more talk of organizing a union at the factory, once I had been fired. He concluded our conversation by stating, "Biomed treated you like an animal, like you're nothing."

Two months later, a couple of days before the beginning of 1984, I phoned Sam to learn more about the current situation at Biomed. "Merry Christmas," Sam said. "I'm glad you called." He told me that he had applied to the University of Wisconsin at Madison at the end of July, was accepted and had left Biomed in the middle of August.

187

"After you were fired, Andy took your job as a utility man. He was after Ben for a raise," Sam told me. "The company tried to hush up your firing," he continued. "I didn't find out about it until a few days later."

"Ben changed stuff. He set up more assembly lines in the back of the factory. Most of the people were still there when I left. Everyone looked for other work but nobody found it. More people were hired, about three a week. Many of them were Spanish people."

I asked Sam if Pedro and Juan were still at Biomed in the summer. He said that they were.

"Because of the hot weather, we worked from 6:30 in the morning to 2:30 in the afternoon starting in the middle of July. Sometimes we'd be forced to work overtime until 6:00. Those extra three and a half hours really seemed like a long time. Although the factory was not air-conditioned, Ben's new office was."

I continued to pump Sam for more information. "At the end of July, Lori got fired for being a lush," he continued. "Everyone began to hate Ben, even Steve. On my last day at Biomed, Steve gave some construction workers "krazy glue" to put in Ben's car door locks. Ben tried to get people to work faster for the same wages. Leopoldo found a new job in a warehouse for $4.00 an hour."

Mike, another young worker, also had left Biomed to attend the University of Wisconsin. He was a friend of Lou's so he kept Sam informed of new developments at Biomed. "Mike told me that Lou isn't a supervisor anymore. He's just another electronic technician," Sam stated. "The factory is all automated now except for the gelling department. There are about one-hundred people currently working at Biomed."

I had been talking with Sam on the phone for nearly half an hour. He had nothing left to say. "Look, I've got to go now," he said. "It's been good talking with you. Have a happy new year."

THE RETURN OF THE DESPOTIC FACTORY REGIME?

In *The Politics of Production,* Burawoy constructs two general types of "factory regimes," the despotic regime and the hegemonic regime, the emergence of which he discusses in historical terms. By "factory regime," Burawoy is referring to two political elements of production—the labor process as a unique arrangement of tasks and the political apparatuses of production that control production relations. For example, one type of a despotic regime that emerged in the New England cotton mills after 1860, "market despotism," was characterized by four conditions—competition between firms; workers being subordinated to capital, meaning that there was a separation of conception from execution in performing tasks; the worker's dependency on wage employment for survival; and state protection of the independent operation of market forces. In terms of the New England cotton mills after 1860, Burawoy points out that in this despotic factory regime the women workers were "entirely dependent" on selling their labor power for survival, piece rates were unilaterally established by the cotton mill managers in the area, and the male supervisors had complete control over hiring and were able to arbitrarily fire the women workers.[1]

However, while despotic factory regimes were much more prevalent in the competitive capitalism of the nineteenth century, this does not mean that *modified* forms of despotic factory regimes do not exist in the monopoly capitalism of the late twentieth century. "Pure" despotic factory regimes do not exist today, according to Burawoy, because of the provision of two important forms of government intervention. The first form is the passage of "social insurance legislation," which provides workers with the opportunity to reproduce labor power, at least at a minimal level, without having to depend on selling their labor power in the marketplace for physical survival. In addition, "social insurance legislation" has also established a minimum wage, which prevents employers from utilizing piece rates to pay workers below this state-guaranteed minimum. The second form of government intervention that has attenuated managerial domination in the workplace is the passage of labor legislation that has provided workers with the legal right to organize unions and to engage in collective bargaining, limiting management from arbitrarily disciplining and firing workers, as well as from reducing their wages.[2]

Although the worker no longer is required to sell his or her labor power in the marketplace in order to eke out an existence at the subsistence level, I would argue that a modified form of the despotic factory regime has arisen (or never disappeared) in certain sectors of the economy that have been left virtually untouched by unionization, one of them being high-tech industries. According to Burawoy, the sine qua non of the despotic factory regime is that coercion dominates consent at the point of production, while in the hegemonic regime consent prevails over coercion although (some) coercion is still present.[3] Although coercion does not prevail over consent in modern-day high-tech industries to the same extent as it did in the Lowell cotton mills of 1860, it certainly leans heavily in that direction. Thus, the despotic factory regime of the nineteenth century has reemerged during the late twentieth century in a modified form in nonunion high-tech factories such as Biomed.

THE MAINTENANCE OF THE MODIFIED DESPOTIC FACTORY REGIME

In the late twentieth century and as we head into the twenty-first century, there are several forces, besides the lack of unionization, that are contributing to the maintenance of a modified form of the despotic factory regime in many high-tech manufacturing companies, such as Biomed. Competition from "black market garage operations" and high-tech homeworkers, as well as from global competition, helps to insure the survival of this modified form of the despotic factory regime within high-tech industries.

Located in Silicon Valley there are "garage sweatshops" that employ a variety of forms of "cheap labor," including housewives, welfare recipients, refugees, and illegal aliens who are paid less than the minimum wage and do not receive the benefits of either Social Security or workers' compensation. These sweatshops, which are primarily engaged in "stuffing" printed circuit boards and operate entirely on a cash basis, employ thousands of illegal Mexican and Vietnamese immigrants who cannot legally obtain work. Although these operations are underground and cannot easily be detected, one Silicon Valley executive estimates that there are approximately two-hundred of these "garage sweatshops" involved in the assembly of printed circuit boards.[4]

Industrial homework is also proliferating in high-tech industries, and the working conditions are just as bad as those of the "garage sweatshops" in Silicon Valley. Based on interviews that Dangler conducted with home-based electronics subassemblers who work on piece rate in central New York, she discovered that even though they were producing finished products for multinational firms such as IBM, Ford, Magnavox, Kodak, and Squibb, half of the workers stated that it was almost impossible for them to earn the minimum wage, with the lowest average wage being reported at $1.20 per hour.[5]

According to a California Division of Labor Standards Investigator, most industrial homeworkers are subjected to a variety of abuses:

Most people who work at home are not paid the minimum wage. The laborers suffer. It also creates unfair competition. In homework, the pervasive violation of minimum wage and overtime laws is chronic.[6]

In a study of homeworkers in the San Francisco Bay area, Lozano found that child labor was reemerging in the home assembly of printed circuit boards. She quotes a home assembler who describes how this system operated in her family's home for five years:

I trained my kids. They were, oh, five, seven, and nine years old. They would stuff the boards and I would solder them, and we made $2.50 a board, or some outrageously low rate like that. Later, my two sons and a friend of theirs worked on it, so I had three boys working in one room. All I was doing at that point was supervising—making sure they got it done.

It was like having contract people working in my home. All of it was in my name. I wouldn't pay them by the hour, because kids have no tolerance for sitting long periods of time. But if I paid them by the piece, they would work for hours, because they'd figure, "If I do twenty-five of these at ten cents each"—well, they would just go crazy. And any rejects, they would not get paid for. Consequently, my children are just fantastic workers now that they are grown.[7]

And this is not an isolated case. Lozano reports how another couple who manufactured electrical transformer cores in their home organized their work:

The whole family does it. We get the kids—they're in third and sixth grade—in on it. Even Grandpa works on it. He's ninety-two and half-blind, but he has this great big magnifying glass with a neon light. It's like a family event.[8]

In addition, global competition in high-tech industries has exerted considerable downward pressure on wages as well as working conditions in domestic high-tech factories. Hundreds of thousands of young women work in semiconductor assembly plants in Asian nations that are owned by electronics companies in Silicon Valley. They are paid wage rates that are a fraction of those earned by high-tech assembly workers in the United States. For example, according to figures published in 1984, microelectronic workers in Malaysia earned sixty cents per hour, while the rate was fifty cents per hour in the Philippines and $1.20 per hour in Hong Kong.[9] The working conditions are worse in these foreign plants than in the high-tech factories located in the United States. For example, in the Malaysian electronics factories, most of the women assemblers voluntarily leave after three to four years of work due to "rapid exhaustion." This extreme level of exhaustion is due to the high production quotas, three-shift cycles, many hours of mandatory overtime, and constant employer surveillance. In addition, the unionization of electronics workers has been thwarted due to a turnover rate of 5 to 6 percent every month in some of these electronics firms, due to the lack of long-term employment for the women assemblers, and due to labor code amendments that severely limit unionization. For example, one amendment states that workers with less than three years of employment in their industry cannot join unions, while another one prevents unions from organizing strikes to force management's recognition of a union.[10]

WHAT IS TO BE DONE?

What can be done to improve the situation of Biomed production workers, as well as that of virtually all U.S. high-tech manufacturing workers, who labor under some of the poorest working conditions, lowest wages, and worst job security? Certainly, a *serious* attempt at unionizing the nation's high-tech production workers would go a long way toward alleviating some of the worst aspects of these problems. However, it is clear that unions interested in organizing high-tech factory workers must take a radically different approach from the dominant strategies used in the 1970s and the 1980s.

Hayes argues that "U.S. labor unions are in fact among the least effective allies of electronics workers" because of their "conservative and meager organizing efforts." Early and Wilson attribute the unions' lack of success in organizing high-tech workers to their focus on single-plant campaigns rather than on building "community-labor coalitions." They point out that these coalitions would be able to provide more services to unorganized workers and would be more effective vehicles for the long-term struggle toward unionization. Noting the transience of high-tech workers, Hayes advocates the adoption of an organizing strategy in which high-tech workers would be represented by an industrywide union that would provide workers with collective bargaining protection regardless of their employer.[11]

The building of industrywide unions using organizing strategies based on providing workers with collective bargaining representation regardless of employer is a realistic strategy for organizing high-tech production workers because it has been used to unionize several industries throughout the United States. For example, in the 1990s, non-NLRB election organizing strategies have been successfully utilized by both the Service Employees International Union (SEIU) in unionizing janitors through its "Justice for Janitors" campaign and by the Laborers' Union in organizing asbestos-abatement workers in New York City. Unions interested in pursuing such strategies to organize high-tech production workers should consult two articles: one written by Banks and one written by Howley. However, the conducting of such campaigns may be problematic and unions using such strategies should make sure that they follow certain guidelines in order to increase their probability of success. In addition, since high-tech manufacturing workers are predominantly low-wage workers, Needleman's article on this topic also would be helpful in devising tactics to organize high-tech production workers.[12]

In addition, because of the dramatic increase in the number of "contingent" workers (temporary, part-time, and contract workers) in high-technology industries, new models of union organization along the lines of Early/Wilson and Hayes are being developed in Silicon Valley. Amy Dean, the head of the South Bay Labor Council (AFL-CIO), has founded an organization called Working Partnerships USA, a labor-community alliance whose goal is to provide employment protection for Silicon Valley's high-tech production workers.[13]

The idea behind Working Partnerships USA is to promote labor unions that organize high-tech workers based on general occupational categories within regional labor markets. The major goal of such organizations would be to develop "career or employment security" within the industry, as opposed to promoting job security at any one individual high-tech firm. Specifically, such unions' functions would include at least the following four basic points.[14]

First, these unions must become involved with the coordination of training programs that will provide workers with the necessary training to enable them to obtain better jobs in the industry. Second, even without the obtaining of a formal contract, such organizations must become involved with the defense of employee rights, insuring that employers are abiding by both occupational safety and health and antidiscrimination legislation by providing members with education and representation concerning their legal rights. Third, the union must aim toward the negotiation of multiemployer regional collective bargaining agreements. Such contracts would prevent firms within the same industry from competing against one another through the slashing of labor costs and would force them to compete against one another through developing ways to increase productivity. Finally, the union would be responsible for administering portable health care and pension benefits that workers could take with them as they moved from employer to employer; such a program would be obtained through collective bargaining and would partially depend upon employer contributions.[15]

While these strategies are excellent ideas and represent significant advances over the single-plant campaigns of the 1970s and the 1980s, I believe that unions interested in organizing high-tech production workers must go one step farther. Because of the significant effects of global competition, union organizing of high-tech production workers must be attempted not only on the national level but on the *international* level as well. While it would be virtually impossible for U.S. trade unions to organize high-tech production workers in, for example, Malaysia and the Philippines, it is certainly possible for these unions to make contacts with their trade union counterparts in these countries. Since a significant portion of production workers in the domestic high-tech industries are Third World immigrants, trade union coordination on an international basis only makes sense for the workers of both countries.

In order to attempt to organize high-tech production workers internationally, U.S. unions should consider further developing the innovative cross-national labor organizing strategies, outlined by Armbruster, that have been utilized in Central and North America throughout the 1980s and 1990s.[16] Three distinct strategies that have been developed will be discussed below.

One strategy involves forming organizations such as the Coalition for Justice in the Maquiladoras (CJM), a trinational organization composed of ninety-five religious, labor (including the AFL-CIO), environmental, and human rights groups, that pressures transnational corporations to adopt corporate codes of conduct. A second organizing strategy, utilized by the U.S./Guatemalan Labor Education Project and the International Labor

Rights and Education Research Fund, attempts to limit exports to the United States from other countries that have violated "basic worker rights standards" through the filing of workers' rights petitions. Finally, a third strategy involves actual attempts at cross-border union organizing by U.S. and Mexican unions in maquiladoras (which will be discussed in more detail later in this chapter).[17]

Because of the number of workers laboring in the electronics assembly plants in Mexico only a few miles from the U.S. border, a serious attempt at utilizing international organizing strategies is certainly worth a shot. According to Tiano, approximately 45 percent of the labor force in the Mexican maquiladoras in 1985 were involved in electronics assembly. Of the manufacturing sector in the maquiladoras, the electronics industry is the most heavily represented, with the apparel industry a distant second, involving only 14 percent of the labor force. Thus, based on the above figure, there are tens of thousands of Mexican high-tech production workers who labor only a few miles outside of the U.S. border.[18]

The number of high-tech workers laboring in maquiladoras will only increase in the future. According to Kopinak, the expansion and proliferation of maquiladoras is predicted to continue well into the twenty-first century. In addition, Shaiken argues that because of the passage of the North American Free Trade Agreement (NAFTA) in 1993, Mexico will continue to be an attractive environment for investment in high-tech manufacturing.[19]

One U.S. union is attempting to organize these Mexican high-tech production workers. In 1992, the UE formed a "strategic organizing alliance" with the Mexican Frente Autentico de Trabajadores (Authentic Workers Front), which is known by its acronym FAT, to organize high-tech production workers in the maquiladora plants, especially those owned by companies with which the UE negotiates collective bargaining agreements. The FAT actually conducts the organizing drives in Mexico with the UE providing both financial support and research assistance.[20]

With the help of the UE, the FAT appears to be an appropriate vehicle for organizing these workers. The organization is independent of the Confederation of Mexican Workers, a trade union federation that has government-controlled unions as members with poor records for representing workers and a history of often supporting management actions as well. In addition, the FAT has more than three decades of experience in representing manufacturing workers at both small and medium-sized companies. Shortly after the formation of this strategic alliance with the UE in 1992, the FAT began organizing campaigns at Honeywell's 500-worker plant in Chihuahua and at General Electric's (GE) Compania Armadora plant in Juarez, which has 950 workers.[21]

However, within weeks of the passage of the NAFTA by the U.S. Congress in November 1993, Honeywell discharged twenty-three women workers involved in the FAT's organizing drive in its Chihuahuas facility, while GE dismissed ten workers who were active in the unionization drive at the Juarez factory. These firings have led to international protests among Honeywell workers in Canada, Mexico, and the United States, as well as to the launching of a solidarity campaign in order to get these workers reinstated. Unions participating in these actions include the UE, the Teamsters, the Canadian Auto Workers, and the Amalgamated Clothing and Textile Workers Union (now called the Union of Needletrades, Industrial and Textile Employees after its merger with the International Ladies Garment Workers Union), as well as the Coalition for Justice in the Maquiladoras. After a letter-writing campaign organized by the UE and the Teamsters generated sufficient pressure on both Clinton administration officials and GE and Honeywell executives, six of the terminated GE employees were rehired, although "the most active and tenured workers" were refused reinstatement.[22]

In the United States, the UE's ties to these Mexican trade unions have begun to pay off. When the UE was having trouble organizing a workforce that was composed of many Mexican immigrants in a major campaign in Milwaukee, the union enlisted the aid of Mexican organizers to help win the unionization drive.[23]

In addition to the UE, another union that has attempted to organize high-tech production workers in the United States in the 1980s has been moving in the direction of trade union internationalism. Although not engaged in internationally organizing high-tech production workers, the Communication Workers of America (CWA) participated in October 1992 in the founding conference of the eleven-union Northern Telecom Solidarity Coalition in Toronto, which involved both workers and union representatives from Canada, Japan, Malaysia, Turkey, the United States, and Western Europe. Although Northern Telecom (NT) employs twenty-three-thousand workers in the United States, due to the company's sophisticated anti-union labor relations policies and a series of decertification elections, only 2 percent of the workforce is represented by the CWA. In Third World countries such as Malaysia, where the company has been rapidly expanding its manufacturing facilities, these jobs are so poorly paid and the working conditions are so bad that local workers refused to take these jobs, forcing NT to recruit Indonesian and Bangladeshi immigrants to fill these positions.[24]

The unions that participated in this conference agreed to put together a "common organizing brochure," which would be translated into seven languages. The purpose of this brochure is to publicize the firm's labor relations record as well as to describe its plans for global expansion. The coalition plans to distribute this brochure to both NT's unionized and nonunionized workplaces around the world in order to build support for a petition-signing campaign among the workers for "management neutrality and non-interference in all organizing drives, and negotiations with a multi-national union committee" concerning the establishment of a "global code of conduct" for NT.[25]

One might argue that a union that has organized only 2 percent of a company's workforce and is conducting a campaign based on written appeals in support of a corporate code of conduct would be notoriously ineffective in achieving its goals. In fact, Armbruster claims that although worker rights petitions have "been successful at opening up political space for workers to organize," they "have had uneven success" and have failed to increase class consciousness or to raise wages when they have not been accompanied by the mass mobilization of workers.[26] Therefore, just *how* effective are these international organizing strategies, and do they ever have a chance of succeeding?

Through his examination of individual case studies concerning the implementation of various cross-national labor organizing strategies, Armbruster acknowledges that although each particular strategy contains strengths and weaknesses, the uniqueness and constraints of each particular organizing situation have resulted in organizations experiencing differential levels of success when using such tactics. However, he concludes that successful international organizing efforts have contained "community-labor coalitions, consciousness-raising, covert/discreet organizing, methodical planning, worker rights petitions, media campaigns, opposition research, combining class and identity-oriented issues, utilizing the resources of complex organizations, and building established relationships with organizations internationally."[27]

While many trade unionists and trade union supporters have argued that the NAFTA labor side accord, named the North American Agreement on Labor Cooperation (NAALC), negotiated in mid-1993, is useless for improving the situation of unions under NAFTA, Compa argues that this side agreement "contains several positive features for labor rights advocacy that ought to be appreciated, or at least tested over a long term, before drawing any conclusions about its worth." Although Compa acknowledges that the six cases filed under the NAALC since the agreement went into effect at the beginning of 1994 have not resulted in either the rehiring of terminated workers or the organization of new unions, he believes that this should not be considered the definitive test of the labor accord's potential usefulness. Specifically, Compa views the NAALC as providing opportunities for unions to establish "labor rights-trade linkage as a matter of policy in trade agreements," to defend workers' rights under the accord's eleven "Labor Principles," and to engage in international labor cooperation "in support of workers' rights." Cook concurs with Compa's analysis, arguing that "the NAALC creates a framework for concrete work" in cross-national labor organizing that includes activities such as "developing strategies, drafting submissions, planning testimony, mounting press conferences, (and) meeting with government officials."[28]

Can the above-mentioned international organizing strategies and the implementation of the NAALC be fruitfully used to organize and improve the situation of high-tech production workers in the United States and throughout the world? Maybe not, but since the trend concerning globalization of the world economy will continue unabated as we move into the twenty-first century, there is not much choice but to seriously consider the use of such strategies.

CONCLUSION: EMERGING FROM THE HISTORICAL RUINS OF THE 1980S

This book has dealt with the past; let us end with the future. But before "ending with the future," I will briefly review what has already been discussed. The industrial ethnography presented in this book is one that is rooted in a certain historical time and geographic place; a time when U.S. manufacturing was undergoing a transformation from the "heavy" manufacturing of the automobile, steel, and rubber industries, to the "light" manufacturing of high-tech production work. This was also a time of extremely high levels of unemployment, as well as an era when a very conservative, anti-union administration occupied the corridors of power, although the Carter era of the mid to late 1970s and the two Clinton administrations of the 1990s have hardly been better. As I have illustrated in this book through my case study, high-tech factory work in the late twentieth century is not an enlightened and progressive departure from industrial factory production as a whole but is a mere continuum to the factory work of the late nineteenth and early twentieth centuries. Although I worked in a medical electronics factory in the early 1980s, my experience appears to be representative of high-tech factory work even in the late 1990s.

Organizing in a high-tech factory in the 1980s, as with all union organizing during this time period, was, needless to say, considerably tougher than organizing in the 1930s and the 1940s, the halcyon days of the American labor movement. In 1980, the annual union certification election success rate in NLRB elections had dipped to 47.8 percent and the 1982–1987 annual average was 46.1 percent, compared with a peak of 86.3 percent in 1942. Although the number of new workers organized into unions through NLRB elections was over 150,000 in 1980, that number had slipped to under 70,000 for 1982. From 1983 to 1987, yearly totals of new workers organized into unions through NLRB elections fluctuated between 65,000 and 82,000.[29]

Union membership density also drastically declined throughout the 1980s, from 22.7 percent in 1980 to 16.3 percent in 1989. This downward trend continued in 1990 with union membership density declining to 16.1 percent. Although public sector union membership density remained fairly steady at approximately 36 percent from 1983 through 1991, the overall decline in union membership density was driven by the decline in private sector union membership density, which steadily fell, from 16.5 percent in 1983 to 11.7 percent in 1991.[30]

However, throughout the decade of the 1980s, unions were not only taking a beating with respect to organizing defeats and declines in union membership density. Many unions were also being hammered at the bargaining table by being forced to engage in "concession bargaining." In addition, unions were confronted with a variety of employee involvement (EI) programs designed, in many situations, to undermine or weaken the union. These EI programs also were used in nonunion companies as a successful union avoidance strategy. According to Jacoby and Verma, "many of the most elaborate and far-reaching" EI programs have been developed by nonunion companies in high-tech industries.[31]

Finally, unions suffered serious losses on the picket lines during the 1980s. Beginning with the Professional Air Traffic Controllers Organization (PATCO) strike in 1981, unions were on the losing side in important strikes such as the Phelps Dodge copper miners' strike in Arizona in 1983, the Hormel strike in Minnesota in 1985, and the nationwide Greyhound bus strikes of 1983 and 1990.[32]

Now, however, we must move on to the future. For trade unions in the late 1990s, there have been a number of positive developments in the last few years (to be discussed later in this chapter), in spite of the fact that both union membership and union membership density continued to decline as the U.S. economy began to recover in 1994 and 1995. Although union membership density slipped to 15.8 percent in 1992, one year later (1993), the union membership density was still 15.8 percent with an additional 208,000 workers having become members of unions, bringing total union membership to 16,598,000 for 1993. Although private-sector union membership density continued to decline, from 11.5 percent in 1992 to 11.2 percent in 1993, this increase in total union membership ended fourteen straight years of membership decreases.[33]

Union membership density dipped once more in 1994, however. Although union membership increased to 16,748,000, union membership density fell to 15.5 percent. In 1995, both union membership and union membership density declined, to 16,360,000 and 14.1 percent, respectively. In 1996 and 1997, this trend continued. In 1996 union membership fell to 16,269,000 members and union membership density slipped to 14.5 percent, while in 1997 membership and density declined to 16,100,000 members and 14.1 percent, respectively.[34]

What can unions do in the face of this continually declining union membership density? Clearly, unions must devote more of their organizational resources to organizing; for example, a survey from the mid-1980s indicated that only 2 percent of union officials devoted any time to union organizing. In addition, unions must discover methods that will increase union certification election win rates. Admittedly, finding these techniques will not be an easy task. However, Morrissey and Coventry suggest that one key toward improving the win rates in union representation elections and revitalizing U.S. trade unionism lies with local labor unions becoming much more innovative and creative in attracting unrepresented workers who have not sufficiently been courted by labor organizations in the past.[35]

In spite of the continuing decline in union membership density, a number of unions have captured the imagination of the labor movement by beginning to achieve significant success in union organizational drives in the 1990s. For example, in Southern California, as well as in a few cities across the nation, the SEIU's "Justice for Janitors" campaign, albeit long and costly, has been successful in organizing immigrant workers by utilizing mass protests, as well as community and ethnic organizations, to obtain signed collective bargaining agreements with "major cleaning companies" in both Los Angeles and Washington.[36]

Another group of largely undocumented immigrant workers has employed tactics similar in spirit to those of the SEIU's "Justice for Janitors" campaign. Mexican drywall workers, who successfully organized in Los Angeles in 1992 after a five-month strike, have utilized "roving pickets" who travel to job sites throughout the area to recruit workers. In the summer of 1993, they successfully spread their organizing drive from Los Angeles to San Diego and recruited thousands of new members.[37]

Although the United Rubber Workers and the United Auto Workers (UAW) experienced major defeats in their respective strikes against Bridgestone-Firestone and Caterpillar in the mid-1990s, a series of strikes by the UAW against General Motors during approximately the same time period have been successful, largely due to the firm's adoption of lean production. The Teamsters strike against the United Parcel Service in the summer of 1997 garnered widespread public support and was viewed by virtually all labor analysts as a major victory for the beleaguered U.S. labor movement.[38]

In addition, labor achieved other minor "victories" during the mid-1990s. For example, an earlier Teamsters strike in April 1994 resulted in a new collective bargaining agreement with the trucking companies that eliminated the use of part-time, nonunion drivers. During the same month, the CWA was able to get Nynex to drop their plans to lay off twenty-two-thousand workers. Under this signed collective bargaining agreement, the company agreed not lay off any workers over the next four years but instead stated that it would try to entice workers to retire early by providing them with six years of "extra pension benefits."[39]

In addition, there have been some positive developments occurring within the highest echelons of the U.S. trade union movement. In October 1995, John Sweeney, the former president of the SEIU, was elected AFL-CIO president, to replace what was viewed by many unions as the increasingly moribund leadership of the Kirkland administration. In one of his first moves as AFL-CIO president, Sweeney promised to significantly increase the federation's organizing department's budget to $20 million.[40]

In October 1996, the AFL-CIO, in an alliance with progressive intellectuals, sponsored a "Teach-In with the Labor Movement" at Columbia University's Low Library which resulted in overflowing crowds jamming the library's rotunda and adjacent rooms to hear the conference's speakers. Finally, the AFL-CIO's sponsorship of "Union Summer," in 1996 explicitly modeled after the civil rights movement's "Freedom Summer" of 1964, was designed to build enthusiastic support among college students and young workers for trade unions.[41] All of these efforts, in spite of their limitations, were designed to demonstrate that the U.S. labor movement is alive and kicking and still possesses enough energy to generate some original ideas.

Even public opinion seems to be more favorable to certain aspects of unionism. A nationwide telephone poll conducted for Time/CNN on 1 June 1994, that asked "With whom do you most often side in labor disputes—the striking workers or management?" indicated that 50 percent sided with the workers while 24 percent sided with management. In addition, 42 percent of the respondents stated that it would be good for the U.S. economy if more workers joined unions, while 36 percent said that such an action would be bad for the economy. However, by a nearly two to one margin, 55 percent of the respondents believed that union leaders were "more interested in their own personal concerns," while 30 percent believed that they were "more interested in helping members."[42]

Nevertheless, employer opposition to unions is still fierce and unions can expect little help from either Democratic or Republican lawmakers in Washington, D.C. Although it has taken a substantial amount of work and the use of innovative tactics, the Amalgamated Clothing and Textile Workers Union (now the Union of Needletrades, Industrial and Textile Employees) has been able to successfully organize the type of workers that often work in high-tech factories—undocumented and documented Third World immigrants. And although they have not made an attempt to organize, a significant number of professional workers at Apple, the computer manufacturer, have considered the option of unionization in response to massive layoffs at the company.[43]

In July 1997, Amy Dean, the chief executive officer of the South Bay AFL-CIO Central Labor Council, publicly stated that it was time to make a concerted effort to organize Silicon Valley's high-tech firms. The future of the U.S. labor movement might just depend on how it relates to high-tech production workers in the coming years. For example, Hossfeld believes that "[I]f organized labor is once again to become viable in the United States, it must come to grips with the types of challenges and failures it faces in Silicon Valley." As we approach the twenty-first century with the continuing ascendancy of "high tech capitalism" and with high-tech manufacturing occupying a position as a fast-growing sector of U.S. manufacturing, isn't it time that the unions made a concerted effort to organize these industries?[44]

Endnotes

PREFACE

1. See P. Thompson, *The Nature of Work: An Introduction to Debates on the Labour Process* (London: Macmillan, 1983), 227.

2. For example, see P. J. Pelto and G. H. Pelto, *Anthropological Research: The Structure of Inquiry* (Cambridge: Cambridge University Press, 1978) in terms of the social and cultural anthropological literature. For sociology, see J. Madge, *The Origins of Scientific Sociology* (New York: Free Press, 1962) and M. Bulmer, *The Chicago School of Sociology: Institutionalization, Diversity and the Rise of Sociological Research* (Chicago: University of Chicago Press, 1985). For industrial sociology, see D. Roy, "Quota Restriction and Goldbricking in a Machine Shop," *American Journal of Sociology* 57, no. 5 (March 1952): 427–42, and M. Burawoy, *Manufacturing Consent: Changes in the Labor Process under Monopoly Capitalism* (Chicago: University of Chicago Press, 1979).

3. United States Department of Commerce, *Census of Manufactures* (Washington D.C.: U.S. Government Printing Office, 1992), 178.

4. Two industrial ethnographies depicting work in the service industry are G. F. Paules, *Dishing It Out: Power and Resistance among Waitresses in a New Jersey Restaurant* (Philadelphia: Temple University Press, 1991) and R. Leidner, *Fast Food, Fast Talk: Service Work and the Routinization of Everday Life* (Berkeley: University of California Press, 1993). For an industrial ethnography of work in a small factory, see T. Juravich, *Chaos on the Shop Floor: A Worker's View of Quality, Productivity, and Management* (Philadelphia: Temple University Press, 1985). With respect to industrial ethnographies of work in large factories,

both unionized and nonunion, see R. Balzer, *Clockwork: Life in and Outside an American Factory* (Garden City, N.Y.: Doubleday, 1976); R. M. Pfeffer, *Working for Capitali$m* (New York: Columbia University Press, 1979); R. Linhart, *The Assembly Line* (Amherst: University of Massachusetts Press, 1981); R. Cavendish, *Women on the Line* (London: Routledge and Kegan Paul, 1982); S. Kamata, *Japan in the Passing Lane: An Insider's Account of Life in a Japanese Auto Factory* (New York: Pantheon, 1983); and L. Graham, *On the Line at Suburu-Isuzu: The Japanese Model and the American Worker* (Ithaca, N.Y.: Cornell University Press, 1995).

5. G. Colclough and C. M. Tolbert, *Work in the Fast Lane: Flexibility, Divisions of Labor, and Inequality in High-Tech Industries* (Albany: State University of New York Press, 1992), 11.

6. Pfeffer, *Working for Capitali$m;* Linhart, *The Assembly Line;* Cavendish, *Women on the Line.*

7. D. Hembree, "Dead End in Silicon Valley: The High-Tech Future Doesn't Work," *Progressive* 49, no. 10 (October 1985): 18.

8. M. Goss, "Smokestacks Revisisted: The Future of High-Tech Workers," *Management Review* 74, no. 5 (May 1985): 26.

CHAPTER 1

1. G. Colclough and C. M. Tolbert, *Work in the Fast Lane: Flexibility, Divisions of Labor, and Inequality in High-Tech Industries* (Albany: State University of New York Press, 1992), 1.

2. Colclough and Tolbert, *Work in the Fast Lane,* 2; S. Thore, *The Diversity, Complexity and Evolution of High-Tech Capitalism* (Boston: Kluwer Academic Publishers, 1995), 1, 3.

3. J. Hage and C. H. Powers, *Post-Industrial Lives: Roles and Relationships in the 21st Century* (Newbury Park, Calif.: Sage, 1992), 26.

4. Ibid., 47.

5. A. Etzioni and P. Jargowsky, "High Tech, Basic Industry, and the Future of the American Economy," *Human Resource Management* 23, no. 3 (fall 1984): 231; J. U. Burgan, "Cyclical Behavior of High Tech Industries," *Monthly Labor Review* 108, no. 5 (May 1985): 9; J. A. Alic and M. C. Harris, "Employment Lessons from the Electronics Industry," *Monthly Labor Review* 109, no. 2 (February 1986): 28; S. Early and R. Wilson, "Do Unions Have a Future in High Technology?" *Technology Review* 89, no. 7 (October 1986): 65.

6. Early and Wilson, "Do Unions Have a Future," 59.

7. T. Mahon, *Charged Bodies: People, Power and Paradox in Silicon Valley* (New York: New American Library Books, 1985), 4–5.

8. N. Solomon, *The Trouble with Dilbert: How Corporate Culture Gets the Last Laugh* (Monroe, Maine: Common Courage Press, 1997), 38.

9. T. Abate, "Laboring in the Silicon Jungle," *San Francisco Chronicle,* 25 April 1993, sec. E; E. Kadetsky, "High-Tech's Dirty Little Secret," *Nation* 256, no. 15 (19 April 1993): 519; J. Greenbaum, "The Forest and the Trees," *Monthly Review* 46, no.6 (November 1994): 67.

10. R. Howard, "Second Class in Silicon Valley," *Working Papers for a New Society* 8, no. 5 (September–October 1981): 21–22.

11. Mahon, *Charged Bodies,* 24.

12. S. Rosegrant and D. R. Lampe, *Route 128: Lessons From Boston's High-Tech Community* (New York: Basic Books, 1992); A. Saxenian, *Regional Advantage: Culture and Competition in Silicon Valley and Route 128* (Cambridge: Harvard University Press, 1994); E. M. Rogers and J. K. Larsen, *Silicon Valley Fever: Growth Of High-Technology Culture* (New York: Basic Books, 1984), 230–51.

13. A. R. Markusen, P. Hall, and A. Glasmeier, *High-Tech America: The What, How, Where, and Why of the Sunrise Industries* (Boston: Allen and Unwin, 1986), 16.

14. P. Hadlock, D. Hecker, and J. Gannon, "High Technology Employment: Another View," *Monthly Labor Review* 114, no. 7 (July 1991): 26.

15. Markusen, Hall, and Glasmeier, *High Tech America,* 18–19; Hadlock, Hecker, and Gannon, "High Technology Employment," 27.

16. A. J. Scott, "Low-Wage Workers in a High-Technology Manufacturing Complex: The Southern California Electronics Assembly Industry," *Urban Studies* 29, no. 8 (December 1992): 1231; S. Early and R. Wilson, "Organizing High Tech: Unions and Their Future," *Labor Research Review* no. 8 (spring 1986): 48; R. Snow, "The New International Division of Labor and the U.S. Work Force: The Case of the Electronics Industry," in *Women, Men and the International Division of Labor,* ed. J. Nash and M. P. Fernandez-Kelly (Albany: State University of New York Press, 1983), 56–57.

17. California Employment Development Department, "State of California Employment by Industry: 1993 Annual Average and 2005 Projected Employment," in *Labor Market Information,* [Online]. Available: http://www.calmis.cahwnet.gov/file/indproj/calstb2.txt [21 June 1997]; T. Abate, "High-Tech Jobs Are Booming: State Enjoying Strong Manufacturing Growth," *San Francisco Chronicle,* 5 June 1997, sec. B; California Employment Development Depart-

ment, "San Jose MSA (Santa Clara County) Labor Force and Industry Employment," In *Labor Market Information*, [Online]. Available: http://www.calmis.
cahwnet.gov/file/indcur/sanjspr.txt [21 June 1997].

18. S. S. Green, "Silicon Valley's Women Workers: A Theoretical Analysis of Sex-
Segregation in the Electronics Industry Labor Market," in *Women, Men and
the International Division of Labor*, ed. J. Nash and M. P. Fernandez-Kelly (Albany: State University of New York Press, 1983), 286; B. Lozano, *The Invisible Work Force: Transforming American Business with Outside and Home-Based
Workers* (New York: Free Press, 1989), 25–26; E. M. Rogers and D. V. Gibson,
"Technology Transfer in High-Technology Industries: Entrepreneurs and Research and Development Consortia in the United States," in *Technology Companies and Global Markets*, ed. D. V. Gibson (Savage, Md.: Rowman and
Littlefield Publishers, 1991), 43; A. J. Scott, *Technopolis: High Technology Industry and Regional Development in Southern California* (Berkeley: University of
California Press, 1993), 180–81.

19. R. Howard, *Brave New Workplace* (New York: Viking Penguin, 1985), 133;
Rogers and Larsen, *Silicon Valley Fever*, 189.

20. California Employment Development Department, "Income in 1989 for
Places in Santa Clara to Trinity Counties," in *Labor Market Information*,
[Online]. Available: http://www.calmis.cahwmet.gov/file/demoinc/
INC90PT7.TXT [21 June 1997].

21. M. Rogers, "Trouble in the Valley," *Newsweek*, 25 February 1985, 93.

22. Green, "Silicon Valley's Women Workers," 305–6; Rogers and Larsen, *Silicon
Valley Fever*, 190; Howard, *Brave New Workplace*, 134; Snow, "The New International Division," 61; Early and Wilson, "Organizing High Tech," 49; California Employment Development Department, "Occupational Wages for
Santa Clara County," in *Labor Market Information*, [Online]. Available: http:
//www.calmis.cahwnet.gov/file/occups/central.htm [21 June 1997].

23. J. Henderson, *The Globalisation of High Technology Production: Society, Space,
and Semiconductors in the Restructuring of the Modern World* (London: Routledge,
1989), 46–47; Colclough and Tolbert, *Work in the Fast Lane*, 18–19; N.
Mohseni, "The Labor Process and Control of Labor in the U.S. Computer
Industry," in *The Labor Process and Control of Labor: The Changing Nature of
Work Relations in the Late Twentieth Century*, ed. B. Berberoglu (Westport,
Conn.: Praeger Publishers, 1993), 71–72.

24. D. T. Cook, "High-Tech vs. U.S. Labor Unions; Loss of Jobs and Clout," *Christian Science Monitor*, 12 September 1983, Monday edition; P. Mattera, "The

Underside of the Computer Age," *Thought* 61, no. 243 (December 1986): 453; Early and Wilson, "Organizing High Tech," 48; S. Armstrong, "Labor Organizing: Growing Blip on High-Tech Screen," *Christian Science Monitor,* 17 May 1983, Tuesday edition; M. Goldfield, *The Decline of Organized Labor in the United States* (Chicago: University of Chicago Press, 1987), 91.

25. K. Sawyer, "Unions Striking Out in High-Tech Firms," *Washington Post,* 18 March 1984, sec. A; J. F. Keller, "The Division of Labor in Electronics," in *Women, Men and the International Division of Labor,* ed. J. Nash and M. P. Fernandez-Kelly (Albany: State University of New York Press, 1983), 361; Green, "Silicon Valley's Women Workers," 309.

26. Rogers and Larsen, *Silicon Valley Fever,* 189–90; Henderson, *The Globalisation of High Technology Production,* 40; Mohseni, "The Labor Process," 71; Keller, "The Division of Labor," 367; K. J. Hossfeld, "'Their Logic Against Them': Contradictions in Sex, Race, and Class in Silicon Valley," in *Women Workers and Global Restructuring,* ed. K. Ward (Ithaca, N.Y.: ILR Press, 1990), 155.

27. Mohseni, "The Labor Process," 71; N. Katz and D. S. Kemnitzer, "Fast Forward: The Internationalization of Silicon Valley," in *Women, Men and the International Division of Labor,* ed. J. Nash and M. P. Fernandez-Kelly (Albany: State University of New York Press, 1983), 333.

28. R. Grossman, "Women's Place in the Integrated Circuit," *Radical America* 14, no. 1 (January-February 1980): 29–49; R. Taplin, "Women in World Market Factories: East and West," *Ethnic and Racial Studies* 9, no. 2 (April 1986): 168–95; Snow, "The New International Division," 55, 60–61; Green, "Silicon Valley's Women Workers," 284.

29. Colclough and Tolbert, *Work in the Fast Lane,* 21.

30. Mohseni, "The Labor Process," 71.

31. Colclough and Tolbert, *Work in the Fast Lane,* 21.

32. Ibid., 34.

33. Ibid., 9, 29; A. K. Glasmeier, "High-Tech Industries and the Regional Division of Labor," *Industrial Relations* 25, no. 2 (spring 1986): 199.

34. Mohseni, "The Labor Process," 69; Colclough and Tolbert, *Work in the Fast Lane,* 29.

35. R. Hodson, "Good Jobs and Bad Management: How New Problems Evoke Old Solutions in High-Tech Settings," in *Industries, Firms and Jobs: Sociological and Economic Approaches,* ed. G. Farkas and P. England (New York: Plenum Press, 1988), 247–79.

36. Ibid.

37. Ibid., 270.

38. For references on high-tech industry as one of the most union-resistant sectors of the U.S. economy, see H. Juris and M. Roomkin, "The Shrinking Perimeter: Unions and Collective Bargaining in Manufacturing," in *The Shrinking Perimeter: Unionism and Labor Relations in the Manufacturing Sector,* ed. H. A. Juris and M. Roomkin (Lexington, Mass.: D.C. Heath, 1980), 197–211; A. Fuentes and B. Ehrenreich, *Women in the Global Factory* (Boston: South End Press, 1983); R. Hodson, "Working in 'High-Tech': Researchers and Opportunities for the Industrial Sociologist," *Sociological Quarterly* 26, no. 3 (September 1985): 351–64; G. Gamst and C. M. Otten, "Job Satisfaction in High Technology and Traditional Industry: Is There a Difference?," *Psychological Record* 42, no. 3 (summer 1992): 413–25; and Mohseni, "The Labor Process," 59–77. Information on high-tech firms' vigorous opposition to union organizing drives can be found in A. B. Shostak, "High Tech, High Touch and Labor," *Social Policy* 13, no. 3 (winter 1983): 23; W. Patterson, "Why Organized Labor Likes High Tech," *Industry Week* 227, no. 3 (11 November 1985): 46; K. J. Hossfeld, "Why Aren't High-Tech Workers Organized? Lessons in Gender, Race and Nationality from Silicon Valley," in *Working People of California,* ed. D. Cornford (Berkeley: University of California Press, 1995), 408, 410; and Early and Wilson, "Organizing High Tech," 52.

39. Early and Wilson, "Do Unions Have a Future," 61–62.

40. Rogers and Larsen, *Silicon Valley Fever,* 190.

41. M. Goss, "Smokestacks Revisited: The Future of High-Tech Workers," *Management Review* 74, no. 5 (May 1985): 30; "High Tech Lures Union Organizers," *Business Week,* 11 April 1983, 101; T. Engstrom, "Union Dues: High Tech Meets Organized Labor," *Electronic Business* 9 (December 1983): 102.

42. J. G. Robinson and J. S. McIlwee, "Obstacles to Unionization in High-Tech Industries," *Work and Occupations* 16, no. 2 (May 1989): 115–36.

43. Early and Wilson, "Organizing High Tech," 51. After spending ten years as an organizer attempting to unionize Silicon Valley high-tech workers, Mike Eisenscher provides an excellent and perceptive analysis of high-tech industry and its prospects for being organized. See M. Eisenscher, "Silicon Valley High Tech Industry: Ready for Organizing. A Discussion Paper for Unions," Draft #3 (San Jose, Calif., 25 July 1985, photocopy) and M. Eisenscher, "Chasing the High-Tech Rainbow: Reality and Fantasy in the Valley of the Silicon Giants" (San Jose, Calif., 1985, photocopy).

44. Early and Wilson, "Organizing High Tech," 51–52.

45. K. Schellenberg, "Taking It or Leaving It: Instability and Turnover in a High-Tech Firm," *Work and Occupations* 23, no. 2 (May 1996): 191; Mohseni, "The Labor Process," 73.

46. Keller, "The Division of Labor," 354.

47. Hodson, "Good Jobs and Bad Management," 261; Green, "Silicon Valley's Women Workers," 301–3.

48. S. Aronowitz and W. DiFazio, *The Jobless Future: Sci-Tech and the Dogma of Work* (Minneapolis: University of Minnesota Press, 1994), 94; S. Aronowitz and W. DiFazio, "High Technology and Work Tomorrow," *Annals of the American Academy of Political and Social Science*, no. 544 (March 1996): 53.

49. P.S. Foner, *Women and the American Labor Movement: From Colonial Times to the Eve of World War I* (New York: Free Press, 1979), 260.

50. Markusen, Hall, and Glasmeier, *High Tech America,* 114; D. J. Braddock, "Scientific and Technical Employment, 1990–2005," *Monthly Labor Review* 115, no. 2 (February 1992): 34.

CHAPTER 2

1. L. Poole and G. Poole, *Electronics in Medicine* (New York: McGraw-Hill Book Company, 1964), 116–17.

2. E. M. Rogers and J. K. Larson, *Silicon Valley Fever: Growth of High-Technology Culture* (New York: Basic Books, 1984), 63.

3. T. Mahon, *Charged Bodies: People, Power and Paradox in Silicon Valley* (New York: New American Library Books, 1985), 95.

CHAPTER 3

1. R. M. Pfeffer, *Working for Capitali$m* (New York: Columbia University Press, 1979), 18, 21. In the first chapter, "Looking for a Job," 17–28, Pfeffer provides an excellent and detailed analysis of what it is like to search for unskilled factory work in the United States in the late twentieth century.

2. Ibid., 23.

3. Ibid., 22.

4. Ibid., 28.

CHAPTER 4

1. D. Hembree, "Dead End in Silicon Valley: The High-Tech Future Doesn't Work," *Progressive* 49, no. 10 (October 1985): 18–24; R. Cavendish, *Women on the Line* (London: Routledge and Kegan Paul, 1982).
2. Hembree, "Dead End in Silicon Valley," 25; Cavendish, *Women on the Line*, 119.
3. K. Kusterer, *Know-How on the Job: The Important Working Knowledge of Unskilled Workers* (Boulder, Colo.: Westview, 1978). I find Kusterer's work to be one of the best commentaries on analyzing the significant amount of "skill" that actually is involved in the successful completion of many different types of work that are deemed to be "unskilled."
4. Ibid., 138–40, 143–45.
5. Ibid., 138–39.
6. Ibid., 140.
7. Ibid., 143.
8. R. Balzer, *Clockwork: Life in and Outside an American Factory* (Garden City, N.Y.: Doubleday, 1976), 127.
9. Ibid.
10. R. Hodson, "Good Jobs and Bad Management: How New Problems Evoke Old Solutions in High-Tech Settings," in *Industries, Firms and Jobs: Sociological and Economic Approaches*, ed. G. Farkas and P. England (New York: Plenum Press, 1988), 247–79.
11. R. M. Pfeffer, *Working for Capitali$m* (New York: Columbia University Press, 1979), 52.
12. Ibid., 77–78.
13. Cavendish, *Women on the Line*, 113.
14. Pfeffer, *Working for Capitali$m*, 78.
15. Ibid., 86.
16. T. Mahon, *Charged Bodies: People, Power and Paradox in Silicon Valley* (New York: New American Library Books, 1985).

CHAPTER 5

1. G. Colclough and C. M. Tolbert, *Work in the Fast Lane: Flexibility, Divisions of Labor, and Inequality in High-Tech Industries* (Albany: State University of New York Press, 1992), 29; N. Mohseni, "The Labor Process and Control of Labor in the U.S. Computer Industry," in *The Labor Process and Control of Labor: The Changing Nature of Work Relations in the Late Twentieth Century*, ed. B.

Berberoglu (Westport, Conn.: Praeger Publishers, 1993), 70; R. Hodson, "Good Jobs and Bad Management: How New Problems Evoke Old Solutions in High-Tech Settings," in *Industries, Firms and Jobs: Sociological and Economic Approaches*, ed. G. Farkas and P. England (New York: Plenum Press, 1988), 266.

2. Mohseni, "The Labor Process," 59–77.

3. S. P. Vallas and J. P. Beck, "The Transformation of Work Revisited: The Limits of Flexibility in American Manufacturing," *Social Problems* 43, no. 3 (August 1996): 339; M. Piore and C. F. Sabel, *The Second Industrial Divide: Possibilities for Prosperity* (New York: Basic Books, 1984).

4. For detailed information on the debate over whether there is a substantive difference between Fordist and post-Fordist production regimes, please see R. Hyman, "Flexible Specialization: Miracle or Myth?" in *New Technology and Industrial Relations,* ed. R. Hyman and W. Streeck (Oxford: Blackwell, 1988), 48–60; A. Sayer, "Post-Fordism in Question," *International Journal of Urban and Regional Research,* 13, no. 4 (December 1989): 666–95; J. P. Womack, D. T. Jones, and D. Roos, *The Machine That Changed the World* (New York: Harper, 1990); and P. Hirst and J. Zeitlin, "Flexible Specialization Versus Post-Fordism: Theory, Evidence, and Policy Implications," *Economy and Society* 20, no. 1 (February 1991): 1–52. For the argument that flexible specialization in post-Fordist regimes leads to an intensification of worker effort, see A. Pollert, *Farewell to Flexibility?* (Oxford: Blackwell, 1991) and V. Smith, "New Forms of Work Organization," in *Annual Review of Sociology,* vol. 23, ed. J. Hagan (Palo Alto, Calif.: Annual Reviews, 1997), 315–39. Empirical evidence on the intensification of worker effort under flexible specialization in the clothing industry has led Taplin to view post-Fordist regimes as a kind of neo-Fordism. See I. Taplin, "Flexible Production, Rigid Jobs: Lessons From the Clothing Industry," *Work and Occupations* 22, no. 4 (November 1995): 412–38 and I. Taplin, "Rethinking Flexibility: The Case of the Apparel Industry," *Review of Social Economy* 54, no. 2 (summer 1996): 191–220.

5. Colclough and Tolbert, *Work in the Fast Lane,* 29; Mohseni, "The Labor Process," 70; Hodson, "Good Jobs and Bad Management," 247–79.

6. P. Thompson, *The Nature of Work: An Introduction to Debates on the Labour Process,* 2d ed. (London: Macmillan, 1989), 57.

7. Ibid., 92.

8. Thompson, *The Nature of Work,* 108; K. Kusterer, *Know-How on the Job: The Important Working Knowledge of Unskilled Workers* (Boulder, Colo.: Westview, 1978).

9. E. Applebaum, "Winners and Losers in the High-Tech Workplace," *Challenge*

26, no. 4 (September-October 1983): 52–55; W. Form and D. B. McMillen, "Women, Men and Machines," *Work and Occupations* 10, no. 2 (May 1983): 147–78; P. G. Schervish, *The Structural Determinants of Unemployment: Vulnerability and Power in Market Relations* (New York: Academic Press, 1983).

10. H. Braverman, *Labor and Monopoly Capital: The Degradation of Work in the Twentieth Century* (New York: Monthly Review Press, 1974); Thompson, *The Nature of Work*, 94. One also should consult J. B. Foster, "*Labor And Monopoly Capital* Twenty Years After: An Introduction," *Monthly Review* 46, no. 6 (November 1994): 1–13; P. Meiksins, "*Labor And Monopoly Capital* for the 1990s: A Review and Critique of the Labor Process Debate," *Monthly Review* 46, no. 6 (November 1994): 45–51; and V. Smith, "Braverman's Legacy: The Labor Process Tradition at 20," *Work and Occupations* 21, no. 4 (November 1994): 403–21, for excellent discussions of the continuing relevance of Braverman's ideas for analyzing the labor process in the 1990s and beyond.

11. N. Shapiro-Perl, "The Piece Rate: Class Struggle on the Shop Floor. Evidence from the Costume Jewelry Industry in Providence, Rhode Island," in *Case Studies on the Labor Process*, ed. A. Zimbalist (New York: Monthly Review Press, 1979), 282–83.

12. W. Baldamus, *Efficiency and Effort: An Analysis of Industrial Administration* (London: Tavistock Institute of Human Relations, 1961), 59.

13. For comprehensive literature reviews concerning workplace automation and its effect on the skill levels of workers, please see R. Hodson and R. E. Parker, "Work in High-Technology Settings: A Review of the Empirical Literature," in *Research in the Sociology of Work*, vol. 4, ed. R. L. Simpson and I. H. Simpson (Greenwich, Conn.: JAI Press, 1988), 1–29; G. Gamst and C. M. Otten, "Job Satisfaction in High Technology and Traditional Industry: Is There a Difference?" *Psychological Record* 42, no. 3 (1992): 413–25; Smith, "Braverman's Legacy," 403–21. For a discussion of this debate as applied to the banking industry, see P. S. Adler, "Rethinking the Skill Requirements of New Technologies," in *High Hopes for High Tech: Microelectronics Policy in North Carolina*, ed. D. Whittington (Chapel Hill: University of North Carolina Press, 1985), 85–112.

14. Hodson and Parker, "Work in High-Technology Settings," 8.

15. For information on suggestion programs, Scanlon Plans, and employee involvement programs, see chapter 15, "Incentive Plans" and chapter 21, "Participative Strategies for Organization Improvement" in W. L. French, *Human Resources Management*, 4th ed., (Boston: Houghton Mifflin, 1998), 397–423, 568–600; T. Juravich, *Chaos on the Shop Floor: A Worker's View of Quality, Productivity, and Management* (Philadelphia: Temple University Press, 1985), 51.

16. R. Edwards, *Contested Terrain: The Transformation of the Workplace in the Twentieth Century* (New York: Basic Books, 1979), 167–68. J. Storey, *Managerial Prerogative and the Question of Control* (London: Routledge and Kegan Paul, 1983), 153.

17. S. S. Green, "Silicon Valley's Women Workers: A Theoretical Analysis of Sex-Segregation in the Electronics Industry Labor Market," in *Women, Men and the International Division of Labor,* ed. J. Nash and M. P. Fernandez-Kelly (Albany: State University of New York Press, 1983), 301–2.

18. I. Taplin, "Flexible Production, Rigid Jobs," 412–38; I. Taplin, "Rethinking Flexibility," 191–220; Vallas and Beck, "The Transformation of Work Revisited," 339–361.

CHAPTER 6

1. G. Colclough and C. M. Tolbert, *Work in the Fast Lane: Flexibility, Divisions of Labor, and Inequality in High-Tech Industries* (Albany: State University of New York Press, 1992), 34; R. Hodson, "Good Jobs and Bad Management: How New Problems Evoke Old Solutions in High-Tech Settings," in *Industries, Firms and Jobs: Sociological and Economic Approaches,* ed. G. Farkas and P. England (New York: Plenum Press, 1988), 247–79.

2. Hodson, "Good Jobs and Bad Management," 269–71.

3. R. M. Veigel-Cooper, telephone conversation with author, 25 March 1997.

4. P. Thompson, *The Nature of Work: An Introduction to Debates on the Labour Process,* 2d ed. (London: Macmillan, 1989), 234; R. Edwards, *Contested Terrain: The Transformation of the Workplace in the Twentieth Century* (New York: Basic Books, 1979), 18.

5. For a detailed discussion of the different types of managerial strategies used to control labor, see J. Storey, *Managerial Prerogative and the Question of Control* (London: Routledge and Kegan Paul, 1983) and P. Thompson, "Crawling from the Wreckage: The Labour Process and the Politics of Production," in *Labour Process Theory,* ed. D. Knights and H. Willmott (London: Macmillan Press, 1990), 95–124.

6. Edwards, *Contested Terrain,* 35; Storey, *Managerial Prerogative,* 129–33, 148–50.

7. Edwards, *Contested Terrain,* 19, 34, 35, 178–79.

8. Ibid., 34–36; M. Burawoy, *Manufacturing Consent: Changes in the Labor Process under Monopoly Capitalism* (Chicago: University of Chicago Press, 1979), 194; M. Burawoy, *The Politics of Production: Factory Regimes Under Capitalism and Socialism* (London: Verso, 1985), 126.

9. T. Nichols and H. Beynon, *Living with Capitalism: Class Relations and the Modern Factory* (London: Routledge and Kegan Paul, 1977), 49.

10. J. G. Robinson and J. S. McIlwee, "Obstacles to Unionization in High-Tech Industries," *Work and Occupations* 16, no. 2 (May 1989): 115–36; R. M. Pfeffer, *Working for Capitali$m* (New York: Columbia University Press, 1979), 96; R. Cavendish, *Women on the Line* (London: Routledge and Kegan Paul, 1982), 90.

11. D. Hembree, "Dead End in Silicon Valley: The High-Tech Future Doesn't Work," *Progressive* 49, no. 10 (October 1985): 20.

12. Cavendish, *Women on the Line*, 90, 111.

13. Hodson, "Good Jobs and Bad Management," 247–79; J. Brecher, "Roots of Power: Employers and Workers in the Electrical Products Industry," in *Case Studies on the Labor Process*, ed. A. Zimbalist (New York: Monthly Review Press, 1979), 214.

14. For discussions of worker manipulation of piecework or incentive systems, please see A. Friedman, *Industry and Labor: Class Struggle at Work and Monopoly Capitalism* (London: Macmillan, 1977), 221; Brecher, "Roots of Power," 214; Burawoy, *Manufacturing Consent*, 48–62.

15. Cavendish, *Women on the Line*, 111–12.

16. Thompson, *The Nature of Work*, 2d ed., 153.

17. Evidence of workers engaging in "games" during production work is a fascinating aspect of the labor process and production politics. For excellent discussions and analyses of this phenomenon, see A. Gouldner, *Patterns of Industrial Bureaucracy* (New York: Free Press, 1954), 45–69; T. Lupton, *On the Shop Floor* (Oxford: Pergamon Press, 1963); Burawoy, *Manufacturing Consent*, 77–94.

18. M. Foucault, *Discipline and Punish: The Birth of the Prison* (London: Allen Lane, 1977), 201.

19. R. Sakolsky, "'Disciplinary Power' and the Labor Process," in *Skill and Consent: Contemporary Studies in the Labour Process*, ed. A. Sturdy, D. Knights, and H. Willmott (London: Routledge, 1992), 240.

20. Foucault, *Discipline and Punish*, 201.

21. H. Braverman, *Labor and Monopoly Capital: The Degradation of Work in the Twentieth Century* (New York: Monthly Review Press, 1974). For a discussion of resistance strategies to managerial control, please see J. M. Jermier, D. Knights, and W. R. Nord, "Resistance and Power in Organizations: Agency, Subjectivity and the Labour Process," in *Resistance and Power in Organizations*, ed. J. M. Jermier, D. Knights, and W. R. Nord (London: Routledge, 1994), 1–24.

22. R. Hodson, "The Active Worker: Compliance and Autonomy at the Work-

place," *Journal of Contemporary Ethnography* 20, no. 1 (April 1991): 47–78; J. V. Johnson, "Collective Control: Strategies for Survival in the Workplace," *International Journal of Health Services* 19, no. 3 (1989): 469–80; R. Hodson, "Workplace Behaviors: Good Soldiers, Smooth Operators and Saboteurs," *Work and Occupations* 18, no. 3 (August 1991): 271–90; J. Kimery, "Labor Process and Race Relations in a Shampoo Factory: The Differential Distribution of Help," *Humboldt Journal of Social Relations* 20, no. 1 (1994): 65–85; R. Hodson, "Cohesion or Conflict? Race, Solidarity and Resistance in the Workplace," in *Research in the Sociology of Work,* vol. 5, ed. by R. L. Simpson and I. H. Simpson (Greenwich, Conn.: JAI Press, 1995), 135–59.

23. On different kinds of unorganized resistance, see Storey, *Managerial Preroga-tive,* 160. On the concept of the "pencil bonus," see R. Balzer, *Clockwork: Life in and Outside an American Factory* (Garden City, N.Y.: Doubleday, 1976), 127. Concerning the role of worker production knowledge as a weapon in the struggle over shop floor control, see V. G. Devinatz, "Rationalizing the Irra-tionality of the Shop Floor: A Reinterpretation of Juravich's *Chaos on the Shop Floor,*" *Labor Studies Journal* 18, no. 1 (spring 1993): 3–16.

24. For a summary of the role of gender in the labor process, see J. West, "Gen-der and the Labour Process: A Reassessment," in *Labour Process Theory,* ed. D. Knights and H. Willmott (London: MacMillan Press, 1990), 244–73. For specific examples of gendered resistance strategies, see C. K. Lee, "Familial Hegemony: Gender and Production Politics on Hong Kong's Electronics Shopfloor," *Gender and Society* 7, no. 4 (December 1993), 529–47; V. Smith, "Braverman's Legacy: The Labor Process Tradition at 20," *Work and Occupa-tions* 21, no. 4 (November 1994): 403–21; C. K. Lee, "Engendering the Worlds of Labor: Women Workers, Labor Markets, and Production Politics in the South China Economic Miracle," *American Sociological Review* 60, no. 3 (June 1995): 378–97.

25. For a discussion of organized resistance strategies, see Storey, *Managerial Pre-rogative,* 167; and Hodson, "Cohesion or Conflict?" 145. On the restriction of output in industrial settings, see D. Roy, "Quota Restriction and Gold-bricking in a Machine Shop," *American Journal of Sociology* 57, no. 5 (March 1952): 427–42; D. Roy, "Work Satisfaction and Social Reward in Quota Achievement," *American Sociological Review* 18, no. 5 (October 1953): 507–14; D. Roy, " Efficiency and the Fix: Informal Intergroup Relations in a Piece-work Machine Shop," *American Journal of Sociology* 60, no. 3 (November 1954): 255–66; and S. B. Mathewson, *Restriction of Output among Unorganized Work-ers* (Carbondale: Southern Illinois University Press, 1969).

26. Edwards, *Contested Terrain*, 16.
27. For a comprehensive historical treatment of the emergence of the "employment at will doctrine" in the United States, see D. A. Ballam, "The Traditional View on the Origins of the Employment-at-Will Doctrine: Myth or Reality?" *American Business Law Journal* 33, no. 1 (fall 1995): 1–50; R. N. Covington and K. H. Decker, *Individual Employee Rights in a Nutshell* (St. Paul, Minn.: West Publishing Company, 1995), 221, 239–40.
28. Pfeffer, *Working for Capitali$m*, 103–4.
29. Colclough and Tolbert, *Work in the Fast Lane*, 34; Hodson, "Good Jobs and Bad Management," 269–71; Robinson and McIlwee, "Obstacles to Unionization," 115–136.

CHAPTER 7

1. T. Juravich, *Chaos on the Shop Floor: A Worker's View of Quality, Productivity, and Management* (Philadelphia: Temple University Press, 1985), 20.
2. C. Geertz, *The Interpretation of Cultures* (New York: Basic Books, 1973), 6–7.
3. A. Pollert, *Girls, Wives, Factory Lives* (London: Macmillan, 1981).
4. P. E. Willis, *Learning for Labour: How Working Class Kids Get Working Class Jobs* (Farnborough, England: Saxon House, 1977).
5. R. Hodson, "Cohesion or Conflict? Race, Solidarity, and Resistance in the Workplace," in *Research in the Sociology of Work*, vol. 5, ed. R. L. Simpson and I. H. Simpson, (Greenwich, Conn.: JAI Press, 1995), 135–59.
6. A. J. Scott, *Technopolis: High-Technology Industry and Regional Development in Southern California* (Berkeley: University of California Press, 1993), 190–91.

CHAPTER 8

1. J. Storey, *Managerial Prerogative and the Question of Control* (London: Routledge and Kegan Paul, 1983); K. J. Hossfeld, "'Their Logic Against Them': Contradictions in Sex, Race, and Class in Silicon Valley," in *Women Workers and Global Restructuring*, ed. K. Ward (Ithaca, N.Y.: ILR Press, 1990), 149–78.
2. R. Erlich, "Rare Employee Strike at Silicon Valley Plant; Job Action at Versatronex May Foreshadow New Drive to Organize Immigrant Workers in High-Tech Industry," *Christian Science Monitor*, 24 November 1992, Tuesday edition; E. Kadetsky, "High-Tech's Dirty Little Secret," *Nation*, 19 April 1993, 517–20.
3. K. J. Hossfeld, "Why Aren't High-Tech Workers Organized? Lessons in Gen-

der, Race and Nationality from Silicon Valley," in *Working People in California,* ed. D. Cornford (Berkeley: University of California Press, 1995), 415; Kadetsky, "High-Tech's Dirty Little Secret," 517.

4. Erlich, "Rare Employee Strike"; Kadetsky, "High-Tech's Dirty Little Secret," 517.

5. Kadetsky, "High-Tech's Dirty Little Secret," 518.

6. Hossfeld, "Why Aren't High-Tech Workers Organized," 415; Kadetsky, "High-Tech's Dirty Little Secret," 519.

7. Kadetsky, "High-Tech's Dirty Little Secret," 517, 519.

8. For more detailed discussions of these components of group solidarity, see D. Roy, "Efficiency and the Fix: Informal Intergroup Relations in a Piecework Machine Shop," *American Journal of Sociology* 60, no. 3 (November 1954): 255–66; C. Vaught and D. L. Smith, "Incorporation and Mechanical Solidarity in an Underground Coal Mine," *Work and Occupations* 7, no. 2 (May 1980): 159–87; D. Halle, *America's Working Man: Work, Home and Politics among Blue Collar Property Owners* (Chicago: University of Chicago Press, 1984); R. Fantasia, *Cultures of Solidarity: Consciousness, Action and Contemporary American Workers* (Berkeley: University of California Press, 1988); C. Molstad, "Control Strategies Used by Industrial Brewery Workers: Work Avoidance, Impression Management and Solidarity," *Human Organization* 47, no. 4 (winter 1988): 354–60.

9. R. Hodson, "Cohesion or Conflict? Race, Solidarity, and Resistance in the Workplace," in *Research in the Sociology of Work,* vol. 5, ed. R. L. Simpson and I. H. Simpson (Greenwich, Conn.: JAI Press, 1995), 150.

10. Ibid., 155.

11. M. Guttman, "Primary (Informal) Work Groups," *Radical America* 6, no. 3 (May-June 1972): 78–91.

12. M. Davis, "The Stop Watch and the Wooden Shoe: Scientific Management and the Industrial Workers of the World," *Radical America* 9, no. 1 (January-February 1975): 71–72.

13. J. A. Blake, "Internal Dynamics, Definition of the Situation and Emerging Organization During a Wildcat Strike," *Humboldt Journal of Social Relations* 4, no. 2 (1977): 60–73. Besides journalistic accounts of nonunion wildcat strikes, there is virtually no scholarly research on this phenomenon.

14. D. M. Byrne and R.H. King, "Wildcat Strikes in U.S. Manufacturing, 1960–1977," *Journal of Labor Research* 7, no. 4 (fall 1986): 387–401.

15. Fantasia, *Cultures of Solidarity.* In chapter 3, "The Internal Dynamics of Wildcat Strikes: Routinization and Its Discontents," 75–120, of this book, Fanta-

sia provides a particularly insightful analysis of the unfolding and dynamics of two wildcat strikes in which he served as a participant observer.

CHAPTER 9

1. For information on high-tech industries being particularly union-resistant, see H. Juris and M. Roomkin, "The Shrinking Perimeter: Unions and Collective Bargaining in Manufacturing," in *The Shrinking Perimeter: Unionism and Labor Relations in the Manufacturing Sector*, ed. H. A. Juris and M. Roomkin (Lexington, Mass.: D.C. Heath, 1980), 197–211; A. Fuentes and B. Ehrenreich, *Women in the Global Factory* (Boston: South End Press, 1983); R. Hodson, "Working in 'High-Tech': Researchers and Opportunities for the Industrial Sociologist," *Sociological Quarterly* 26, no. 3 (1985): 351–64; and N. Mohseni, "The Labor Process and Control of Labor in the U.S. Computer Industry," in *The Labor Process and Control of Labor: The Changing Nature of Work Relations in the Late Twentieth Century*, ed. B. Berberoglu (Westport, Conn.: Praeger Publishers, 1993), 59–77. On high-tech firms' vigorous opposition to unionization, see A. B. Shostak, "High Tech, High Touch and Labor," *Social Policy* 13, no. 3 (1983): 23; and W. Patterson, "Why Organized Labor Likes High Tech," *Industry Week* 227, no. 3 (11 November 1985): 46. The two case studies of organizing attempts at high-tech firms during 1982–83 can be found in S. Early and R. Wilson, "Do Unions Have a Future in High Technology?" *Technology Review* 89, no. 7 (October 1986): 56–65f; and S. Early and R. Wilson, "Organizing High Tech: Unions and Their Future," *Labor Research Review* no. 8 (spring 1986): 47–65. In these two articles, Early and Wilson compare and contrast the dynamics of two unsuccessful unionization attempts: the Glaziers Union's "hot shop" campaign at Atari and the Communications Workers Union's (CWA) strategic organizing drive at Wavetek.

2. K. Gagala, *Union Organizing and Staying Organized* (Reston, Va.: Reston Publishing Company, 1983). For information on how a union should handle unfair labor practice charges, see "What to Do about Unfair Labor Practices" (pp. 31–36) in Gagala's book.

3. Ibid., 36.

4. K. Bronfenbrenner, "The Role of Union Strategies in NLRB Certification Elections," *Industrial and Labor Relations Review* 50, no. 2 (January 1997): 208.

5. H. L. Delgado, *New Immigrants, Old Unions: Organizing Undocumented Workers in Los Angeles* (Philadelphia: Temple University Press, 1993).

6. R. Hodson, "Cohesion or Conflict? Race, Solidarity, and Resistance in the Workplace," in *Research in the Sociology of Work*, vol. 5, ed. R. L. Simpson and I. H. Simpson (Greenwich, Conn.: JAI Press, 1995), 151.
7. W. H. Holley and K. M. Jennings, *The Labor Relations Process*, 6th ed. (New York: Dryden Press, 1997), 279, 282.
8. R. B. Peterson, T. W. Lee, and B. Finnegan, "Strategies and Tactics in Union Organizing Campaigns," *Industrial Relations* 31, no. 2 (spring 1992): 374; J. J. Lawler, *Unionization and Deunionization: Strategy, Tactics, and Outcomes* (Columbia: University of South Carolina Press, 1990), 143–50.
9. Holley and Jennings, *The Labor Relations Process*, 6th ed., 190.
10. W. H. Holley and K. M. Jennings, *The Labor Relations Process*, 5th ed. (New York: Dryden Press, 1994), 174.
11. Early and Wilson, "Do Unions Have a Future in High Technology?" 62; Gagala, *Union Organizing and Staying Organized*, 36.
12. J. G. Robinson and J. S. McIlwee, "Obstacles to Unionization in High-Tech Industries," *Work and Occupations* 16, no. 2 (May 1989): 126.
13. Ibid., 128.
14. K. J. Hossfeld, "Why Aren't High-Tech Workers Organized? Lessons in Gender, Race, and Nationality from Silicon Valley," in *Working People of California*, ed. D. Cornford (Berkeley: University of California Press, 1995), 407.

CHAPTER 10

1. M. Burawoy, *The Politics of Production: Factory Regimes under Capitalism and Socialism* (London: Verso, 1985), 87, 89, 102.
2. Ibid., 125–26.
3. Ibid., 126.
4. E. M. Rogers and J. K. Larsen, *Silicon Valley Fever: Growth of High-Technology Culture* (New York: Basic Books, 1984), 193.
5. J. F. Dangler, "Electronic Subassemblers in Central New York: Nontraditional Homeworkers in a Nontraditional Homework Industry," in *Homework: Historical and Contemporary Perspectives on Paid Labor at Home*, ed. E. Boris and C. R. Daniels, (Urbana: University of Illinois Press, 1989), 150–51.
6. Rogers and Larsen, *Silicon Valley Fever*, 193.
7. B. Lozano, *The Invisible Work Force: Transforming American Business with Outside and Home-Based Workers* (New York: Free Press, 1989), 117–18.
8. Ibid., 36.

9. Rogers and Larsen, *Silicon Valley Fever,* 194–95.

10. A. Ong, *Spirits of Resistance and Capitalist Discipline: Factory Women in Malaysia* (Albany: State University of New York Press, 1987), 148.

11. D. Hayes, *Behind the Silicon Curtain: The Seductions of Work in a Lonely Era* (Boston: South End Press, 1989), 59, 61; S. Early and R. Wilson, "Do Unions Have a Future in High Technology?" *Technology Review* 81, no. 7 (October 1986), 56–65f.

12. For a comment on the SEIU's "Justice for Janitors" campaign, see P. Johnston, *Success While Others Fail: Social Movement Unionism and the Public Workplace* (Ithaca, N.Y.: ILR Press, 1994), 166. For information on the impressive success of the Laborers' Union in organizing asbestos-abatement workers in New York City, see M. H. Cooper, "LIUNA Organizes Asbestos Industry in Model Campaign," *AFL-CIO News* 41, no. 8 (1996): 1, 13; K. C. Crowe, "A Unionized Victory For Asbestos Workers," *Newsday,* 21 April 1996; A. Banks, "The Power and Promise of Community Unionism," *Labor Research Review* 10, no. 2 (1991–92): 17–31; and J. Howley, "Justice For Janitors: The Challenge of Organizing in Contract Services," *Labor Research Review* 9, no. 1 (1990): 61–71. For guidelines that unions should use in non-NLRB election organizing campaigns in order to increase their probability for success, see V. G. Devinatz, "The Fair Deal Campaign: The Evolution of a Non-NLRB Election Organizing Strategy for Unionizing Milwaukee Asbestos-Abatement Workers," *Labor Studies Journal* 22, no. 3 (fall 1997): 74–91; and R. Needleman, "Organizing Low-Wage Workers," *Working USA* (May–June 1997): 45–59.

13. Early and Wilson, "Do Unions Have a Future," 65, 79; Hayes, *Behind the Silicon Curtain,* 61; C. Benner, "Computer Workers Feel the Byte: Temp Jobs in Silicon Valley," *Dollars and Sense,* September/October 1996, 23–25, 44.

14. Benner, "Computer Workers Feel the Byte," 25.

15. Ibid.

16. R. Armbruster, "Cross-National Labor Organizing Strategies," *Critical Sociology* 21, no. 2 (1995): 75–89. For a discussion of internationalizing union practice across many different countries and industries, see K. Moody, *Workers in a Lean World: Unions in the International Economy* (London: Verso, 1997).

17. Armbruster, "Cross-National Labor Organizing Strategies," 75–89.

18. S. Tiano, "Maquiladora Women: A New Category of Workers," in *Women Workers and Global Restructuring,* ed. K. Ward (Ithaca, N.Y.: ILR Press, 1990), 197.

19. K. Kopinak, "Transitions in the Maquilization of Mexican Industry: Move-

ment and Stasis from 1965 to 2001," *Labour, Capital and Society* 28, no. 1 (1995): 68–94; H. Shaiken, "Advanced Manufacturing and Mexico: A New International Division of Labor?" *Latin American Research Review* 29, no. 2 (1994): 68.

20. D. Ohmans, "Seeds of Solidarity: Union Initiatives Towards Mexico," *OCAW Reporter,* 49 nos. 5–6 (1993): 11; "Teamsters, UE Launch Historic Solidarity Campaign with Fired Mexican Workers," *Working Together: Labor Report on the Americas,* no. 5 (March-April 1994): 1.

21. M. McGinn, "After NAFTA . . . Honeywell, G. E. Fire Mexican Workers for Organizing Unions," *Labor Notes* 178 (January 1994): 1, 14.

22. McGinn, "After NAFTA," 1, 14; "Teamsters, UE Launch," 1; Armbruster, "Cross-National Labor Organizing Strategies," 85.

23. D. Moberg, "The Resurgence of American Unions: Small Steps, Long Journey," *Working USA* (May-June 1997): 30.

24. S. Early, "Northern Telecom: Telephone Workers' Campaign Promotes Labor," *Labor Notes* 154 (January 1992): 8.

25. Ibid.

26. Armbruster, "Cross-National Labor Organizing Strategies," 80.

27. Ibid., 87.

28. L. Compa, "Another Look at NAFTA," *Dissent* 44, no. 1 (winter 1997): 46, 48; M. L. Cook, "Cross-Border Labor Solidarity," *Dissent* 44, no. 1 (winter 1997): 49.

29. Statistics on union success in NLRB certification elections, as well as the actual number of workers organized, in the 1980s can be found in G. N. Chaison and D. G. Dhavale, "A Note on the Severity of the Decline in Union Organizing Activity," *Industrial and Labor Relations Review* 43, no. 4 (July 1990): 369. The 1942 statistic for union success in NLRB certification elections is from M. Goldfield, *The Decline of Organized Labor in the United States* (Chicago: University of Chicago Press, 1987): 90.

30. For union density statistics from the 1980s, see M. A. Curme, B. T. Hirsch, and D. A. MacPherson, "Union Membership and Contract Coverage in the United States, 1983–1988," *Industrial and Labor Relations Review* 44, no. 1 (October 1990): 9. For union density statistics from 1990 and 1991, see B. T. Hirsch and D. A. MacPherson, "Union Membership and Coverage Files from the Current Population Surveys: Note," *Industrial and Labor Relations Review* 46, no. 3 (April 1993): 577.

31. For discussions of concession bargaining in the 1980s, see J. Slaughter, *Con-*

cessions and How to Beat Them (Detroit: Labor Education and Research Project, 1984); and P. Capelli, "Plant-Level Concession Bargaining," *Industrial and Labor Relations Review* 39, no. 1 (October 1985): 90–104. For a collection of short articles on union experiences with different types of EI programs, see M. Parker, *Inside the Circle: A Union Guide to QWL* (Boston: Labor Notes/South End Press, 1985). Two detailed case studies of EI programs in unionized settings can be found in D. Wells, *Empty Promises: Quality of Working Life Programs and the Labor Movement* (New York: Monthly Review Press, 1987). A fascinating case study on the use of an EI program to combat unionization can be found in G. J. Grenier, *Inhuman Relations: Quality Circles and Anti-Unionism in American Industry* (Philadelphia: Temple University Press, 1988). Concerning the reference to high-tech firms using EI programs, see S. M. Jacoby and A. Verma, "Enterprise Unions in the United States," *Industrial Relations* 31, no. 1 (winter 1992): 137.

32. For detailed information on the PATCO strike, see H. R. Northrup, "The Rise and Demise of PATCO," *Industrial and Labor Relations Review* 37, no. 2 (January 1984): 167–84; and A. B. Shostak and D. Skocik, *The Air Controllers' Controversy: Lessons from the PATCO Strike* (New York: Human Sciences Press, 1986). Two accounts of the Phelps Dodge copper miners' strike can be found in B. Kingsolver, *Holding the Line: Women in the Great Arizona Mine Strike of 1983* (Ithaca, N.Y.: ILR Press, 1989); and J. D. Rosenblum, *Copper Crucible: How the Arizona Miners' Strike of 1983 Recast Labor-Management Relations in America*, 2d ed. (Ithaca, N.Y.: Cornell University Press, 1998). For detailed analyses of the Hormel strike, see H. Green, *On Strike at Hormel: The Struggle for a Democratic Labor Movement* (Philadelphia: Temple University Press, 1990); and P. Rachleff, *Hard-Pressed in the Heartland: The Hormel Strike and the Future of the Labor Movement* (Boston: South End Press, 1993).

33. United States Department of Labor, Bureau of Labor Statistics, *Employment and Earnings* (Washington, D.C.: U.S. Government Printing Office, January 1994), 248.

34. Union density and membership figures for 1994 can be found in United States Department of Labor, Bureau of Labor Statistics, *Employment and Earnings* (Washington, D.C.: U.S. Government Printing Office, January 1995), 214. For comparable figures from 1995, 1996, and 1997, see United States Department of Labor, Bureau of Labor Statistics, *Employment and Earnings* (Washington, D.C.: U.S. Government Printing Office, January 1996), 210; United States Department of Labor, Bureau of Labor Statistics, *Employment and Earnings*, (Washington, D.C.: U.S. Government Printing Office, January 1997), 211; and

United States Department of Labor, Bureau of Labor Statistics, "News Release," 30 January 1998: 1.

35. H. Meyerson, "Labor Pains: Toward Less Imperfect Unions," *New Yorker,* 30 October 1995, 7; M. Morrissey and B. T. Coventry, "Divided Against Itself: Local vs. International Union Interests in a Toledo Supermarket Strike," *Critical Sociology* 22, no. 1 (1996): 53–71.

36. P. Rachleff, "A Page From History: Seeds of a Labor Resurgency," *Nation* 258, no. 7 (21 February 1994): 226.

37. D. Brody, "Criminalizing the Rights of Labor," *Dissent* 42, no. 3 (summer 1995): 363–67; Rachleff, "A Page from History," 226.

38. Information concerning the strikes of the United Rubber Workers and the UAW against Bridgestone-Firestone and Caterpillar is contained in M. H. Cimini, "Labor-Management Bargaining in 1995," *Monthly Labor Review* 119, nos. 1 and 2 (January-February 1996): 25–46. The comment concerning the success of the UAW's series of strikes against General Motors (GM) is based on J. Mills, "A Truce, for Now, at G.M.," *New York Times,* 24 March 1996, sec. 3. The relationship between UAW strike success and GM's adoption of lean production can be found in G. Sharma-Jensen and R. Romell, "UAW, GM Locked in Jobs Struggle," *Milwaukee Journal Sentinel,* 8 June 1997, sec. D. For details on the Teamsters' successful strike against UPS, see P. Dine, "Unions Find Rare Reason to Rejoice," *St. Louis Post-Dispatch,* 20 August 1997, sec. A and M. Tran, "UPS Caves in After 15-day Teamsters Strike," *Guardian* (London), 20 August 1997, sec. 1.

39. G. J. Church, "Unions Arise—With New Tricks," *Time,* 13 June 1994, 56.

40. J. Fine and R. Locke, "Unions Get Smart: New Tactics for a New Labor Movement," *Dollars and Sense,* September/October 1996, 16.

41. S. Fraser and J. Freeman, "Labor and the Intellectuals: Rebuilding the Alliance," *Dissent* 44, no. 1 (winter 1997): 29; A. Scher, "Union Summer: Young Activists Discover Unions Aren't History," *Dollars and Sense,* September/October 1996, 20.

42. Church, "Unions Arise—With New Tricks," 58.

43. H. L. Delgado, *New Immigrants, Old Unions: Organizing Undocumented Workers in Los Angeles* (Philadelphia: Temple University Press, 1993); G. P. Zachary, "Apple Workers Mull Collective Bargaining Push," *Wall Street Journal,* 19 June 1991, sec. B.

44. M. Simon, "Joe Hill Meets the Microchip: Amy Dean, Chief Executive Director of the South Bay AFL-CIO Central Labor Council, Thinks It's Time for Labor to Make a Hard Drive in Silicon Valley," *San Francisco Chronicle,* 13 July

1997, sec. S; K. J. Hossfeld, "Why Aren't High-Tech Workers Organized? Lessons in Gender, Race and Nationality from Silicon Valley," in *Working People of California,* ed. D. Cornford (Berkeley: University of California Press, 1995), 407; S. Thore, *The Diversity, Complexity, and Evolution of High-Tech Capitalism* (Boston: Kluwer Academic Publishers, 1995), 3.

Bibliography

Abate, T. "Laboring in the Silicon Jungle." *San Francisco Chronicle,* 25 April 1993, sec. E.

———. "High-Tech Jobs Are Booming: State Enjoying Strong Manufacturing Growth." *San Francisco Chronicle,* 5 June 1997, sec. B.

Adler, P. S. "Rethinking the Skill Requirements of New Technologies." In *High Hopes for High Tech: Microelectronics Policy in North Carolina*, edited by D. Whittington, 85–112. Chapel Hill: University of North Carolina Press, 1985.

Alic, J. A., and M. C. Harris. "Employment Lessons from the Electronics Industry." *Monthly Labor Review* 109, no. 2 (February 1986): 27–36.

Applebaum, E. "Winners and Losers in the High-Tech Workplace." *Challenge: Magazine of Economic Affairs* 26, no. 4 (September-October 1983): 52–55.

Armbruster, R. "Cross-National Labor Organizing Strategies." *Critical Sociology* 21, no. 2 (1995): 75–89.

Armstrong, S. "Labor Organizing: Growing Blip on High-Tech Screen." *Christian Science Monitor,* 17 May 1983, Tuesday edition.

Aronowitz, S., and W. DiFazio. *The Jobless Future: Sci-Tech and the Dogma of Work.* Minneapolis: University of Minnesota Press, 1994.

———. "High Technology and Work Tomorrow." *Annals of the American Academy of Political and Social Science* no. 544 (March 1996): 52–67.

Baldamus, W. *Efficiency and Effort: An Analysis of Industrial Administration.* London: Tavistock Institute of Human Relations, 1961.

Ballam, D. A. "The Traditional View on the Origins of the Employment-at-Will

Doctrine: Myth or Reality?" *American Business Law Journal* 33, no. 1 (fall 1995): 1–50.

Balzer, R. *Clockwork: Life in and Outside an American Factory.* Garden City, N.Y.: Doubleday, 1976.

Banks, A. "The Power and Promise of Community Unionism." *Labor Research Review* 10, no. 2 (1991–92): 17–31.

Benner, C. "Computer Workers Feel the Byte: Temp Jobs in Silicon Valley." *Dollars and Sense,* September/October 1996, 23–25, 44.

Blake, J. A. "Internal Dynamics, Definition of the Situation and Emerging Organization During a Wildcat Strike." *Humboldt Journal of Social Relations* 4, no. 2 (1977): 60–73.

Braddock, D. J. "Scientific and Technical Employment, 1990–2005." *Monthly Labor Review* 115, no. 2 (February 1992): 28–41.

Braverman, H. *Labor and Monopoly Capital: The Degradation of Work in the Twentieth Century.* New York: Monthly Review Press, 1974.

Brecher, J. "Roots of Power: Employers and Workers in the Electrical Products Industry." In *Case Studies on the Labor Process,* edited by A. Zimbalist, 206–27. New York: Monthly Review Press, 1979.

Brody, D. "Criminalizing the Rights of Labor." *Dissent* 42, no. 3 (summer 1995): 363–67.

Bronfenbrenner, K. "The Role of Union Strategies in NLRB Certification Elections." *Industrial and Labor Relations Review* 50, no. 2 (January 1997): 195–212.

Bulmer, M. *The Chicago School of Sociology: Institutionalization, Diversity and the Rise of Sociological Research.* Chicago: University of Chicago Press, 1985.

Burawoy, M. *Manufacturing Consent: Changes in the Labor Process under Monopoly Capitalism.* Chicago: University of Chicago Press, 1979.

———. *The Politics of Production: Factory Regimes under Capitalism and Socialism.* London: Verso, 1985.

Burgan, J. U. "Cyclical Behavior of High Tech Industries." *Monthly Labor Review* 108, no. 5 (May 1985): 9–15.

Byrne, D. M., and R. H. King. "Wildcat Strikes in U.S. Manufacturing, 1960–1977." *Journal of Labor Research* 7, no. 4 (fall 1986): 387–401.

California Employment Development Department. "State of California Employment by Industry: 1993 Annual Average and 2005 Projected Employment." In *Labor Market Information,* [Online]. Available: http://www.calmis.cahwnet.gov/file/indproj/calstb2.txt [21 June 1997].

California Employment Development Department. "San Jose MSA (Santa Clara County) Labor Force and Industry Employment." In *Labor Market Informa-*

tion, [Online]. Available: http://www.calmis.cahwnet.gov/file/indcur/ sanjspr.txt [21 June 1997].

California Employment Development Department. "Income in 1989 for Places in Santa Clara to Trinity Counties." In *Labor Market Information,* [Online]. Available: http://www.calmis.cahwmet.gov/file/demoinc/INC90PT7.TXT [21 June 1997].

California Employment Development Department. "Occupational Wages for Santa Clara County." In *Labor Market Information,* [Online] Available: http:// www.calmis.cahwnet.gov/file/occups/central.htm [21 June 1997].

Cappelli, P. "Plant-Level Concession Bargaining." *Industrial and Labor Relations Review* 39, no. 1 (October 1985): 90–104.

Cavendish, R. *Women on the Line.* London: Routledge and Kegan Paul, 1982.

Chaison, G. N., and D. G. Dhavale. "A Note on the Severity of the Decline in Union Organizing Activity." *Industrial and Labor Relations Review* 43, no. 4 (July 1990): 366–73.

Church, G. J. "Unions Arise—With New Tricks." *Time,* 13 June 1994, 56–58.

Cimini, M. H. "Labor-Management Bargaining in 1995." *Monthly Labor Review* 119, nos. 1 and 2 (January-February 1996): 25–46.

Colclough, G. and C. M. Tolbert. *Work in the Fast Lane: Flexibility, Divisions of Labor, and Inequality in High-Tech Industries.* Albany: State University of New York Press, 1992.

Compa, L. "Another Look at NAFTA." *Dissent* 44, no.1 (winter 1997): 45–48, 50.

Cook, D. T. "High-Tech vs. U.S. Labor Unions; Loss of Jobs and Clout." *Christian Science Monitor,* 12 September 1983, Monday edition.

Cook, M. L. "Cross-Border Labor Solidarity." *Dissent* 44, no. 1 (winter 1997): 49.

Cooper, M. H. "LIUNA Organizes Asbestos Industry in Model Campaign." *AFL-CIO News* 41, no. 8 (1996): 1, 13.

Covington, R. N. and K. H. Decker. *Individual Employee Rights in a Nutshell.* St. Paul, Minn.: West Publishing Company, 1995.

Crowe, K. C. "A Unionized Victory For Asbestos Workers." *Newsday,* 21 April 1996.

Curme, M. A., B. T. Hirsch, and D. A. MacPherson. "Union Membership and Contract Coverage in the United States, 1983–1988." *Industrial and Labor Relations Review* 44, no. 1 (October 1990): 5–33.

Dangler, J. F. "Electronic Subassemblers in Central New York: Nontraditional Homeworkers in a Nontraditional Homework Industry." In *Homework: Historical and Contemporary Perspectives on Paid Labor at Home,* edited by E. Boris and C. R. Daniels, 147–64. Urbana: University of Illinois Press, 1989.

Davis, M. "The Stop Watch and the Wooden Shoe: Scientific Management and the

Industrial Workers of the World." *Radical America* 9, no. 1 (January-February 1975): 69–95.

Delgado, H. L. *New Immigrants, Old Unions: Organizing Undocumented Workers in Los Angeles*. Philadelphia: Temple University Press, 1993.

Devinatz, V. G. "Rationalizing the Irrationality of the Shop Floor: A Reinterpretation of Juravich's *Chaos on the Shop Floor*." *Labor Studies Journal* 18, no. 1 (spring 1993): 3–16.

———. "The Fair Deal Campaign: The Evolution of a Non-NLRB Election Organizing Strategy for Unionizing Milwaukee Asbestos-Abatement Workers." *Labor Studies Journal* 22, no.3 (fall 1997): 74–91.

Dine, P. "Unions Find Rare Reason to Rejoice," *St. Louis Post-Dispatch*, 20 August 1997, sec. A.

Early, S. "Northern Telecom: Telephone Workers' Campaign Promotes Labor." *Labor Notes* 154 (January 1992): 8.

Early, S., and R. Wilson. "Do Unions Have a Future in High Technology?" *Technology Review* 89, no. 7 (October 1986): 56–65f.

———. "Organizing High Tech: Unions and Their Future." *Labor Research Review* no. 8 (spring 1986): 47–65.

Edwards, R. *Contested Terrain: The Transformation of the Workplace in the Twentieth Century*. New York: Basic Books, 1979.

Eisenscher, M. "Silicon Valley High Tech Industry: Ready for Organizing. A Discussion Paper for Unions." Draft #3, San Jose, California, 25 July 1985. Photocopy.

———. "Chasing the High Tech Rainbow: Reality and Fantasy in the Valley of the Silicon Giants." San Jose, California, 1985. Photocopy.

Engstrom, T. "Union Dues: High Tech Meets Organized Labor." *Electronic Business* 9 (December 1983): 100–3.

Erlich, R. "Rare Employee Strike at Silicon Valley Plant; Job Action at Versatronex May Foreshadow New Drive to Organize Immigrant Workers in High-Tech Industry." *Christian Science Monitor,* 24 November 1992, Tuesday edition.

Etzioni, A., and P. Jargowsky. "High Tech, Basic Industry, and the Future of the American Economy." *Human Resource Management* 23, no. 3 (fall 1984): 229–40.

Fantasia, R. *Cultures of Solidarity: Consciousness, Action and Contemporary American Workers*. Berkeley: University of California Press, 1988.

Fine, J., and R. Locke. "Unions Get Smart: New Tactics for a New Labor Movement." *Dollars and Sense,* September/October 1996, 16–19, 42.

Foner, P. S. *Women and the American Labor Movement: From Colonial Times to the Eve of World War I*. New York: Free Press, 1979.

Form, W., and D. B. McMillen. "Women, Men and Machines." *Work and Occupations* 10, no. 2 (May 1983): 147–78.

Foster, J. B. *"Labor And Monopoly Capital* Twenty Years After: An Introduction." *Monthly Review* 46, no. 6 (November 1994): 1–13.

Foucault, M. *Discipline and Punish: The Birth of the Prison.* London: Allen Lane, 1977.

Fraser, S., and J. Freeman. "Labor and the Intellectuals: Rebuilding the Alliance." *Dissent* 44, no. 1 (winter 1997): 29–30.

French, W. L. *Human Resources Management,* 4th ed. Boston: Houghton Mifflin, 1998.

Friedman, A. *Industry and Labor: Class Struggle at Work and Monopoly Capitalism.* London: Macmillan, 1977.

Fuentes, A., and B. Ehrenreich. *Women in the Global Factory.* Boston: South End Press, 1983.

Gagala, K. *Union Organizing and Staying Organized.* Reston, Va.: Reston Publishing Company, 1983.

Gamst, G., and C. M. Otten. "Job Satisfaction in High Technology and Traditional Industry: Is There a Difference?" *Psychological Record* 42, no. 3 (summer 1992): 413–25.

Geertz, C. *The Interpretation of Cultures.* New York: Basic Books, 1973.

Glasmeier, A. K. "High-Tech Industries and the Regional Division of Labor." *Industrial Relations* 25, no. 2 (spring 1986): 197–211.

Goldfield, M. *The Decline of Organized Labor in the United States.* Chicago: University of Chicago Press, 1987.

Goss, M. "Smokestacks Revisited: The Future of High-Tech Workers." *Management Review* 74, no. 5 (May 1985): 26–32.

Gouldner, A. *Patterns of Industrial Bureaucracy.* New York: Free Press, 1954.

Graham, L. *On the Line at Suburu-Isuzu: The Japanese Model and the American Worker.* Ithaca, N.Y.: Cornell University Press, 1995.

Green, H. *On Strike at Hormel: The Struggle for a Democratic Labor Movement.* Philadelphia: Temple University Press, 1990.

Green, S. S. "Silicon Valley's Women Workers: A Theoretical Analysis of Sex-Segregation in the Electronics Industry Labor Market." In *Women, Men and the International Division of Labor,* edited by J. Nash and M. P. Fernandez-Kelly, 273–331. Albany: State University of New York Press, 1983.

Greenbaum, J. "The Forest and the Trees." *Monthly Review* 46, no. 6 (November 1994): 60–70.

Grenier, G. J. *Inhuman Relations: Quality Circles and Anti-Unionism in American Industry.* Philadelphia: Temple University Press, 1988.

Grossman, R. "Women's Place in the Integrated Circuit." *Radical America* 14, no. 1 (January–February 1980): 29–49.

Guttman, M. "Primary (Informal) Work Groups." *Radical America* 6, no. 3 (May–June 1972): 78–91.

Hadlock, P., D. Hecker, and J. Gannon. "High Technology Employment: Another View." *Monthly Labor Review* 114, no. 7 (July 1991): 26–30.

Hage, J., and C. H. Powers. *Post-Industrial Lives: Roles and Relationships in the 21st Century.* Newbury Park, Calif.: Sage, 1992.

Halle, D. *America's Working Man: Work, Home and Politics among Blue Collar Property Owners.* Chicago: University of Chicago Press, 1984.

Hayes, D. *Behind the Silicon Curtain: The Seductions of Work in a Lonely Era.* Boston: South End Press, 1989.

Hembree, D. "Dead End in Silicon Valley: The High-Tech Future Doesn't Work." *Progressive,* 49, no. 10 (October 1985): 18–24.

Henderson, J. *The Globalisation of High Technology Production: Society, Space and Semiconductors in the Restructuring of the Modern World.* London: Routledge, 1989.

"High Tech Lures Union Organizers." *Business Week,* 11 April 1983, 101–2.

Hirsch, B. T., and D. A. MacPherson. "Union Membership and Coverage Files from the Current Population Surveys: Note." *Industrial and Labor Relations Review* 46, no. 3 (April 1993): 574–88.

Hirst, P., and J. Zeitlin. "Flexible Specialization Versus Post-Fordism: Theory, Evidence, and Policy Implications." *Economy and Society* 20, no. 1 (February 1991): 1–52.

Hodson, R. "Working in 'High-Tech': Researchers and Opportunities for the Industrial Sociologist." *Sociological Quarterly* 26, no. 3 (September 1985): 351–64.

———. "Good Jobs and Bad Management: How New Problems Evoke Old Solutions in High-Tech Settings." In *Industries, Firms and Jobs: Sociological and Economic Approaches,* edited by G. Farkas and P. England, 247–79. New York: Plenum Press, 1988.

———. "The Active Worker: Compliance and Autonomy at the Workplace." *Journal of Contemporary Ethnography* 20, no. 1 (April 1991): 47–78.

———. "Workplace Behaviors: Good Soldiers, Smooth Operators, and Saboteurs." *Work and Occupations* 18, no. 3 (August 1991): 271–90.

———. "Cohesion or Conflict?: Race, Solidarity, and Resistance in the Workplace." In *Research in the Sociology of Work,* vol. 5, edited by R. L. Simpson and I. H. Simpson, 135–59. Greenwich, Conn.: JAI Press, 1995.

Hodson, R., and R. E. Parker. "Work in High-Technology Settings: A Review of the

Empirical Literature." In *Research in the Sociology of Work,* vol. 4, edited by R. L. Simpson and I. H. Simpson, 1–29. Greenwich, Conn.: JAI Press, 1988.

Holley, W. H., and K. M. Jennings. *The Labor Relations Process,* 5th ed. New York: Dryden Press, 1994.

———. *The Labor Relations Process,* 6th ed. New York: Dryden Press, 1997.

Hossfeld, K. J. "'Their Logic Against Them': Contradictions in Sex, Race, and Class in Silicon Valley." In *Women Workers and Global Restructuring,* edited by K. Ward, 149–78. Ithaca, N.Y.: ILR Press, 1990.

———. "Why Aren't High-Tech Workers Organized? Lessons in Gender, Race and Nationality from Silicon Valley." In *Working People of California,* edited by D. Cornford, 405–32. Berkeley: University of California Press, 1995.

Howard, R. "Second Class in Silicon Valley." *Working Papers for a New Society* 8, no. 5 (September-October 1981): 21–26.

———. *Brave New Workplace.* New York: Viking Penguin, 1985.

Howley, J. "Justice For Janitors: The Challenge of Organizing in Contract Services." *Labor Research Review* 9, no. 1 (1990): 61–71.

Hyman, R. "Flexible Specialization: Miracle or Myth?" In *New Technology and Industrial Relations,* edited by R. Hyman and W. Streeck, 48–60. Oxford: Blackwell, 1988.

Jacoby, S. M., and A. Verma. "Enterprise Unions in the United States." *Industrial Relations* 31, no. 1 (winter 1992): 137–58.

Jermier, J. M., D. Knights, and W. R. Nord. "Resistance and Power in Organizations: Agency, Subjectivity and the Labour Process." In *Resistance and Power in Organizations,* edited by J. M. Jermier, D. Knights and W. R. Nord, 1–24. London: Routledge, 1994.

Johnson, J. V. "Collective Control: Strategies for Survival in the Workplace." *International Journal of Health Services* 19, no. 3 (1989): 469–80.

Johnston, P. *Success While Others Fail: Social Movement Unionism and the Public Workplace.* Ithaca, N.Y.: ILR Press, 1994.

Juravich, T. *Chaos on the Shop Floor: A Worker's View of Quality, Productivity, and Management.* Philadelphia: Temple University Press, 1985.

Juris, H., and M. Roomkin. "The Shrinking Perimeter: Unions and Collective Bargaining in Manufacturing." In *The Shrinking Perimeter: Unionism and Labor Relations in the Manufacturing Sector,* edited by H. A. Juris and M. Roomkin, 197–211. Lexington, Mass.: D.C. Heath, 1980.

Kadetsky, E. "High-Tech's Dirty Little Secret." *Nation* 256, no. 15 (19 April 1993): 517–20.

Kamata, S. *Japan in the Passing Lane: An Insider's Account of Life in a Japanese Auto Factory*. New York: Pantheon, 1983.

Katz, N., and D. S. Kemnitzer. "Fast Forward: The Internationalization of Silicon Valley." In *Women, Men and the International Division of Labor*, edited by J. Nash and M. P. Fernandez-Kelly, 332–45. Albany: State University of New York Press, 1983.

Keller, J. F. "The Division of Labor in Electronics." In *Women, Men and the International Division of Labor*, edited by J. Nash and M. P. Fernandez-Kelly, 346–73. Albany: State University of New York Press, 1983.

Kimery, J. "Labor Process and Race Relations in a Shampoo Factory: The Differential Distribution of Help." *Humboldt Journal of Social Relations* 20, no. 1 (1994): 65–85.

Kingsolver, B. *Holding the Line: Women in the Great Arizona Mine Strike of 1983*. Ithaca, N.Y.: ILR Press, 1989.

Kopinak, K. "Transitions in the Maquilization of Mexican Industry: Movement and Stasis from 1965 to 2001." *Labour, Capital and Society* 28, no. 1 (1995): 68–94.

Kusterer, K. *Know-How on the Job: The Important Working Knowledge of Unskilled Workers*. Boulder, Colo.: Westview, 1978.

Lawler, J. J. *Unionization and Deunionization: Strategy, Tactics, and Outcomes*. Columbia: University of South Carolina Press, 1990.

Lee, C. K. "Familial Hegemony: Gender and Production Politics on Hong Kong's Electronics Shopfloor." *Gender and Society* 7, no. 4 (December 1993): 529–47.

———. "Engendering the Worlds of Labor: Women Workers, Labor Markets, and Production Politics in the South China Economic Miracle." *American Sociological Review* 60, no. 3 (June 1995): 378–97.

Leidner, R. *Fast Food, Fast Talk: Service Work and the Routinization of Everyday Life*. Berkeley: University of California Press, 1993.

Linhart, R. *The Assembly Line*. Amherst: University of Massachusetts Press, 1981.

Lozano, B. *The Invisible Work Force: Transforming American Business with Outside and Home-Based Workers*. New York: Free Press, 1989.

Lupton, T. *On the Shop Floor*. Oxford: Pergamon Press, 1963.

Madge, J. *The Origins of Scientific Sociology*. New York: Free Press, 1962.

Mahon, T. *Charged Bodies: People, Power and Paradox in Silicon Valley*. New York: New American Library Books, 1985.

Markusen, A. R., P. Hall, and A. Glasmeier. *High-Tech America: The What, How, Where, and Why of the Sunrise Industries*. Boston: Allen & Unwin, 1986.

Mathewson, S. B. *Restriction of Output among Unorganized Workers*. Carbondale: Southern Illinois University Press, 1969.

Mattera, P. "The Underside of the Computer Age." *Thought* 61, no. 243 (December 1986): 452–59.

McGinn, M. "After NAFTA . . . Honeywell, G.E. Fire Mexican Workers for Organizing Unions." *Labor Notes* 178 (January 1994): 1, 14.

Meiksins, P. "*Labor And Monopoly Capital* for the 1990s: A Review and Critique of the Labor Process Debate." *Monthly Review* 46, no. 6 (November 1994): 45–59.

Meyerson, H. "Labor Pains: Toward Less Imperfect Unions." *New Yorker,* 30 October 1995, 7–8.

Mills, J. "A Truce, for Now, at G.M." *New York Times,* 24 March 1996, sec. 3.

Moberg, D. "The Resurgence of American Unions: Small Steps, Long Journey." *Working USA* (May-June 1997): 20–31.

Mohseni, N. "The Labor Process and Control of Labor in the U.S. Computer Industry." In *The Labor Process and Control of Labor: The Changing Nature of Work Relations in the Late Twentieth Century,* edited by B. Berberoglu, 59–77. Westport, Conn.: Praeger Publishers, 1993.

Molstad, C. "Control Strategies Used by Industrial Brewery Workers: Work Avoidance, Impression Management and Solidarity." *Human Organization* 47, no. 4 (winter 1988): 354–60.

Moody, K. *Workers in a Lean World: Unions in the International Economy.* London: Verso, 1997.

Morrissey, M., and B. T. Coventry. "Divided Against Itself: Local vs. International Union Interests in a Toledo Supermarket Strike." *Critical Sociology* 22, no. 1 (1996): 53–71.

Needleman, R. "Organizing Low-Wage Workers." *Working USA* (May–June 1997): 45–59.

Nichols, T. and H. Beynon. *Living with Capitalism: Class Relations and the Modern Factory.* London: Routledge and Kegan Paul, 1977.

Northrup, H. R. "The Rise and Demise of PATCO." *Industrial and Labor Relations Review* 37, no. 2 (January 1984): 167–84.

Ohmans, D. "Seeds of Solidarity: Union Initiatives Towards Mexico." *OCAW Reporter* 49, nos. 5–6 (1993): 11.

Ong, A. *Spirits of Resistance and Capitalist Discipline: Factory Women in Malaysia.* Albany: State University of New York Press, 1987.

Parker, M. *Inside the Circle: A Union Guide to QWL.* Boston: Labor Notes/South End Press, 1985.

Patterson, W. "Why Organized Labor Likes High Tech." *Industry Week* 227, no. 3 (11 November 1985): 46–48.

Paules, G. F. *Dishing It Out: Power and Resistance among Waitresses in a New Jersey Restaurant.* Philadelphia: Temple University Press, 1991.

Pelto, P. J., and G. H. Pelto. *Anthropological Research: The Structure of Inquiry,* 2d ed. Cambridge, Mass.: Cambridge University Press, 1978.

Peterson, R. B., T. W. Lee, and B. Finnegan. "Strategies and Tactics in Union Organizing Campaigns." *Industrial Relations* 31, no. 2 (spring 1992): 370–81.

Pfeffer, R. M. *Working for Capitali$m.* New York: Columbia University Press, 1979.

Piore, M., and C. F. Sabel. *The Second Industrial Divide: Possibilities for Prosperity.* New York: Basic Books, 1984.

Pollert, A. *Girls, Wives, Factory Lives.* London: Macmillan, 1981.

———. *Farewell to Flexibility?* Oxford: Blackwell, 1991.

Poole, L., and G. Poole. *Electronics in Medicine.* New York: McGraw-Hill Book Company, 1964.

Rachleff, P. *Hard-Pressed in the Heartland: The Hormel Strike and the Future of the Labor Movement.* Boston: South End Press, 1993.

———. "A Page From History: Seeds of a Labor Resurgency." *Nation* 258, no. 7 (21 February 1994): 226–29.

Robinson, J. G., and J. S. McIlwee. "Obstacles to Unionization in High-Tech Industries." *Work and Occupations* 16, no. 2 (May 1989): 115–36.

Rogers, E. M., and D. V. Gibson. "Technology Transfer in High-Technology Industries: Entrepreneurs and Research and Development Consortia in the United States." In *Technology Companies and Global Markets,* edited by D. V. Gibson, 39–60. Savage, Md.: Rowman and Littlefield Publishers, 1991.

Rogers, E. M., and J. K. Larsen. *Silicon Valley Fever: Growth of High-Technology Culture.* New York: Basic Books, 1984.

Rogers, M. "Trouble in the Valley." *Newsweek,* 25 February 1985, 92–94.

Rosegrant, S., and D. R. Lampe. *Route 128: Lessons From Boston's High-Tech Community.* New York: Basic Books, 1992.

Rosenblum, J. D. *Copper Crucible: How the Arizona Miners' Strike of 1983 Recast Labor-Management Relations in America,* 2d ed. Ithaca, N.Y.: Cornell University Press, 1998.

Roy, D. "Quota Restriction and Goldbricking in a Machine Shop." *American Journal of Sociology* 57, no. 5 (March 1952): 427–42.

———. "Work Satisfaction and Social Reward in Quota Achievement." *American Sociological Review* 18, no. 5 (October 1953): 507–14.

———. "Efficiency and the Fix: Informal Intergroup Relations in a Piecework Machine Shop." *American Journal of Sociology* 60, no. 3 (November 1954): 255–66.

Sakolsky, R. "'Disciplinary Power' and the Labor Process." In *Skill and Consent: Contemporary Studies in the Labour Process,* edited by A. Sturdy, D. Knights, and H. Willmott, 235–54. London: Routledge, 1992.

Sawyer, K. "Unions Striking Out in High-Tech Firms." *Washington Post,* 18 March 1984, Sunday edition, sec. A.

Saxenian, A. *Regional Advantage: Culture and Competition in Silicon Valley and Route 128.* Cambridge, Mass.: Harvard University Press, 1994.

Sayer, A. "Post-Fordism in Question." *International Journal of Urban and Regional Research* 13, no. 4 (December 1989): 666–95.

Schellenberg, K. "Taking It or Leaving It: Instability and Turnover in a High-Tech Firm." *Work and Occupations* 23, no. 2 (May 1996): 190–213.

Scher, A. "Union Summer: Young Activists Discover Unions Aren't History." *Dollars and Sense,* September/October 1996, 20–22.

Schervish, P. G. *The Structural Determinants of Unemployment: Vulnerability and Power in Market Relations.* New York: Academic Press, 1983.

Scott, A. J. "Low-Wage Workers in a High-Technology Manufacturing Complex: The Southern California Electronics Assembly Industry." *Urban Studies* 29, no. 8 (December 1992): 1231–46.

———. *Technopolis: High-Technology Industry and Regional Development in Southern California.* Berkeley: University of California Press, 1993.

Shaiken, H. "Advanced Manufacturing and Mexico: A New International Division of Labor?" *Latin American Research Review* 29, no. 2 (1994): 39–71.

Shapiro-Perl, N. "The Piece Rate: Class Struggle on the Shop Floor. Evidence from the Costume Jewelry Industry in Providence, Rhode Island." In *Case Studies on the Labor Process,* edited by A. Zimbalist, 277–98. New York: Monthly Review Press, 1979.

Sharma-Jensen, G. and R. Romell. "UAW, GM Locked in Jobs Struggle." *Milwaukee Journal Sentinel,* 8 June 1997, sec. D.

Shostak, A. B. "High Tech, High Touch and Labor." *Social Policy* 13, no. 3 (winter 1983): 20–23.

———, and D. Skocik. *The Air Controllers' Controversy: Lessons from the PATCO Strike.* New York: Human Sciences Press, 1986.

Simon, M. "Joe Hill Meets the Microchip: Amy Dean, Chief Executive Director of the South Bay AFL-CIO Central Labor Council, Thinks It's Time for Labor to Make a Hard Drive in Silicon Valley," *San Francisco Chronicle,* 13 July 1997, sec. S.

Slaughter, J. *Concessions and How to Beat Them.* Detroit: Labor Education and Research Project, 1984.

Smith, V. "Braverman's Legacy: The Labor Process Tradition at 20." *Work and Occupations* 21, no. 4 (November 1994): 403–21.

———. "New Forms of Work Organization." In *Annual Review of Sociology,* vol. 23, edited by J. Hagan, 315–39. Palo Alto, Calif.: Annual Reviews, 1997.

Snow, R. "The New International Division of Labor and the U.S. Work Force: The Case of the Electronics Industry." In *Women, Men and the International Division of Labor,* edited by J. Nash and M. P. Fernandez-Kelly, 39–69. Albany: State University of New York Press, 1983.

Solomon, N. *The Trouble with Dilbert: How Corporate Culture Gets the Last Laugh.* Monroe, Maine: Common Courage Press, 1997.

Storey, J. *Managerial Prerogative and the Question of Control.* London: Routledge and Kegan Paul, 1983.

Taplin, I. "Flexible Production, Rigid Jobs: Lessons From the Clothing Industry." *Work and Occupations* 22, no. 4 (November 1995): 412–38.

———. "Rethinking Flexibility: The Case of the Apparel Industry." *Review of Social Economy* 54, no. 2 (summer 1996): 191–220.

Taplin, R. "Women in World Market Factories: East and West." *Ethnic and Racial Studies* 9, no. 2 (April 1986): 168–95.

"Teamsters, UE Launch Historic Solidarity Campaign with Fired Mexican Workers." *Working Together: Labor Report on the Americas* no. 5 (March–April 1994): 1.

Thompson, P. *The Nature of Work: An Introduction to Debates on the Labour Process.* London: Macmillan, 1983.

———. *The Nature of Work: An Introduction to Debates on the Labour Process,* 2d ed. London: Macmillan, 1989.

———. "Crawling from the Wreckage: The Labour Process and the Politics of Production." In *Labour Process Theory,* edited by D. Knights and H. Willmott. London: Macmillan Press, 1990: 95–124.

Thore, S. *The Diversity, Complexity and Evolution of High-Tech Capitalism.* Boston: Kluwer Academic Publishers, 1995.

Tiano, S. "Maquiladora Women: A New Category of Workers." In *Women Workers and Global Restructuring,* edited by K. Ward, 193–223. Ithaca, N.Y.: ILR Press, 1990.

Tran, M. "UPS Caves in After 15-Day Teamsters Strike," *Guardian* (London), 20 August 1997, sec. 1.

United States Department of Commerce. *Census of Manufactures.* Washington, D.C.: U.S. Government Printing Office, 1992.

United States Department of Labor, Bureau of Labor Statistics. *Employment and Earnings.* Washington, D.C.: U.S. Government Printing Office, January 1994.

——. *Employment and Earnings*. Washington, D.C.: U.S. Government Printing Office, January 1995.

——. *Employment and Earnings*. Washington, D.C.: U.S. Government Printing Office, January 1996.

——. *Employment and Earnings*. Washington, D.C.: U.S. Government Printing Office, January 1997.

——. "News Release," 30 January 1998.

Vallas, S. P., and J. P. Beck. "The Transformation of Work Revisisted: The Limits of Flexibility in American Manufacturing." *Social Problems* 43, no. 3 (August 1996): 339–61.

Vaught, C., and D. L. Smith. "Incorporation and Mechanical Solidarity in an Underground Coal Mine." *Work and Occupations* 7, no. 2 (May 1980): 159–87.

Veigel-Cooper, R. M. Telephone conversation with author, 25 March 1997.

Wells, D. *Empty Promises: Quality of Working Life Programs and the Labor Movement*. New York: Monthly Review Press, 1987.

West, J. "Gender and the Labour Process: A Reassessment." In *Labour Process Theory,* edited by D. Knights and H. Willmott, 244–73. London: Macmillan Press, 1990.

Willis, P. E. *Learning for Labour: How Working Class Kids Get Working Class Jobs*. Farnborough, England: Saxon House, 1977.

Womack, J. P., D. T. Jones, and D. Roos. *The Machine That Changed the World*. New York: Harper, 1990.

Zachary, G. P. "Apple Workers Mull Collective Bargaining Push." *Wall Street Journal,* 19 June 1991, sec. B.

Index

A

advisory boards, Biomed, 24
Amalgamated Clothing and Textile
    Workers Union, 196, 202
American Electronics Association
    (AMA), 8
automation, Biomed, 73–76, 77–78

B

Biomed: advisory boards at, 24;
    attempts to unionize, 154–76;
    attractiveness of to union
    organizers, 182; automation at,
    73–76, 77–78; cable work at,
    70–71; chloriding elements at,
    72–73; corporate history of, 20–
    22, 24–25; cutting plastic
    coverings at, 68; daily routine
    at, 49–51; description of jobs
    at, 61–73; deskilling of produc-
    tion process at, 76–78; drug use
    at, 132–33; ethnic and gender
    segregation at, 62, 116–18;
    factory discipline at, 82–89,
    108; firings at, 104–6, 112;
    foreign markets for, 22, 25;
    fragmentation of production
    process at, 55, 58, 78, 79;
    gelling at, 34–37, 41–44, 49–51,
    61–64; gendered resistance at,
    111; individual worker por-
    traits, 118–28; as industrial
    panopticon, 109–10; issue of
    raises and wages at, 139–42;
    janitorial work at, 73; layoffs at,
    100–4, 112; line foremen at, 90,
    107, 117; management tricks
    at, 98–100; managerial control
    at, 81–106, 107–10, 112, 113;
    managerial incompetence at,
    55; mass walkout at, 143;
    obstacles to collective action at,
    148–50; obstacles to unioniza-
    tion at, 178, 180–83, 184; office
    and plant personnel, 23–24;
    officers and directors of, 22–23;
    opportunities for advancement
    within, 78–79; packing depart-
    ment at, 69–70; politics at,
    129–31; pounding tin at, 64;
    production padding at, 49–50,
    54–55, 72, 111; production
    speedup at, 97–98; production

work reports at, 93–97, 108, 110; racism among workers at, 128, 150, 181; resistance to managerial control at, 110, 111; running at, 63–64; shopfloor revolt of Latino gellers at, 138, 143–47; snap-type electrode assembly work at, 71–72; subassembly work at, 64–68; time studies at, 91–93, 109–10; worker attitudes at, 58–60, 82, 135, 137–38, 139–42; worker innovation at, 60–61, 78, 82; workers' views on unions at, 152–54, 179

Biomedical Electronics Corporation. *See* Biomed

Brotherhood of Railway, Airline and Steamship Clerks (BRAC), 46, 128, 152, 153, 155, 156

Byrne, Jane, 129

C

cable work, Biomed, 70–71
Canadian Auto Workers, 196
capitalism, high-tech, 1–2, 203
child labor, 191
chloriding elements, Biomed, 72–73
Clinton, Bill, 3
Coalition for Justice in the Maquiladoras (CJM), 194
Communication Workers of America (CWA), 151, 196, 201
Confederation of Mexican Workers, the, 195
contingent workers, 193
counting time, 55–56

D

Daly, Richard, 129
Dean, Amy, 193
defibrillators, ventricular, develop-

ment of, 19
despotic factory regimes, 107, 189–92
disciplinary measures, Biomed, 82–89, 108

E

Eisenscher, Mike, 13
electronics assembly industry, 6–7
employee involvement (EI) programs, 199
employment agencies, 28, 38–39
"employment at will" doctrine, 112
Epton, B., 130

F

factory regimes, types, 188–90
factory work: keys to obtaining, 37–39; physical toll of, 51, 52–53, 62–63
firings, Biomed, 104–6, 112
Frente Autentico de Trabajadores (FAT), 195–96

G

Glaziers Union, 151, 152
gendered resistance, Biomed, 111

H

hegemonic factory regimes, 188, 189
Hewlett, William, 4
High Tech Network (HTN), 13
High-tech capitalism, 1–2, 203
high-tech industry: adapting to factory work in, 41–52; analogy to classroom setting, 86, 108; "average" production worker in, 10; California, 6–7; compared with traditional industry, xv, 3–4, 15, 199; child labor in, 191; contingent workers in,

193; definition of, 4–5;
deskilling of labor process in,
76–78, 79; despotic factory
regime in, 107, 189–90; ethnic
and gender segregation in, 117–
18; and global competition,
191–92; growth predictions for,
1–2; international factory
conditions, 191–92; low wages
for production workers in, 8;
"making out" games in, 109;
managerial control in, 106–7,
108, 109, 111–13; managerial
incompetence in, 11–12, 55,
81; opportunities for advancement within, 14–15, 78–79;
organization of production
process within, 10–12, 57, 81;
percentage of workforce
employed by, 1, 2; proliferation
of throughout U.S., 4; resistance to managerial control in,
110–13; strategies for unionizing, 192–94; sweatshops in,
190; union resistance of, 8, 12–
14, 151, 183–84, 185; venture
capital in, 21; women in
workforce of, 9–10, 14–15;
worker dependence on overtime in, 51, 56; worker innovation in, 78
homeworkers, industrial, 190–91

I
Industrial Workers Local 44, 154
International Ladies Garment
Workers Union, 196

J
"Justice for Janitors" campaign, 193,
201

L
layoffs: Biomed, 100–4, 112; as
dismissal mechanism, 105, 112
line foremen, Biomed, 90, 107, 117

M
"making out" games, 109
managerial control, Biomed, 81–106,
107–10, 112, 113
market despotism, 189
measured daywork, 108–9
Metal Processors' Union Local 16,
154
Microsoft, 3

N
National Labor Relations Board
(NLRB), xiii, 8, 138, 161, 176,
177, 178, 182, 183, 184, 199
North American Agreement on Labor
Cooperation (NAALC), 197–98
Northern Telecom Solidarity Coali-
tion, 196–97
Noyce, Robert, 4

O
organized workplace resistance:
Biomed, 143–47; factors in,
147–48
overtime, worker dependence on, 51,
56

P
pacemaker, development of, 19
Packard, David, 4
packing department, Biomed, 69–70
"pencil bonus," 54, 111
Pfeffer, R. M., xv, 38–39
plastic coverings, cutting, Biomed, 68
post-Fordism, 57

pounding tin, Biomed, 64
primary work groups, importance of, 148
Professional Air Traffic Controllers Organization (PATCO), 200
production process,: deskilling of, 76–78, 79; fragmentation of, Biomed, 55, 58, 78, 79
production work reports: controlling of, 95; as management control tactic, 93–97, 108, 109, 110; padding of, 49–50, 54–55, 72, 111
production workers, small firms, xiii–xv

R

rank and file intensive strategies, 178

S

secondary labor market, 9, 78
Service Employees International Union (SEIU), 193, 201
Silicon Valley:
Silicon Valley: economic division of workforce in, 7; electronics assembly industry employment in, 6; as embodiment of high-tech industry, 3; regional versions of, 4; unionization rates in, 8–9, 12; women in workforce of, 9, 14–15; workforce segregation in, 9
simple control, 107
skill, 76
snap-type electrode assembly, Biomed, 71–72
social insurance legislation, 189
South Bay Labor Council, 193, 202
strikes: economic, 182; unfair labor practice, 182; use of in obtaining collective bargaining

agreement, 182; Versatronex, 138–39; wildcat, 149
subassembly work, Biomed, 64–68
sweatshops, garage, 190
Sweeney, John, 201–2

T

Taylorism, 11
Teamsters Union, 149, 153, 196, 201
time studies: at Biomed, 91–93, 109–10; in high-tech industry, 11, 57
top-down hierarchy, in high tech industry, 10, 81
Toyworkers Union, 149
traction, 77
Transportation Communication Union, 46

U

Unfair labor practice charge, 176–78
Union of Needletrades, Industrial and Textile Employees (UNITE), 196, 202
unions: and undocumented workers, 179
unions: benefits of, xiv; decline in membership of, 199–200; industry-wide, 192–94; international, 194–98; management tactics to avoid, 182, 183, 199; recent successes among, 200–2; strategies for organizing, 178–80
United Auto Workers (UAW), 201
United Electrical Workers (UE), 12, 138, 155, 156, 159, 160, 161, 169, 176, 178, 182, 195, 196
United Farm Workers of America (UFWA), 159
United Rubber Workers, 201

V

venture capital, 20–21
Versatronex, strike at, 138–39

W

Washington, Harold, 129, 130, 131
wildcat strikes, 149
women: in high-tech industry, 9–10,
    14–15; in Silicon Valley
    workforce, 9, 14–15
worker innovation: Biomed, 60–61,
    78, 82; disincentives to, 60, 61
worker resentment, Biomed, 82, 135,
    137–38, 139–42
working knowledge, 53–54
Working Partnerships USA, 193

Z

Zoll, Paul, 19